INSIGHT GUIDES

alsace

Edited by Gaby Lefèvre
Photography by Patrice Astier and others
Editorial Director: Dieter Vogel
Translated by Susan James

APA
PUBLICATIONS

aLsace

ABOUT THIS BOOK

alsace is one of the few regions in the world that has been blessed with a wealth of beautiful scenery, culture, art and cuisine, so much so that any excessive hype for Alsace would be really superfluous. The decision to open APA Publications' new series of regional guides with this particular book was therefore not a difficult one.

The regional guides, as their name implies, are intended to cover a somewhat smaller area than the famous *Insight Guides* and can therefore provide information in much more detail.

After the publication of *Insight Guide: France* there was a great demand for more detailed descriptions of the country, and Alsace, because of its individual culture and its position as a buffer zone between France and Germany, is an obvious choice for the new series of regional guides.

The great attractions of this country lie not in its famous half-timbered houses, the romantic castle ruins and the legendary Wine Route, but in the fact that it is a real European cultural mosaic of Celtic, Gallic, Roman, Germanic and Alemannic elements. It is a fascinating place, not only for Europeans.

This travel guide is more than just another contribution to the already long list of books about Alsace. It fits in well with the rest of the *Insight Guides*, which began in 1970 with **Hans Höfer's** detailed description of his experiences in Bali.

Since 1970 the list of *Insight Guides* has been constantly expanding with books following Hans Höfer's model and covering the countries of Asia, the Pacific, North America, the Antilles, Europe, Africa and the Middle East.

While **Gaby Lefèvre** was translating *City Guide: Paris*, Dr. Heinz Vestner of the APA Munich office suggested to her that she take over the responsiblity for the Alsace guide. Gaby Lefèvre, a North German by birth and a translator and interpeter by profession, has lived in Paris for 16 years and feels quite comfortable in her role as "immigrant." She took on the job with great enthusiasm. Alsace, the meeting point of German and French history and culture, is a subject that fits in well with her interests.

The Written Word

Grace Coston is "an American in Paris." She works as an author, translator and language teacher. The chapters on Paris and the Loire valley in *Insight Guide: France* are her work, and she came up with the concept for *City Guide: Paris*. You will recognise her enthusiasm for everything that she has come to know and love about France in the articles on Strasbourg.

Marton Radkai, too, is a familiar face at APA. He wrote the history section for the Paris guide and edited *Insight Guide: Hungary* which was published in May 1989. His father is Hungarian, his mother German. He grew up in Paris, London, Geneva and America, and speaks a corresponding number of languages. His knowledge of languages came in handy when leafing through the history books, trying to trace the course of Alsatian history obscured by patriotic and emotional wishful thinking.

G.Lefèvre

G. Coston

M. Radkai

E. Hagedorn

G. Gockel

Eliane Hagedorn writes book reviews, adapts the plots of novels for screenplays, and can often be found at book fairs. She also has a passion for translating comics and crime stories, so she is a real bookworm. She lives in Munich and is married to a Frenchman who lives in Grenoble: they often meet at a "halfway house", in Paris, Cannes or Colmar, the city she describes in this book.

Gabriele Gockel also lives in Munich. She doesn't have a husband in France, but has many friends there. She has close ties with the country and the people, as you can tell from reading her articles on Mulhouse, the Sundgau, the Route Joffre and the Picturesque Villages Route. Gabriele Gockel is an author, translator and teacher and loves travelling; she is a frequent visitor to Alsace.

Dr. Reiner Stephan works as an author in Munich and is one of those people who can digest the printed word in large quantities, but like to wash it down with a glass of good (preferably Alsatian) wine. The gourmet among our authors, Stephan, who knows Alsace well, will point out the restaurants along the Route du vin and in the Munster valley where you can eat and drink to your heart's content.

Another author from Munich, **Dr. Bernhard Jendricke**, is a writer and translator of books. Together with Gabriele Gockel, he founded the translators' collective *Druckreif*. A passionate traveller, who knows France well, he did not want to miss the opportunity of taking a close look at the areas around Saverne, between Strasbourg and Sélestat and around the Kochersberg.

Another German *emigré* in France is **Barbara Reynaud**. Originally a secondary school teacher by profession, she has now changed her career; she translates and writes *à domicile*. Her own personal hobbies are costume, traditional dress and arts and crafts. It's a pity that work and children leave her so little time. Her contribution, covering Alsatian traditional dress, is brief but excellent.

Monique Gilbert is quite a different kind of bookworm. She spends all her time in libraries looking for forgotten works on icons and paintings, her own specialty. As she spends nearly every day turning archives upside down, Gaby Lefèvre asked her to do it this time for the purpose of this book. Monique Gilbert has been familiar with Alsace since the last world war, and she thought that the job was not a bad idea at all. The result is the practical *Travel Tips* section at the end of the book.

Captured in Colour

Patrice Astier, a busy Paris photographer, could hardly imagine working as a landscape photographer when Gaby Lefèvre offered him the job. For him, photographing Alsace was a break from studio work, dark room and flashlights. "It was a holiday…" he says. We think Patrice should treat himself to "holidays" like this more often.

We wish to thank all those who have been helpful to us. The Bibliothèque Forney, the magazine *Spiegel*, the Maison d'Alsace and the Musée Carnevalet in Paris opened their archives for us. Everywhere we went in Alsace we found friendly assistance and support.

–Apa Publications

| *R. Stephan* | *B. Jendricke* | *B. Reynaud* | *M. Gilbert* | *P. Astier* |

INTRODUCTION

HISTORY AND CULTURE

MAPS

PLACES

PLACES

TRAVEL TIPS

"WHAT A BEAUTIFUL GARDEN…"

Louis XIV was obviously pleasantly surprised when he crossed the Vosges and saw Alsace for the first time.

Alsace—isn't that the really lovely place with the storks and the half-timbered houses, where the people wear traditional costumes, speak German, eat sauerkraut and drink beer or *Gewürztraminer*? Clichés survive for a long time but then again, they are never entirely wrong either.

We wanted to see what Alsace was really like and to take a close look at the country and the people. To start with the external appearance of Alsace: it consists of the two departments Bas-Rhin (Lower Rhine) to the north and Haut-Rhin (Upper Rhine) to the south. It lies wedged between the Alpine foothills to the south and the Vosges range to the west and north. Alsace is a neatly separated, long strip of land in the easternmost corner of France, along the river Rhine, which has always played a more or less disputed role as a national boundary. Natural boundaries rarely acted as obstacles to "nomadic peoples". Alsace is a living example of this fact: it may be a region with good natural borders, yet it has been sought out again and again by invaders, for Louis XIV was not the only one attracted by the "beautiful garden".

For a long time Alsace has been a melting pot of different cultures and influences. Its long history and its geographic position have had a corresponding influence. Alsace is a mosaic, right in the heart of Europe, of different peoples, religious denominations, economic systems and cultures. Strasbourg as the capital of Europe? Why not?

Alsace first: Yet this country, whose people are so vehement in the defence of their independent culture, is now part of France with its centralised government. A number of

Preceding pages: the blue line of the Vosges; typical Alsatian wine-growing country; overlooking the rooftops of Strasbourg; the colorful *Schlupfkappen* of the Catholics. <u>Left</u>, a welcome smile to the good life.

problems result from this. Paris has little understanding of any desire for regional identity and cultural independence. Alsatian dance groups may get state support, but if there's too much cultivation of regional traditions, and particularly when the issue of teaching Alsatian as well as French in schools is raised, the government fears the break-up of national culture and the rise of separatist tendencies. Whatever Alsace may "propose", it's Paris that "disposes". Paris even dumped the atomic power station of Fessenheim on the Alsatians, but by now they seem to be reconciled to their fate. The French papers claim that the only people who still get upset about it are the German "Greens". And anyway, claims the government, an atomic power station does have its good side: jobs!

People have settled from all over in Alsace. The Alsatian towns may be expanding, but that doesn't entail any depopulation of rural areas. Every corner of Alsace is part of the great jigsaw made up of different kinds of agriculture, forests and hills, together with the villages, large or small but in all cases cosy with that "operetta look" typical for Alsace—clean, half-timbered houses decorated with flowers. Such houses are incidentally still being built and decorated in the traditional style; Alsatian masons and carpenters have obviously not forgotten their old skills. This doesn't mean that time has stood still; traditional and modern lifestyles exist side by side in Alsace.

Now is the time to take the opportunity of working your way through this jigsaw. We hope that our travel guide can help you.

In the first part, a short summary will acquaint you with the history of the country and its people. This is followed by several articles which will inform you about the economy and the geography, the vernacular architecture, the traditional costume, festivals and language of the country.

The second part contains descriptions of the most important cities: Strasbourg, Colmar and Mulhouse. The section deals with the countryside and will show you the most beautiful routes through Alsace, where you can get to know the beauty of the countryside and its culinary, oenologocal and artistic specialties.

The third part contains practical information and important facts about important places and their interesting sights.

A final word before you set out: you will need a good temper and some patience. You will have to put up with some long waits and traffic jams in the most popular areas such as the Wine Route, for tourism is as essential to Alsace as fat bacon is to sauerkraut. Alsace is particularly popular for weekend breaks and short holidays.

The region is attractive at any time of year. There is plenty of snow in winter, and winter sports fans can enjoy the danger-free downhill and the very popular cross-country skiing to their hearts' content, particularly in the Vosges. You can also enjoy the winter with much less elaborate equipment, such as a toboggan or simply a pair of weatherproof shoes. There are plenty of trails for walking and hiking. Spring is very attractive to ramblers from March to May, as the weather is mainly dry, the fruit trees and the famous fields of daffodils are in bloom.

Alsace flourishes in summer and, apart from the very pleasant weather, offers everything you need in the way of activities and recreation to make a perfect summer holiday. The autumn is also an excellent time to travel, with its splendid colours, the wine harvests and of course the wine festivals which take place in many of the villages.

There is no real "high season" for Alsace, but something for everyone. Nature lovers will appreciate the many nature reserves and the unique flora and fauna of the Alsace. Gourmets and lovers of fine arts will also find plenty to satisfy them. As far as the latter group is concerned, Alsace offers many interesting museums, magnificent churches, monasteries, chapels and other historic buildings.

We would like to wish you a very enjoyable trip through an Alsace rich in traditions.

Right, few places have as many medieval buildings and walls as the towns of Alsace.

25

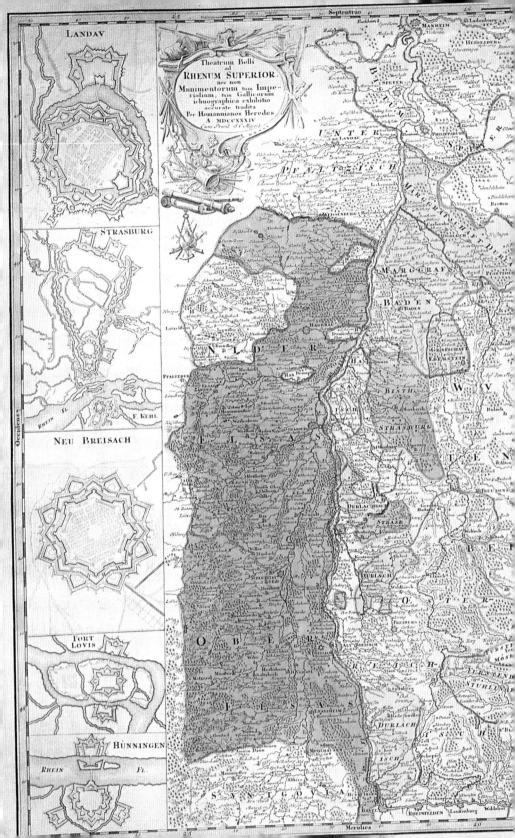

Origins: Alsace, it must be admitted, was never either the tribal grounds of a particular people or a true province. Rather, it represents an attitude of mind which has developed over many battles and over the centuries. Squeezed between the Rhine in the east and the Vosges in the west, Alsace has served many masters. It has been the buffer zone between different empires, the meeting place of vagabond armies, a football in the game of European politics, a yoyo in the hands of many a tyrant.

Alsace was rich and industrialisation came early. The Alsatians and their rulers were obliged to fill state coffers, either by means of trade taxes or simply by plundering the country. In this way Alsace has contributed to the contents of cupboards, cellars, wardrobes and factories in many European countries, from Göteborg via Rome and Budapest to London. Small wonder, then, that this little province in the plain, just 20 km (12.4 miles) broad and lying between the west bank of the Rhine and the eastern slopes of the Vosges, was desired by many and was always an interesting piece of booty.

Back to the question of origins: where exactly does Alsace belong, anyway? The languages of the Alsatians provide no answer. Apart from French, Romance, Germanic and Alemannic dialects survive. Is there any way of deciding where the country belongs? Even the origin of the name Alsace is puzzling. Which is the true explanation: the Germanic *Alis-lauti-sat* (those people from over there), the Celtic *Alis-atin* (at the foot of the hills), or the Germanic *Ell-sass* (those who live on the banks of the Ill)?

Alsace was densely populated in Celtic times and famed as far as the Balkans for the artistic skill of its inhabitants. Already by this time the Germanic tribes had done well out of the power struggles among the Celts (Sequani, Mediomatrici and Raurici) and

had settled in the northern and eastern parts of Gaul by the time Caesar's legions arrived. The Germanic tribes, with their warpaint and savage battle cries, broke Gallic resistance without too much trouble. However, these "savages" made little impression on the well-organised Roman legions. After an unsuccessful attempt in 58 B.C. to deal with the German leader Ariovistus, Caesar switched to attack and taught the stubborn tribes a lesson in a battle which is believed to

have taken place on the shores of the Rhine.

Alsace and Rome: Alsace flourished under the Pax Romana. Old roads were improved and new ultra-modern ones built, complete with contemporary "motels" such as Tres Tabernae (Three Taverns). Trade also began to flourish at about this time. By A.D. 3, Roman families could enjoy Alsatian wines and sausages. Alsace was one of the most important strategic centres of the Roman Empire. This was the place where armies gathered to prepare for attacks on Germanic territory. It was also the place where the Germans made their first camp when it was

Left, Alsace in the 18th century (1734): the Sundgau is still an independent region. **Above**, Celtic jewellery.

their turn to attack the Roman armies and their vassals.

Of course the presence of the Roman armies also brought cultural progress and the benefits of civilisation. Complete garrison towns such as Argentoratum (Strasbourg), Mons Brisiacus (Brisach) and Saletio (Seltz) were built practically from nothing, and probably possessed baths, amphitheatres, taverns, markets and temples, although unfortunately no notable remains have survived. In the cities, Roman and Gaulish religions either existed side by side or merged.

even got as far as Spain. In A.D. 355 Constantine II sent his son Julian to check the dangerous tribes of the Alemanni. Julian moved his headquarters to Saverne and in A.D. 357 he defeated the invaders near Strasbourg. However, this victory brought a brief respite to the Roman rulers.

A colourful succession of Vandals, Goths, Franks and Alemanni invaded and flattened cities and villages. Anything left standing was stormed by Attila's hordes. In A.D. 451 all the combined forces of Aetius, the last of the great Roman generals, were able to de-

Druidism survived long in rural areas. In such places, old traditions were passed down to the present day. The summer and winter solstices are still celebrated. Christianity spread quickly through the Empire. In A.D. 3, Strasbourg became the centre of the Mithras cult, that mysterious religion from the Middle East by the *legionnaires*.

After a long pause, broken here and there by attacks from an easterly direction, and also by periods of peace and co-operation, pressure from the Germanic tribes began to increase. In A.D. 275 the Germans invaded Gaul and in the subsequent campaign they

feat the Huns, but by this time the Roman Empire had been a thing of the past.

Merovingians and Carolingians: The brutal king of the Salian Franks, whose name Chlodwig was latinised as Clovis, prepared his way to power over western Europe by defeating the Alemanni and other tribes in A.D. 496 and eliminating real or imagined rivals. He made Paris his capital. The dynasties of the Carolingians and Merovingians controlled the fate of Europe for almost 500 years, yet they produced few outstanding leaders during this time. Clovis, however, was one of them. He delegated his authority to counts, and used them together with his military leaders and dukes to set up a powerful and independent aristocracy. He soon recognised the advantages of an alliance with the Church and was converted to Christianity, also converting himself into a powerful "enemy of the heathen".

After Clovis' death in A.D. 511 his three sons divided the kingdom into Austrasia, Neustria and Burgundy. Alsace was pushed from one to the other until it finally became part of Austrasia. However, the succession, which was never straightforward, kept the

personalities. However, by the middle of the 8th century, their power was broken once more, for reasons unknown.

With the spread of Christianity, many missionaries appeared in the province, persuading the still partially pagan population of the advantages of Christianity. In the 6th century St. Argobastes became the first Bishop of Alsace. He was followed by a line of Irish priests. During this time the church of St. Martin was built in Strasbourg. Monasteries, chapels and oratories were built all over the province. Eticho's daughter Odilia,

various members of the royal family busy putting paid to each other's chances. Provincial matters did not receive enough attention. The Alsatian nobility, led by its dukes, developed into an independent power, as it no longer had to suffer curbs or controls. In the 7th century Eticho I manoeuvred skilfully and successfully at getting the ducal status to become hereditary. The Etichonian dynasty provided Alsace with a number of important

Left, the Heathen Wall (St. Odile), a relic of Alsatian ancient history. **Above**, Roman relief near Horbourg.

later canonised and made patron saint of Alsace in 1807, founded a monastery near Obernai. Although marked by centuries of war and destruction and by much rebuilding, the place is still opened to visitors.

The Merovingian dynasty was at its last gasp when interest in Alsace of the inhabitants on the opposite bank of the Rhine revived once more. They too knew all about the wealth of Alsace. In A.D. 742 rebellious Alemanni and Bavarians had to be expelled. Pippin the Younger, the first of the Carolingians, began his campaign of subjugation. His successor Charlemagne fought the Saxons in the "Germany" of the time for more than 20 years.

The new Carolingian dynasty was considerably more effective than the old one. However, in A.D. 829 quarrels within the dynasty and the empire caused an unfortunate situation which was to have long-lasting consequences for Alsace. Louis the Pious had three sons: Lothar, Pippin and Louis the German. After the death of his wife, Louis the Pious married Judith of Bavaria, who gave him another son, Charles the Bald. Each member of the family was eyeing the between Colmar and Kayersberg. The Pope attempted to deal with Louis the Pious, while the three brothers intrigued, tried to get their father's army to withdraw their support for him. The Field of Red entered the chronicles as the "Field of Lies". Eventually, Alsace fell into the hands of Louis the German, who put his parents and his half-brother in prison.

In A.D. 837 Louis the Pious was freed again, but instead of sitting back to enjoy his retirement, he freed Charles the Bald and his mother and put his property back in order. Two years later, just as order was returning

inheritance of the others. A power struggle developed and drained the strength of the ruling house. Hugo, one of the Dukes of Alsace and a descendant of Eticho, former right hand of Charlemagne, smoothed over the family quarrel by marrying one of his daughters to Lothar and promising another daughter to Judith's brother.

At first Alsace was part of Lothar's inheritance, but in A.D. 829 his father changed his will and gave the province to the six-year-old Charles. The three elder sons were not inclined to take this lying down, and so in A.D. 833 the Battle of the Field of Red was fought to Louis' kingdom, Lothar reappeared in Alsace to claim his original inheritance.

Louis the Pious had barely been buried when Lothar tried to take Charles the Bald's inheritance by force. Charles turned to his half-brother Louis the German for help. The latter left for Alsace at once and got there in A.D. 842. However, the Treaty of Verdun gave Alsace back to Lothar in A.D. 843. His German-speaking brother Louis was now to the east of Alsace, and his French-speaking half-brother Charles to the west. This was how the shape of Western Europe came to be, with Alsace practically in the middle.

Eticho's successor Hugo had died in A.D. 837. After the death of Lothar (A.D. 855), Lothar II inherited the northern part of the former's lands, which included Alsace, by now heavily buffeted by fate. Lothar II's wife soon proved to be barren, but his mistress Walrade bore him a son, who was baptised Hugon. Lothar II spent a great deal of his political career trying to have his first marriage annulled, but with no success. One needed influential connections to obtain an annulment in those days. Lothar asked for help from all sides and in utmost secrecy he

forced to look to their borders, as Vikings, Saracens, Moldavians and Magyars invaded the country from all sides. No wonder Hugon saw his chance of achieving independence for Alsace and Lorraine. But his attempt failed because the Carolingians for once were in agreement on one point: they did not want "islands" ruled by strangers within their territories. So they had Hugon taken prisoner, blinded and incarcerated in the monastery of St. Gallen. Alsace was once more under the direct control of the Carolingians. In 912, 917 and 921 France tried

offered Alsace as the prize. After Lothar II's death Charles the Bald repeated his claim to the lands on the west bank of the Rhine. However, in Meersen in A.D. 870 the cunning Louis produced the records of Lothar's deal involving Alsace from his pocket and walked off with the province.

German Alsace: Louis left the ruling of Alsace to the son of Lothar II, Hugon. Meanwhile, the last of the Carolingians were

Left, Charlemagne and an early Christian ceiling fresco in La Petite Pierre. **Above,** a ceiling mosaic in St. Odile depicting the Holy Family.

repeatedly to annex Alsace but the rulers of the Teutonic empire reconquered it every time. Henry I, of the Hohenstaufen dynasty, proved particularly stubborn. In 925 Alsace was incorporated into the *Regnum teutonicorum* as part of the Duchy of Swabia and Alsace. Then, when the Magyars rode through Western Europe, Henry signed an agreement with them which obviously did not include Alsace. In A.D. 926 he watched nonchalantly as the nobility of Alsace, led by Luitfried II, fought the Magyars in a battle as bloody as it was senseless.

It was Otto II who finally defeated the

31

Magyars near Augsburg in A.D. 955. This battle earned him the title "the Great". He also kept the quarrelsome, power-hungry princes in his provinces down, including those of Alsace.

The great cities: At the end of the first millenium Alsace looked forward to a rosy future. The furious invasions of the barbarian tribes had ended. France was more interested in stabilising the rule of the Capets than in the events on its eastern borders. The nobility of Alsace had to pay tribute to the Empire, but they could decide local issues for themselves, and the Bishop of Strasbourg was even allowed to mint coins. In 1002 a certain Werner, from the upper ranks of Alsatian society, first made a name for himself. Later he had a castle built and called it *Habichtsburg* (Hawk Castle) which then changed to *Habsburg*, the name of the dynasty which was to play a decisive role in Alsatian history.

Once again, a long period of peace ended in strife and warfare. The house of Eguisheim, who ruled northern Alsace, backed the wrong side in the long drawn out dispute between the secular rulers and Rome. In 1048 Bruno of Eguisheim was elected, with the help of Emperor Henry II, as Pope Leo IX. He showed himself to be a follower of the Cluny movement and planned church reforms. (Leo IX's fame is also due to the following incident: he had led an army against the Normans in Sicily, which was under the administration of Constantinople. The Patriarch of the church in Constantinople complained of this unjustified intervention, whereupon Leo IX simply excommunicated him and laid the foundations for the later schism between the Roman Catholic and Orthodox churches). Henry II's heir Henry IV viewed the influence of Rome with unease. In the end, he handed Alsace over to his confidant, Frederick of Hohenstaufen, who placed his own brother in the bishopric of Strasbourg and divided the wealth of the Eguisheims among others.

Apart from the struggles of power politics, there was peace, and the German noble families such as the Werds, Oettingens and Geroldsecks could continue to increase their fortunes. Many fortified castles, once they had served their wartime purposes, were turned into residences for counts and princes. It was the flowering of the Middle Ages. Troubadours came from France to share in the wealth. Colmar, Haguenau and Strasbourg later became centres of the famous medieval minstrels, the Minnesänger and Meistersänger. It was around this time

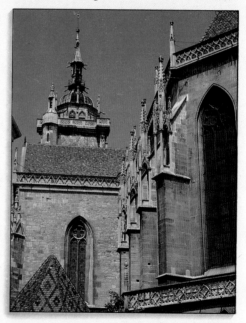

that Gottfried of Strasbourg put the Celtic legend of Tristan and Isolde into German.

Decapolis: Medieval developments in economics and politics brought about the rise of a new, wealthy class in the cities—the bourgeoisie. This class of merchants and craftsmen organised and supported powerful guilds. They soon began to rival the upper classes and the aristocracy. The Hohenstaufen dynasty at once recognised the value of this new class and offered them tasks and opportunities for income, thus encouraging them to defy the clerics and the aristocrats, both controlled by Rome.

Left, one of the Hohenstaufen castle ruins. **Above**, Gothic cathedral of St. Martin in Colmar.

33

In 1201 Strasbourg achieved the status of Imperial City. It was followed by Sélestat, Colmar, Kaysersberg and others. Once Strasbourg had established a city council and had been given the right to mint coins by the Bishop of Strasbourg, it became a Free Imperial City. The church followed these developments with anxiety, and the Bishop of Strasbourg soon had to defend himself against so much wordly power. The aristocracy was divided. When the episcopal army occupied Colmar in 1263, Rudolf of Habsburg hastened to free the city.

There was renewed trouble when rival factions among the upper bourgeoisie tried to maintain control of the guilds, the legal system and the right to mint coins entirely to themselves. In 1332 the people of Strasbourg finally had enough, and they drove these rivals out of the city and from the city council. They formed a new government led by *Stettmestres* (city masters). In 1361 the people of Colmar followed suit.

The only way for the towns to gain their independence was to unite. Ten towns joined the union, *Decapolis*, between 1342 and

The development of the cities into new centres of political power came at the right time. In 1268 the Habsburg dynasty replaced the house of Hohenstaufen. The new dynasty abandoned local control of politics in favour of direct control from the centre. They appointed noble families as representatives of government, who above all excelled themselves as tax collectors. Life in Alsace was somewhat anarchic, especially since the families, to get hold of money quickly, fought with each other for the privilege of collecting taxes. The cites were vulnerable when faced with such "robber barons".

1354: Colmar, Haguenau, Rosheim, Landau, Oberehnheim, Wissembourg, Munster, Kaysersberg, Turkheim and St. Gregoriental. Strasbourg remained a free city.

Hard times: The 14th century began with famines and natural catastrophes. During the search for a scapegoat for the misery, a former innkeeper named "King Leatherarm" (he and his followers wore leather sleeves) led a horde of ruffians against Alsatian Jews, who were brutally ill-treated. Such acts of "heroism" were undoubtedly lucrative. In 1337 the oppressors had captured 1,500 Jews and were about to storm the city of

Colmar, but Prince Louis of Bavaria came to the rescue. The average Alsatian had little in common with "King Leatherarm", but as the "black plagues" continued to decimate the the Alsatians, hysteria broke out. Leatherarm's adherents sprang out from behind every street corner, and protest slogans against the Jews were shouted in the cities.

On 14 February 1349 about 2,000 Jews were burned at the stakes in Strasbourg. At the same time, all existing debts to Jewish moneylenders were invalidated, Jewish property was confiscated and the survivors

The dubious figure of one Enguerrand de Coucy, a leader of mercenaries, attacked the province in 1369. After the event, he sent cordial messages of friendship to the towns, but few seemed to want to trust him. After senseless military campaigns which lasted seven years and included an attack on Switzerland, de Coucy moved westwards.

Seventy years later, the French king Charles VII, together with his Dauphin (later Louis XI) and the Armagnacs, tried to incorporate Alsace into France. After a few victories of a military and diplomatic nature, the

of the pogrom were expelled from the towns.

Meanwhile France, after the mixed success of the centuries-old struggle against the English, began to feel a little squeezed within its borders and turned towards the east, to see if a few extra parcels of territory could be gained there. The Habsburgs, by contrast, were showing signs of tiring, having already lost Switzerland to a handful of peasants who opposed them with flails.

war came to a standstill. The French had no desire for a bloody war with the Habsburgs, and their army—known to the Alsatians as "butchers"—had done nothing to gain the affections of the people of the country.

One day the Habsburg Frederick II gave the province away to the Burgundian Duke Charles. The Alsatians were not pleased with such a transaction made above their heads, and with the help of the Swiss and the Duke of Lorraine, they waged a war against Charles. Charles died in fighting near Nancy, and Louis XI tried his luck again. He wanted to marry his ten-year-old son to the

Far left, Charles VII, the French king, who wanted to add Alsace to his dominions. **Left**, the baptism of Clovis. **Above**, Louis XI.

18-year-old Burgundian heiress, but she preferred to marry her contemporary, Maximilian of Habsburg, son of Frederick II.

The Reformation: In Italy the Habsburgs were fighting François I. The wars cost many human lives and a great deal of money. But they also brought the splendours of the Renaissance to France. On the other side of the country's eastern border the Reformation began to spread, for the plutocratic tendencies of the church had been making enemies since the 15th century. Johann Geiler, an Alsatian satirist, remarked *"De Pfoaffe*

aim. The Reformation surged through Alsace. At the same time rebellious peasants marched on Saverne, Wissembourg and other towns and seized them.

The Habsburgs were too busy with the French and left the suppression of the peasants to the local nobility, who addressed themselves to the task with great savagery in 1525. For this purpose, Duke Antoine of Lorraine and Claude de Guise were in command of the army. Peasants who had barricaded themselves in Saverne were offered safe conduct if they surrendered, but the trick

han ds' fill" (the priests are too wealthy). Thanks to the invention of the printing press, such radical writings and ideas could be copied and distributed.

In 1491 the Bundschuh rebellion, named after the wooden shoe worn by peasants, broke out. It was a union of country dwellers under the leadership of Johann Ulmann, the *Stettmestre* of Sélestat. He himself was quartered, but the Bundschuh remained. Luther's 95 Theses which he nailed to the church door in Wittenberg were attractive to the Bundschuh and to other groups in revolt, even though rebellion had hardly been Luther's

was as old as the history of warfare itself, and the number of slaughtered and wounded peasants ran into several tens of thousands.

However, around 1525, the Reformation had spread throughout Alsace and the surrounding provinces, despite opposition from the Pope and Charles V. One province after another joined the Schmalkadic League. Charles V may have succeeded in gaining a victory at Mühlberg in the Schmalkadic War, and there may still have been plenty of Catholics, but by this time (between 1561 and 1681) the bishops of Strasbourg could only carry out their duties in Saverne.

Since the Christian world split in two halves, it was inevitable that civil conflict should follow. It was business as usual in Alsace, but the atmosphere was already noticeably more tense. The Reformation made slow headway in France, but after half a century, the Protestants there were also a political power to be counted on.

Paris, that most Catholic of cities, was in turmoil, but between François I (who stirred up Protestant German princes against the Habsburgs) with his relatively tolerant government and Henri II, who was able to ex-

and then on into Germany, where people were friendlier towards them. They took with them their knowledge, their wealth and their love of Renaissance art. Not only that; they brought also the French language to the eastern territories.

The Thirty Years' War: In 1618 the situation was reversed. There was peace once more in France under the wise rule of Henri IV, and the Thirty Years' War had broken out in Central Europe. Armies marched through countries and cities, destroying, burning, raping women and girls. All these were done

pand his empire by skilful alliances but was only interested in upholding law and order at home, the Parisians were hardly able to express their rage.

Civil war broke out after the death of Henri II and plunged the country into turmoil and horror for about 40 years. Thousands of people were killed, and many Protestants with all their belongings moved to Alsace

in the name of Christianity, and of course a soldier could change sides then and again, according to how things were going and who was paying more.

In France, Louis XIII and Cardinal Richelieu watched the developments with interest. When the Swedish king Gustavus Adolphus joined the war on the Protestant side, it was the Protestant-hater Richelieu, of all people, who supported him.

The Swedes overran Alsace. Some towns such as Strasbourg welcomed them, others such as Colmar offered resistance. But all of them had to pay tribute, whichever course

Far left, Louis XIV, who said "The customs of Alsace are not to be interfered with." **Left**, synagogue in Sélestat. **Above**, carpenter's workshop in the early Industrial Age.

37

they took. The Peace of Westfalia assigned Alsace to France. After 49 years and several wars, this treaty was ratified in Rijkswijk in 1697. Mulhouse remained a free city, flirting with Switzerland, until it joined France "of its own free will" during the Revolution.

French Alsace: Military support for the province was one thing, incorporating it was quite another. At first absolutely nothing was done, as the French king was busy restraining rebellious nobility, the Fronde, in his own country. However, Alsace was then put under the rule of Colbert de Croissy, the

aristocrats or other opportunists, who looked for help from the west from time to time in order to advance their own affairs, do not constitute hard evidence. In most cases Alsace minded its own business and occasionally sent out feelers eastwards or in the direction of Switzerland.

Louis XIV knew how to manage his new property. *"Ne pas toucher aux usages d'Alsace."* ("The traditions and customs of Alsace should not be interfered with.") was his maxim. Even when he started to persecute Protestants in France, he left the

brother of the Colbert who was Minister of Finance under Louis XIV. The long wars had decimated the population, and many of the farmers who survived had emigrated to Poland or Hungary, to start a new life there with their families.

Most of the French-Alsatian historians of the 20th century have taken great pains to convince their readership and probably also themselves that the Alsatians had only one idea during the 800 years of Teutonic rule—to become part of France at all costs. Unfortunately there is no proof of such a state of mind. Even the power intrigues of some

followers of the new religion who lived in Alsace in peace. The Bourbon yoke was not too heavy on the little province by the Rhine.

The economy of Alsace, left to its own resources, flourished. Workshops were built and factories opened their gates. Strasbourg became a trade centre for tobacco, beer and metalwork. In Mulhouse, Dollfus, Koechlin and Schmaltzer opened their textile works.

The Enlightenment did not stop at the borders of Alsace, either. Philosophy and politics were discussed in the salons of Alsace too. Influential Jewish families such as Cerfberr and Isaac Beer brought the works of

Moses Mendelssohn and the Haggada into the country and contributed to the emancipation of the Jews during the Revolution. Friedrich Oberlin followed in Pestalozzi's footsteps. In 1769 Conrad Pfeffel set up a literary society in Colmar. The Alsatian universities drew students from all over Europe: Goethe, Herder and Metternich studied at the Protestant university of Strasbourg.

However, dark clouds had begun to gather in the skies over Alsace. As there was no real centralised administration, the local aristocracy and the aristocratic landlords took a

Alsace, and industry moved out. The result was unemployment on a large scale, and the people became more and more impoverished. A peaceful century had its price. The Age of Humanism was drawing to an end.

The Revolution: The Revolution aroused passions in Alsace as much as anywhere else in France. Palaces were burned, monasteries reduced to rubble and ashes. As early as the first year Alsace was appended to France in the form of two departments, and its representatives—one of them was the anti-Semitic François Rebwell—swore loyalty to

fairly free and easy attitude towards taxing the population. The extravagant life at the Bourbon court, which was to provoke the Revolution at the end of the century, needed to be financed. And of course it was the less affluent of society who had to foot the bill for the luxury and extravagance of the rulers. After a while corruption began to spread more and more throughout the towns of

France. The church made vain claims for its state-appropriated properties. The Alsatian resolve did waver: they couldn't get on with the new clergy imposed on them by the state and complained bitterly about the emancipation of the Jews. But Louis XVI's attempt to flee recharged the emotional batteries of the Alsatians. It should also be remembered that the *Marseillaise* was composed by Rouget de l'Isle in Strasbourg.

However, as the Revolution progressed the Alsatians began to waver once again. The time of the Terror, the many invasions, the *Sans-Culottes* with their extermination

Far left, swearing loyalty on the French Tricolore. **Left**, Napoleon won the hearts of the Alsatians. **Above**, Catholics in their traditional clothes on the way to church.

campaign against spies and anyone not of their opinion, the ideological feuds and the endless requisitions were just too much for the average Alsatian. The cathedral in Strasbourg, like many other religious buildings, was turned into a "Temple of Reason". Gerold, the police chief of the city, just managed to save a few statues before the "fundamentalists" among the revolutionaries could demolish them from the facade.

Napoleon not only saw to law and order, but his patriotic message inspired the Alsatians. The general, later consul and finally

tives began to flourish afterwards for trade and business. Many companies reopened their doors. Iron ore, lead and copper were mined, and there was drilling for oil for the production of asphalt. New roads and canals were built. Alsace kept politics at arm's length and gently celebrated all the changes taking place in Paris, while concentrating on its business affairs.

France, controlled from the centre as always, kept the little eastern province on a leash. Those Alsatians who spoke French managed to make sense of the administra-

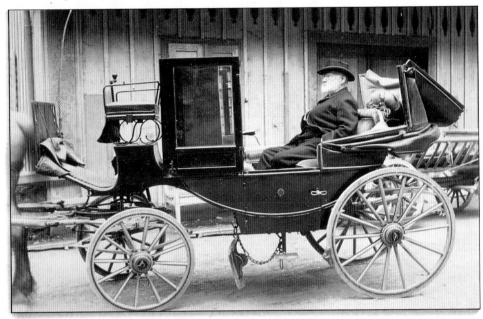

emperor, appointed several efficient generals who came from Alsace, among them Kellermann and Kleber. Napoleon's empire collapsed, but the patriotic spirit remained. When Napoleon returned from Elba to take power once more, he could count on the support of Alsace, even though the city council of Strasbourg had hastily declared its loyalty to the king. Waterloo buried the very last hopes, but Sélestat, Belfort and Huningue bravely resisted the Prussian invaders called in by Louis XVIII.

The Revolution had done great damage to Alsatian industry. However, private initia-

tion, but for the others it was *tant pis* (tough luck). The attempt to get the Alsatians to speak French by force came much too late. When Germany conquered the province in 1871, a referendum was held. Only 12.5 per cent of the population voted to belong to France, a fact which spoke volumes.

In those times life was very hard for the working class. The workers sweated for 11 to 15 hours a day, and their children laboured in the mines and factories. There was no universal education. Social insurance and protection for mothers just didn't exist.

Back in the German empire: Becoming part

of the German empire did not please everyone by any means. In 1870 France declared war on Prussia and lost. The Prussians took Strasbourg without any difficulty. Belfort held out bravely until 18 February 1871, later than Paris. Alsace and Lorraine became new properties for Prussia. Bismarck was not at all sure of himself when he demanded the two provinces. He felt certain that a new war against France would be the inevitable result. Adolphe Thiers had no choice; he was forced to accept the break-up of French territory. The Assemblée grumbled, and Victor

Alsace did not become a German state (Land) such as Württemberg, but remained a Reichsland under the direct control of the emperor. The assembly or Landtag which was created in 1911 did nothing to change this fact. Many Alsatians felt that the Prussians had gone over their heads. Understandably, they wanted more power in the state administration of their own country, and demanded not only the recognition of their dialect but also the respect of the dual Alsatian culture. In 1913, a few insulting remarks by a German lieutenant about the

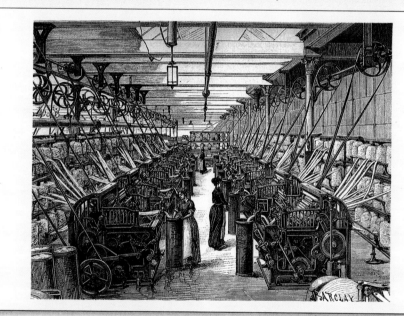

Hugo, then a delegate, thundered words of warning eastwards; revenge was his slogan. Many pondered over what he did.

Prussia made every attempt to Germanise Alsace. Compulsory education was introduced, but French was not on the curriculum. Bismarck brought in social reforms, including the most modern social security system in all of Europe.

Left, the patriot Victor Hugo wanted revenge for the German annexation of Alsace after the Franco-Prussian War in 1871. Above, factory at the end of the 19th century.

the Alsatians led to a revolt in Saverne. However, the rebels' wish to realise their claims for greater self-rule prevented them from supporting an alliance which had the aim of returning Alsace to France. They preferred to achieve more autonomy within the Empire. René Schickele (1883-1940), journalist, poet and author, born of a German father and a French mother, was one of those Alsatians who succeeded in putting their dilemma into words. His trilogy *Erbe am Rhein* (*Inheritance on the Rhine*) makes clear to families what it means to be torn between two nations.

Back in France again: After World War I, Alsace was part of France again. At first an executive council was set up which was supposed to rule the province, but by 1924 it had been dissolved and the two Alsatian departments were added among the "also rans" in the list of French national territory. Representatives of the French government took up administrative posts and indiscriminately imposed all laws made in Paris on the Alsatians. Suddenly the Alsatians found themselves having to pay enormously high taxes and to speak French again. Alsatian banks, railways and industries were administered by France, and that was where the profits went. The government in Paris managed to turn almost all Alsatians against the move, except for those who had returned from France after 1918.

The Catholic church, oppressed by the Protestant Prussians, thought its time had arrived at last, but realised that church and state were now separate in France and that education was a secular activity. Abbé Haegi and Abbé Fassauer founded the *Union Populaire Républicaine* (UPR), which defended the rights of the clergy and kept up political and social traditions.

Other political parties were founded at this time, among them the liberal *Partie du Progrès*, and the Alsatian proletariat supported the Communist party, especially since the French government of the 1920s did not have a progressive set of social security laws similar to the one established by the German administration at the end of the 19th century. The Alsatian Communists fought for more rights in local government and in the decision-making of public affairs, finally demanding the "evacuation" of the whole province. Strasbourg elected a Communist mayor. In 1927 Carl Roos founded the *Partie Autonomiste*. Alsace was swamped with pamphlets and handbills demanding autonomy.

The government in Paris showed no understanding of the causes of the general dissatisfaction of Alsace and blamed the autonomist movement on German agitators, a very naive theory which still surfaces in

serious historical works today.

In 1927 some of the leaders of the autonomist movement were arrested, among them Rickling, Hauss and Fasshauer. Roos escaped to Germany. A trial in Colmar aroused much interest and ended with many not-guilty verdicts, as there was no evidence that the accused had tried to undermine French security. France's politics only made the autonomists more radical than ever and practically forced them to the German side, which also offered financial and moral support. The German influence became even

more marked when Hitler came to power.

New political groups were formed, based on Nazi models, such as Hermann Bickler's *Jungmannschaft*, Josef Bilger's farmers' union *Union Paysanne* and the workers' association *Front National du Travail*. As early as 1933 the Communists decided to withdraw from the Alsatian front, and in 1936 their leader, Maurice Thorez, opposed all separatist tendencies.

The final chapter: All hopes of gaining an independent Alsace were now lost. In addition, the unfortunate experiences of France under Pétain and the collaborators, who formed a government approved by the Nazis in Vichy. Under Nazi rule, Alsace became a colony of Hitler's. Any autonomists who hoped to gain something like an independent state followed the Gauleiter Robert Wagner. Men such as Stürmel and Rossé gained high positions in Nazi Alsace, but were later arrested for not showing confidence in the Third Reich. For the Nazis, they were no more than puppets. Alsatian men fought on the eastern front in World War II. Many fought only because they were forced to, but some believed in Hitler's cause.

The autonomists had begun a dangerous game and finally lost on all sides, with the Nazis and with the French. By co-operating with the Nazis they put Alsace, for whose independence they were fighting, into an extremely difficult position. Two concentration camps had been built in their country—Schirmeck and Struthof—and thousands of French and Alsatians died there. The little province, which also produced a strong resistance group, was split, and in this state it came under the control of France.

After the war, Alsace, destroyed by bombs, had to be rebuilt. The difficult work of restoration cooled off a few separatist hotheads and allowed the image of World War II to pale gradually. However, the economic boom of the 1950s blew a few clouds away from the skies of Alsace.

Now that Germans were almost universally despised everywhere in the world, it was easy for the French government to ensure that the curricula of Alsatian schools contained only the French language, and to impose a French patriotism on the Alsatians.

Ever since the 1960s, the desire of the Alsatians to achieve at least cultural independence has been reviving, but little is happening on the political level. Only high unemployment and economic stagnation have managed to produce a few sparks (mostly on the Right). The racist message of the right-wing radical Jean-Marie Le Pen gained many Alsatian votes in the 1988 presidential elections. His campaign posters showed the cathedral spire in Strasbourg bearing the crescent of Islam, together with an Alsatian woman wearing the *chador*.

In A.D. 842 it was Louis the German and Charles the Bald who split up Europe between them. Ever since then, Alsace has not only been a witness to the eventful political struggles of history, but has also often enough been in the midst of the battles between the "giants".

In Alsace the battlefields of ancient and recent times are greater in number than in many other countries. Many military cemeteries, such as those at Cernay, Orbey, Wattwiller or Froeschwiller, are eternal memorials to the need for peace. In 1949, 1,107 years after the division of Western Europe, Alsace became a symbol for the unification of the continent through the founding of the Council of Europe (with its seat symbolically placed in Strasbourg).

The people of an unified Europe which is still to be created will, of course, need to speak several languages. Let us hope that Alsace will now get its opportunity!

Left, the Botanical Gardens in Strasbourg with the Conservatoire du Musique. **Above**, the Palais d'Europe, seat of the Council of Europe.

43

THE PEOPLE AND LANGUAGES OF ALSACE

May we just clear a few clichés out of the way first? It should really have got around by now that the Alsatians build nothing but half-timbered houses or wear traditional costumes all the time, if only because of the plans for the region's future development—after all, Strasbourg is intended to become the capital of Europe. The Alsatians can't survive on agriculture and tourism alone. Nor do they want a diet solely of sauerkraut washed down by *Gewürztraminer*. The "stage Alsatian" has become a myth.

However, most of the landscape is still very beautiful, and its inhabitants try to keep their natural surroundings unspoilt. There are still storks, and the Alsatians try to protect both them and the landscape that is their habitat, or otherwise to re-settle them with little disturbance in suitable places.

What about the Alsatian language? Alsace has several languages to offer. It is an interesting fact that the Germanic-Romance language border, which has nothing to do with any national borders, runs through Belgium, the northeast of France, Alsace and Switzerland. It runs between the Vosges and the Alsatian plain. The Franks, who settled in the Vosges in the 5th and 6th centuries, took up Romance dialects which are still spoken today. It is not possible to say exactly when the Germanic and Alemannic dialects were first spoken in Alsace, although it is certain that they were spoken as early as the 5th century.

Since dialects are transmitted orally, they differ from area to area, although there are no problems in communicating from one Romance dialect to another. The large Jewish community should not be forgotten. They have lived in Alsace since the Middle Ages and speak their form of Yiddish, a mix of middle-high German and Hebrew. This language is spoken in daily situations, in the village or just within the home. The language of most daily transactions is French, al-

though the Alsatians often use dialects when conversing among themselves. It is said that the dialects are dying out, but few families have entirely abandoned theirs for the national language. Languages that have existed for over 1,500 years don't disappear overnight. The Alsatians have shown themselves to be very strong-minded when the survival of their cultural inheritance was at stake. Who would dare to rob them of their special characteristics?

Alsatian Alsace: A man, drowning in the Rhine near Strasbourg, shouts *"Au secours!"* An Alsatian watches him impassively from the shore and calls out: "You'd have done better to learn swimming instead of French!"

Despite, perhaps even because of, the many invasions from all points of the compass and the subsequent difficulties with which they have had to struggle, the Alsatians have still kept their sense of humour, which sometimes can be quite sarcastic.

Keeping Alsace Alsatian has not been easy over the last few years, for the Alsatians had to battle with bureaucrats who saw sup-

Left, one Alsatian's obliging smile. **Above**, tuba player in one of the countless Alsatian folk festivals.

port for cultural independence as a threat to the integrity of the French state. Programmes which preserved and revived regional languages were turned down by nationalist powers: "They would bring about the collapse of French cultural unity and it would be the end of democracy." Newspapers such as *Figaro* made jokes about bilingualism in their own country: "The farmers speak to their cows in dialect, to their children in French."

The children of France should, so said a former Minister of Education, learn languages which will broaden their perspectives, not dialects. National patriotism was better than the regional variety. Every child had to learn the national anthem, the *Marseillaise*, by heart. The second part of this pronouncement was at least bearable for even the most defiant Alsatian, for the *Marseillaise* was written in Strasbourg by the Alsatian Roget de l'Isle.

The signal for a Renaissance of regional culture was given by President Francois Mitterrand in the electoral campaign of 1981: "It is unworthy of France to continue with this shameful persecution of regional languages and to be the last country in Europe to deny certain sections of the population their fundamental cultural rights."

Well, Mitterrand was re-elected in 1988, and many Alsatians voted for him. Nothing would hinder many others from giving the right-wing extremist Le Pen and his Front National the most votes after Mitterrand in the first round. Of course it is well known that when the economy is in crisis the call for a "strong leader" is raised everywhere. The Alsatian writer René Schikele once called his country a "heavenly garden of pain between the Rhine and the Vosges". Anyone who knows Alsace knows what he means.

The language of the tourist: The cultural and linguistic ties betweeen Alsace and France cannot be denied, and even if various dialects are spoken, the language that unites and is understood by everyone is French. If you can speak German and address an Alsatian in that language, don't expect an enthusiastic reply in German. He may well understand

you, but he will reply in an Alsatian dialect, and you most probably won't understand a word. If you don't speak French, take a phrase book with you. Not all Alsatians learn German at school, so don't make the mistake of thinking that you're going to an "ethnically German" country because you have heard that the Alsatians want to defend their Germanic and Alemannic heritage.

Alsace is a country both blessed and cursed by tourism. This little anecdote may help you to understand its people, whose "lyres accompany Alsatian songs, but whose

swords have mostly been used in the service of the French cockerel", and to exercise a little restraint when you travel. A group of ramblers, looking for *en route* refreshments, were picking some grapes left after the harvest from the vines growing along the path. A vintner ran towards them, brandishing a pitchfork and yelling "Hey, you, what are you doing, that's theft!" The ramblers, all French, were surprised and embarrassed and defended their action. Thereupon the relieved vintner replied: "Oh, you're French! You know, the Germans come along by the coachload and pick great carrier bags full of grapes. Then they vanish over the border without so much as a by-your-leave."

But enough grumbling about tourists. Let's try instead to understand the country and its people better.

Between Germany and France: The Alsatian sense of humour is proverbial. It is the most apt medium for revealing the conflicts within the country, for example in the many jokes that play on German-French relations, the historical conflicts still present in the consciousness of both peoples.

Having the Rhine as a border between two

enced the following misadventures. His German name, Wache (= guard), was re-adapted to French in 1918. Herr Wache became M. Vache (= cow). In 1940 his son was obliged to re-Germanise the name and Vache became Kuh (= cow). In 1945 he had to adapt the name to French once more. The only course left open to M. Cuh (pronounced as in French *cul*, meaning arse) was to plead with the registry office to be allowed to assume the original name Lagarde once more.

It is impossible to decide whether the Germanic tribes in the north and the Aleman-

peoples, as we know, brought about a frequent change of government for Alsace. It might have been painful for the country, but nowadays it makes the Alsatians laugh. The constant changes of citizenship, French one day, German the next, provided opportunities for bureaucracy, as each state in turn required that surnames be adapted to the current national language. The worthy Mr. Lagarde, forced in 1871 to translate his name into German, is supposed to have experi-

Left and above, keeping up their zest for life: relaxing with a good glass of wine.

nic peoples in the south were always unwanted invaders who had to be repulsed on principle. Varied theories have revolved around this topic. The different peoples have left clear traces behind them.

The Alsatian people, just like their languages, have stood up to the passage of time and to outside influences. They go their own ways, which are not always comprehensible to others. At any rate, they have managed to combine their desire for strong government (vide the last presidential elections) with their adamant approach towards authority (to preserve their own culture).

Like the Black Forest on the opposite bank of the Rhine, the Vosges, geologically speaking, could give the Alps quite a few years—they are much older. Their existence goes back to the Variscan orogeny: in Palaeozoic times (300 million years ago), an ocean covered the area where the Rhine plain now lies. Out of the ocean arose a huge, crystalline mountain range, mainly composed of granite and gneiss. In the humid, tropical climate of the time the first plants, similar to the modern horsetails, appeared on earth. About 300 million years later, they grew into huge forests, and the ancestors of today's reptiles crawled through them. But by the end of this geological period the sea was expanding once more, and the forests of cycads and ferns sank beneath the water and later beneath other layers of rock. This was how coal was created.

In the Mesozoic age which followed, this region experienced a desert climate. Mighty layers of sandstone were built up, covering the original crystalline mountain range. While dinosaurs spread over the face of the earth, a long, deep crack in the earth's surface opened up the fault which contains the upper stretch of the Rhine, an earthquake risk zone even nowadays.

The Alps did not appear until the Tertiary period (60 million years ago). When they rose up, they also raised the height of the old Variscan ranges. At the same time the Upper Rhine Fault became deeper, so that the central section of the Variscan ranges collapsed along this fault. Today the Black Forest remains on the eastern bank of the Rhine, and the Vosges on the western.

The present shape of Alsace: Today Alsace consists of the land between the main ridge of the Vosges to the west and the Rhine to the east. The Vosges themselves are divided into a purely crystalline southern part (with the

Grand Ballon at 4,672 feet or 1,424 metres, its highest point) and a mainly sandstone northern part (the highest peak being Donon 3,606 feet or 1,099 metres). The dividing line between the north and the south Vosges follows the valley of the Bruche, which has its source above the forest on the Col des Saales and flows into the Ill in Strasbourg.

Only right in the north does Alsace go beyond the Vosges range, towards the west in the direction of Sarre-Union in Lorraine.

This region is known as Alsace Bossue, the hunchback of Alsace.

The structure of the landscape: The long ridge of the Vosges, dropping steeply down to the plain (Plaine d'Alsace), not only dominates the view of Alsace. The range also has considerable influence on the climate, the landscape and settlement patterns.

While the Ice Age Rhine-Rhône glacier seeped away, piles of gravel were deposited at the foot of the Vosges. Wherever this moraine debris lies under the ground (for instance in the so-called Ox Field in southern Alsace), the soil is hardly arable.

Left, acid rain damage to the forests of Alsace could be catastrophic. Two-thirds of the Vosges are covered with woodland. **Above**, working in the sawmill.

The mountains have had a different effect on northern Alsace. Here, wind and rain have weathered the sandstone rocks, and the resulting fine-grained sand has been brought down into the valleys by the mountain rivers and built up into mighty dunes, providing excellent soil for forest trees. The Haguenau Forest, together with the Pfälzer Wald which borders it to the north, forms the largest continuous stretch of forest in Central Europe. But the sandy soil is also used for agriculture—for instance for growing asparagus, hops or tobacco.

ingly widespread, particularly on the higher parts of the range, on the slopes of Donon and the Grand Ballon d'Alsace.

However, not all parts of the Alsatian forest are equally susceptible to disease. The beech trees on the lower levels have survived well up till now, and in the 2,000–3,600 foot (600–1,100 metre) range it is mostly the conifers which are the worst affected. Broadleaved trees in the higher regions (particularly ash and sycamore) have fared better. Incidentally, in Alsace you often find broad, well-preserved groves of sweet chest-

Even more important for the economy of Alsace than the sand is the loess, blown by the wind into the foothills of the main Vosges ridge. This is the source of Alsace's fame as a wine-growing area. Fruit, vegetables and grain also thrive in this fertile soil.

The forest which covers more than two-thirds of the slopes of the Vosges serves as a protective zone for the vineyards and the grain and vegetable fields below. For this reason, the acid rain damage to forests, which is now afflicting Alsace and many parts of Europe, could have disastrous consequences. The damage is already alarm-

nut trees just above the vineyards. Another attractive feature of the Vosges landscape is formed by the high mountain pastures, the *chaumes* as they are known in French. These lie above the tree line—often above it because medieval landowners needed summer pastures for their cattle and had the higher mountain forests cleared.

The high pastures around the Münster valley are very beautiful. The main stretch of the Route du fromage runs through here. In spring, often until June, a splendid Alpine flora thrives here, from gentian to mountain primrose and the blue Vosges pansy.

The high pastures are interwoven with high moorland, where broad stretches of heather make a delightful contrast to the marshes and water meadows of the Rhine plain. The latter, however, have largely been drained for cultivation, and the environments of many species of animals and plants have been destroyed. Among other species, the storks have been driven from Alsace. To be able to show at least a few of these birds, which are a symbol of the region, a sanctuary (*Centre de Réintroduction des Cigognes*) which plans eventually to resettle storks in

(European) market arrangements, natural sites continued to be exploited agriculturally and industrially. In Alsace, both these factors have resulted in the relatively late realisation of the value of an intact environment. In this context, an important role has been played by movements which have crossed national boundaries, set up in the early 1970s in Alsace, in Baden (across the border into West Germany) and in Switzerland to protest against the planned (and eventually built, with the exception of Wyhl in Baden) nuclear power stations. Today, apart from

Alsace has been opened near Hunawihr. Here you can see the birds in compounds…

A word on the subject of environmental issues in Alsace: the tradition of viniculture and the natural features of the region saw to it that the environment of the upper Vosges slopes has remained reasonably stable, or at least appears to do so. The situation on the lower levels was quite different. Partly because of custom, partly because of senseless

Left, the Vosges have had a formative influence on the pattern of settlement. **Above**, a smithy that has survived the Industrial Revolution.

the important *Club Vosgien*, there are several environmental pressure groups active in Alsace. Among them are the *Association Fédérative Régionale pour la Protection de la Nature* (AFRPN), the *Association Régionale pour l'Initiation à l'Environment et à la Nature en Alsace* (ARIENA), the *Comité Sauvegarde de la Plaine du Rhin* (CSPR) and the small but energetic *Ecologie et Survie* movement. International organisations such as Greenpeace or the World Wildlife Fund are also active in Alsace.

The economic structure of Alsace: Environmental pressure groups have only been really successful in places where economic and ecological interests have not been in conflict. It is a hopeful sign that tourism is still a major industry in Alsace. There are about 550 state classified hotels in the region, with 13,000 rooms between them. In addition, there is private and "part-official" accommodation on offer from the so-called *fermes auberges* (farms which offer refreshments and in many cases accommodation to tourists). There is accommodation available for just under 30,000 people. More than 55 per cent of the working population of Alsace

are involved in the service and trade sectors.

The number of full-time farmers, making their living from agriculture (including viniculture), is surprisingly small. Over the last few years they have only made up five per cent of the working population.

Incidentally, the proportion of the French wine production made up by Alsatian wines is almost always over-estimated. On average, Alsatian vintners produce 800,000 hectolitres (up to a million hectolitres in very productive years), from vineyards which cover only 12,500 hectares (30,888 acres). Compare these figures with the size of the

wine-growing area in the south of France (500,000 hectares–1,235,505 acres), the southwest (200,000 hectares–492,202 acres) and Champagne (20,000 hectares–49,420 acres). In other words, Alsace produces only 1.6 per cent of the French wine harvest. Apart from grapes and hops, the most commonly grown crops in Alsace are fruit, vegetables, wheat, potatoes and various animal feed plants. The prices for these crops (and the economic viablility of the farms that grow them) can in most cases only be maintained by subsidies from the French government or the European Community. As a result, in Alsace—just as in other Western and Central European countries many farmers have given up farming or only keep it going as a sideline.

Industrial production, on the other hand, makes up a relatively high proportion of the Alsatian economy. Today just under 40 per cent of the working population are employed in this sector. Apart from textiles (mainly involving the industrial treatment of cotton), the dominant industries are the motor industry, machine asembly and food processing. The role of the energy sector is increasing in importance: mention should be made here of the great petrochemical works around Wanzenau (to the north of Strasbourg), the potash deposit near Mulhouse, which is one of the largest on earth (and which is mainly used for the manufacture of fertilisers), and also the many hydro-electric and nuclear power stations along the Rhine valley. Alsace, thanks largely to pressure from the central French government in Paris, was given a kind of guinea-pig role for testing the economic uses of nuclear power. Here, electricity from atomic power stations was already in use as early as 1959—a pioneering achievement, which nonetheless makes part of the local population quite uncomfortable these days.

All in all, Alsace boasts a relatively healthy mixed economy. The low unemployment rate in the region is due to these circumstances, and also to the fact that small and medium-sized businesses exist in fairly large numbers.

The administration of Alsace: Politically, the historic region of Alsace is composed of the two Departments Haut-Rhin (Upper Alsace), with its capital Colmar, in the south and Bas-Rhin (Lower Alsace) with its capital Strasbourg to the north. The two Departments cover an area of 3,209 sq miles (8,310 sq km), and have a population of over 1.5 million. This makes Alsace the third most densely populated region in France.

The biggest city in Alsace is Strasbourg with more than 370,000 inhabitants. It is followed by Mulhouse (population 220,000) and Colmar (82,000). About 35,000 of the workforce are commuters: they live in Alsace, but travel to work daily across the borders into Switzerland or Germany.

It is important, in this context, to remember the following: the Alsatians do indeed value their historic and cultural independence, but in general they do not want to be seen as a sort of minority of German extraction under French rule.

The Alsatians are first and foremost Alsatians, but when the chips are down they would definitely prefer to be seen as French than as German.

Climate and the best time to travel: As far as the weather is concerned, you can take your holiday in Alsace at any time of year, but you must of course expect different conditions and different opportunities.

If you want to visit the Rhine valley (including the Route du vin, i.e. the wine-growing areas along the edge of the Vosges), early spring is probably the best time. On the one hand, the natural weather barrier of the Vosges will see to it that the rain clouds approaching from the west will deposit their rain over the mountains (the region around Colmar has an annual rainfall of 50–1,000 millimetres, one of the lowest in France!); on the other, warm air comes up from the south, coming from southwestern Europe through the Burgundian Gap, and it only cools down gradually. These currents of warm air cause

trees, hedges, meadows and flowers here to green and blossom noticeably earlier than in neighbouring central European regions.

The ideal times for rambling in Alsace are late spring and autumn. If you want to walk high up in the Vosges, you can do that in summer as well. It is cool up here, even in July and August—though not free from occasional heavy rain and thunderstorms.

In the Rhine plain it is often hot and humid in high summer. On the other hand, the weather barrier of the Vosges means that travellers visiting the water meadows in the

winter months will have an above average amount of sunshine. However, the Vosges themselves are even better in winter, if you want a winter sports holiday. Plenty of snow falls here, often starting in early December, and there is usually a sharp frost in the first two months of the year. The conditions are ideal, therefore, for cross-country skiing, for downhill skiing and for winter walks.

The most important winter sports centres in Alsace are to be found in the La Bresse region, near Col de la Schlucht, around the Ballon d'Alsace and on the Champ du Feu above Andlau.

Left, in Alsace, too, economic interests are in conflict with conservation. **Above**, an example of state-subsidised market gardening.

The structure of the villages: Scattered individual houses are not to be found in the plain of Alsace, in contrast to the Vosges, where the houses are often reminiscent of the isolated mountain farms of the Alps. The Alsatians love their houses and often hide themselves away in a courtyard surrounded by walls. But they like their neighbours to be near, too. The houses along the single road of the street villages of northern Alsace lie close together. Most of the villages of southern Alsace, however, are cluster villages, which have often developed within a town wall and later around its outer edges.

The villages and the villagers: In earlier times, craftsmen in Alsace also tilled their own (usually modest) patch of ground, and even the vintners were often also craftsmen. They preferred to drink their wine themselves or to sell it to a nearby inn. Apart from these small farmers, wealthy "landed gentry" had larger farms. They grew crops not only for their own use, but also delivered such crops as hops, tobacco or rape seed to the processing industries. They employed casual labourers who did not own any land.

This rural hierarchy is reflected in the villages. Large, impressive houses belonged to the gentry. The smaller houses of the craftsmen-farmers and the even more modest accommodation of the labourers lined the approach roads to the town or village. Yet all the buildings were built with similar methods and materials.

The Alsatian family house: The half-timbered house of the lowlands could be called the typical Alsatian house. A carpenter, who designed and built the wooden structure of the house, was nearly always in charge of the building. The mason was responsible for the foundations, sometimes for the door and window frames, for the chimneys and for the filling of the gaps in the timber frame, which was done with different materials according to regional customs and the nature of the land; with bricks, with a mixture of calf hair, chopped straw and clay, or with blocks of pink Vosges sandstone. To ensure good fortune, a coin was thrown into the filling and built into the foundations of the house.

The houses of the 15th and 16th centuries were simple and functional, but towards the end of the 16th century houses were skilfully decorated, such as the Kammerzell house in Strasbourg. In the country, the carving and

painting was not for decorative purposes alone. Inscriptions and various symbols were intended as a protection, to keep away evil and bring good fortune. The recurring motif of the branch, for instance, symbolises the womb and the wish for an unending line of male heirs, and the horizontal figure eight is a symbol of longevity.

The sun, the essential source of all life, was of course depicted especially in country homes: in fan-shapes above doors, either made of wooden planks or scratched into the plaster, and symbolised the rays of the sun. Some houses were covered from top to

Left, picturesque houses decorated with flowers in a street in Ribeauvillé. **Above**, a typical timber beam decoration using grape motifs.

bottom with "graffiti", not even excepting the roof shingles. However, other buildings only received inscriptions on the support and the corner beams: the year the house was built, the initials of the builders, a meaningful psalm, the initials of Christ (J H S—Jesus Hominum Salvator), or a particular object which represented the trade of the house owner, such as a shoe for a cobbler or a pretzel for a baker. Who knows what more could be discovered if a few layers of plaster were to be removed?

The houses in the Vosges were hardly

had windows opening onto the street and the courtyard. The parlour was the biggest room and the living centre of the house. It was not only the dining and living room, but the reception room for guests. This was where the master of the house slept with his wife and the new-born child, whose cradle would stand in a corner of the room next to the parental alcove. In the evening the family would gather round in the cosy warmth of a tiled or iron stove and knit, spin, play games or tell stories.

This was not all: the room was also often

decorated at all on the outside. Apart from a few inscriptions on the entrance door or the "porthole" above, the typical mountain farmhouse has little to offer by way of ornament. In earlier years the houses were thatched, in contrast to those in the lowlands, which were roofed with typical fired tiles, known as "beavers' tails", which can still be found in Strasbourg. These were also occasionally adorned with symbols of protection and good luck.

House interiors: The most important room in an Alsatian house was the "parlour", which took up the front part of the house and

used for the exercise of a craft or trade. Craftsmen would make pots or shoes, weave or do repair work in their parlours.

The room was even used as a chapel: above the place where the family sat, there would be a crucifix on some corner shelves, flanked by pictures of saints or blessed branches. This "sitting place" with its fixed corner bench, big table and chairs was usually situated in the corner near the windows.

The kitchen: In both town and countryside the kitchen of Alsatian houses was only used for preparing food. It lay right next to the parlour, separated from it by a wall which allowed access to the stove in the parlour, which was fed from the kitchen.

The traditional kitchen had four closed stoves (the Alsatians did not use open fireplaces): one for cooking food, with a flue that did not add a chimney reaching above the roof till the 18th century; another stove for preparing animal feed; the third fed the stove that heated the parlour, and the fourth was used for baking bread.

The kitchen contained plates, kitchen utensils and only those items of furniture necessary for the preparation of food.

above the parlour was the family's "best room", partially heated due to its situation. This was where the family treasures were kept and where the children slept.

Alsatian girls kept the linen for their "bottom drawer" in multicoloured cupboards which were carved from precious woods and very skilfully, individually decorated with carvings, paintings or inlay work. These cupboards, together with the bridal beds, often bore the familiar symbols of protection and good luck which appeared on the outside of the houses. Some motifs of

Other ground floor rooms: Access to the kitchen and the parlour was from the entrance hall, the *Hüsehre*, usually flagged with pink sandstone. This also gave access to the grandparents' "little parlour", which was similar to the parlour opposite but smaller and without alcoves. This room was also heated from a central point, i.e. the kitchen.

The first floor: Stairs led up from the entrance hall to the first floor rooms. Right

Left, facade of L'arsenal in Sélestat. **Above**, a traditional Alsatian kitchen in the Musée Alsacien in Strasbourg.

cooing doves, little heart shapes and wedding rings showed an often pronounced trend towards kitsch. However, this in no way lessened the skill of the craftsmen. Poorer families painted their furniture, which was made of poor quality wood, using colours made from ox blood and potato juice. Above the kitchen lay the larder and drying room. Here preserves of fruit and vegetables were stored, as well as culinary and medicinal herbs. Nowadays, these chambers have another use. Between the two world wars, many Alsatian began replacing their first-floor larders with bathrooms.

TRADITIONAL COSTUMES

To describe the traditional costumes of Alsace is to take a look at the past, to open the doors of history, as if you were unlocking a huge old country cupboard.

What is most fascinating is the splendour of the colours and the many variations of tradition which reflect the creative ability of the rural population. Variations in costume showed from which village or hometown the wearer came, what his or her social status was, and, for a woman, whether she was married or unmarried.

Religious denomination also played a part: Protestant women usually wore a black head-dress, while a visitor in Alsace could tell the young girls from Catholic villages by their white, coloured or patterned headgear. *Joie de vivre*, religious faith, the wisdom of old age, sorrow and grief were reflected in the choice of colours and in the numerous little details of traditional clothes. Traditional costume forms a sort of identity card, often made to last a lifetime and handed on from generation to generation. Traditional costume, therefore, accompanies all the rites of passage in a lifetime and is worn in honour of all the festivals.

Alsatian traditional costume had its hour of glory in the 19th century, when the standard of living of the peasants was rising and, due to the industrial revolution, the manufacture of cloth and accessories became easier. The materials became more valuable; cotton, silk and brocade were embroidered with gold and silver threads, with sequins and glass beads.

The symbolic headgear: The *Schlupfkapp*, symbol of Alsatian women since 1870, is famous all over the world and is often known as the typical Alsatian head-dress. Originally the head covering was held by a ribbon, tied in a small knot on the forehead. This became a little bow, and was later developed into the spectacular butterfly knot which often measured up to a yard across by the end of the 19th century. Wearing this headgear was of course a problem; you were unable to see where you were going, especially if you happen to be in a group. In Upper Alsace this style of headdress soon disappeared, but the new fashion spread to over a quarter of the area of Alsace.

But how was the idea of one single style of tra-ditional dress created, which unenlightened tour-ists still hope to find all over Alsace? When Alsace became German once more in 1870, many

Alsatians moved to other French provinces. In order to publicise their loyalty to France, they wore the red, blue and white rosette in their headgear. This was repeated after the 1918 armi-stice and again after the liberation of Alsace in 1945. In Strasbourg and in Upper Alsace in par-ticular the women wore red skirts with their black butterfly knot headdresses, with red as a symbol of patriotism. In this instance traditional costume was a means of political expression, an effect which lasted so long that the wide variety of tra-ditional Alsatian costume were almost forgotten.

Gradually, people gave up wearing traditional

dress, as it became increasingly difficult to recon-cile it with a contemporary life-style. An old country woman who gave up wearing her head-dress overnight explained her attitude thus: "If I wear the *Schlupfkapp*, people would soon begin to address me "Grandma" instead of "Mrs".

Even if you don't see Alsatian traditional cos-tume on the streets any more, you can be quite sure that many an outfit is hidden away in old farmhouse chests.

Nowadays only the folk music and dance groups revive the arts of the people. They can give their audience some idea of the great variety of traditional costumes in Alsace, costumes which once used to blend so well with the different landscapes and ways of life in the province.

Left, a traditionally dressed couple seems to enjoy each other's company. **Above**, costumed young Alsatian apparently enjoys the publicity.

Just as in the past Christian churches were built on the sites of temples and shrines of older faiths, pagan festivals were given a Christian foundation so that people could continue to celebrate them. After all, nobody's likely to be pleased if traditional festivities are banned overnight just because the rulers have changed their religion. The Alsatians were not always that easy to convert, either. The political games played with religion would need to have concrete improvements) an international standing which it had never had before. However, after the bloodbaths of Saverne and Scherwiller and the defeat of the Schmalkadic League (see also the chapter on the history of Alsace), the period of progessive Protestantism came to an end.

Even so, Alsace remained tolerant in matters of religion, offered a refuge to those Protestants whom Louis XIV would not allow a minute's peace, and became a gather-

advantages to offer if the "true" faith were to find supporters in the villages.

Of course Christianity did not stop at the borders of Alsace, but looking at the remains of pagan customs, it is easy to imagine even nowadays what a difficult job the very first missionaries must have had in their struggle to be heard.

Protestantism spread rapidly in Alsace and was relatively successful, as it was disseminated by progressive men among a people exploited by the Catholic clergy then.

Jakob Sturm gave the movement (which also pressed for moderate policies and social

ing place for people of many faiths.

From these foundations the present-day peaceful co-existence of religious faiths has developed. This is also shown by the many different festivals and customs in Alsace. One thing unites all the Alsatians: they like celebrating. Nearly every village has its own individual festival.

In the country you can still find many remnants of pagan beliefs. They were polished up with a few accessories and a significance for whatever new religious dogma that came along.

There is hardly another country, except for

those which know long, dark winters, where the feast of Christmas has such significance as in Alsace. It is still considered the most important festival in the country and is celebrated with many ancient traditional customs. This festival as it is celebrated today all over central Europe has actually been quite markedly influenced by old Alsatian traditions. During the Thirty Years' War, the Swedes are supposed to have met up with the Alsatian *Christkind* (a supernatural child-figure which brings gifts to children) and the dark, threatening Christmas spirit known to

vals. The candles of the Alsatian Christmas tree are lit before Christmas Eve. The dark time of year around the winter solstice is lit by the blazing tree. Even the Christmas baking has to do with "light" in a symbolic sense: the delicious and definitely "heathen" pretzel was a symbol of good fortune, baked in a kind of sun-wheel shape at the time of the winter solstice. The Christmas market, too, which the Alsatians like to visit in the evenings, is filled with bright lights, a reminder of the strongly sun-orientated worship of pre-Christian times.

much of Europe as Knecht Ruprecht and called Hans Trapp in Alsace. The Christmas tree itself is supposed to be an Alsatian invention. The tree and its decoration are first mentioned in documents as early as the 16th century: mention is made in the account books of the guilds of that time of the money needed to buy fruit and coloured paper to decorate the trees. Light, in the form of fire, played an important role in all pagan festi-

The St John's fires in the summer are a similar case. Wood is piled up on the hills and burned during the days between 21 and 24 June (not always actually on St John's Eve, and not on the longest day of the year either). At this time of year, the summer solstice fires no longer served to bring light into the darkness, but they were lit in honour of the sun, the giver of life. In June you can see the columns of smoke rising in the distance all over the mountains of Alsace. This custom is so popular among young people that it is unlikely to die out in the near future.

Left, the *Schlupfkapp*, famous all over the world as part of Alsatian traditional dress. **Above**, bouquets for the ladies at a festival.

Carnival, too, had to be given its Christian

coat of paint. For ages this had been the feast when winter, which had outstayed its welcome, was driven out. During this time the Alsatians tried to put on some insulating layers of fat, and for this reason the missionaries had a hard time getting them to observe the fasts of Lent. This festival was another "festival of lights", and great fires were lit.

In Offwiller, a village at the foot of the northern Vosges, an old tradition has been kept up. Throughout the winter the people in the village make little disks with a hole in the middle and a flammable edge of beech wood. A huge bonfire is built on a hill near the village. On the day of the festival the fire is lit and the villages hold the disks into the flames, revolve them on a stick until they glow white-hot, and then throw them in a wide arc down into the valley.

By coincidence, the Easter festival falls in that time of year when it was the pagan custom to get rid of winter eventually. Even today, this festival is not celebrated on the same date each year, but on the weekend that follows the first full moon of spring. One pagan custom is the Easter cleaning of the houses, which is, however, not carried out quite as ruthlessly nowadays.

Almost all the contents of the house were put into the street, cleaned and scrubbed. During this spring cleaning, anything that proved to be unwanted and combustible was piled up in front of the church. On the one hand, the subsequent great bonfire was intended to get rid of the bits and pieces that had accumulated over the winter months; on the other, under its "Christianised" aspect, it represented the burning of Judas in the form of a straw figure. This custom soon disappeared, as Judas became *Jud* (= Jew) in the southern Alsatian dialect, and the practice was misunderstood as anti-Semitic.

The Whitsun festivities also have pagan origins. At this time of the year people celebrated the re-awakening of nature, the coming of warm weather and the fertility of the fields. Some villages have kept widely differing traditions, the origins of which can no longer be determined with any certainty. In some places young people disguise themselves and go from door to door, reciting short speeches which they have learned by heart, and are given eggs, bacon and other foodstuffs in return, as a sacrificial offering.

In Soulzbach-les-Bains the idea of "sacrifice" is quite evident. At Whitsun, a boy is locked into a cage and symbolically sacrificed: the cage is flung into the water (the boy is, of course, quickly let out first—a concession to the times and more sensitive natures).

Another fine tradition has survived in some places in Alsace. In earlier years the villagers used to ride through the countryside on horseback, cracking whips and thus driving away all the evil spirits which might have crept into the village during the year and threatened the households and the harvests. This developed into the custom of Whitsun rides, which are still organised in Wissembourg, Hoerdt and Schleithal.

The May bouquets, found in many places, are made of delicate, fragrant green birch twigs and are tied to the doorposts of houses to welcome spring. Christian harvest festivals also still harbour some pagan customs, such as little "thank-you offerings" in the shape of bunches of herbs or grain.

Most of the festivals in the villages of Alsace are based on events that come and go with the seasons. Sometimes festivals also came about to commemorate historical or simply imaginary events. Every year in Marlenheim, for instance, they celebrate the wedding of *Ami Fritz*, a hero of a 19th century novel with whom (almost) every Alsatian can identify. The wedding is very effectively acted out by a folklore group. Often a ceremony commemorates the birth or death of the village saint.

The festivals, which are often prepared and organised with a great deal of care, are spectacular. However, if the stress is on amusing the tourists, the effect is lost, as can be seen in all the areas popular with visitors.

Be sure to see one of these typical festivals if you choose one of the summer months for your visit to Alsace.

The Virgin, by Martin Schongauer (Petit Louvre, Colmar).

Alsace

30km

Saarbrücken
Pirmanens
Hinterweidenthal
DEUTSCHLAND
Bad Bergzabern
Sarreguemines
Wissembourg
Karlsruh
St.Avold
Bitche
Lembach
Lauterbourg
Puttelange
PARC RÉGIONAL DES VOSGES DU NORD
Niederbronn
Woerth
Rastatt
MOSELLE
Sarre-Union
Ingwiller
Soufflenheim
Morhange
Sarre
La Petite-Pierre
Bouxwiller
Haguenau
Bischwiller
Château-Salins
Dieuze
Baden-Bade
Sarrebourg
Saverne
Hochfelden
Brumath
Achern
Marmoutier
Wasselone
BAS- RHIN
Cal de la Marne au Rhin
Wangenbourg
Strasbourg
Kehl
Lunéville
Blâmont
Molsheim
MEURTHE- ET-
MOSELLE
Meurthe
Schirmeck
Bruche
Obernai
Offenburg
Oppena
FRANCE
Ste Odile
Le Hohwald
Barr
Saales
Ville
Andlau
DEUTSCH-
Rambervillers
Moselle
S.t-Dié
LORRAINE
Ste Marie-
aux- Mines
Sélestat
Haslach
Herbolzheim
Elzach
Bruyéres
Fraize
Lapoutroie
Ribeauvillé
Marckolsheim
LAND
Epinal
VOSGES
Kaysersberg
Colmar
Géradmer
Munster
Eguisheim
Neuf- Brisach
Breisach
Freiburg
Remiremont
Cornimont
Rouffach
Bad Krozingen
Titis
Guebwiller
Ensisheim
(FEDERAL REPUBLIC
Le Thillot
HAUTE- RHIN
Badenweiler
Schönau
Luxeuil
Giromagny
Thann
Masevaux
Mulhouse
OF GERMANY)
HAUTE- SAÔNE
Waldshut
Lure
Belfort
Cal du Rhône au Rhin
Altkirch
Lörrach
Rhein
BELFORT
Sochaux
Basel
Bâle
Brugg
Montbeliard
Delle
Ferrette
Sissach
SCHWEIZ
Aarau
Porrentruy
(SWITZERLAND)
Olten
DOUBS
Delémont
Balsthal

72

TOWNS AND THE COUNTRYSIDE

Our journey through Alsace begins in the larger towns, with Strasbourg at their head. If you want to explore this city off your own bat, you will find plenty of suggestions, without our cutting short the description of those sights of the "City of Europe" which are an absolute must. We follow this up with Colmar, the attractive capital of Haut-Rhin, with the Unterlinden Museum or Petit Louvre as the cultural centre. Mulhouse, *Mülhausen* in German, is the subject of the third city tour. It was an Imperial City in the 13th century and is today a metropolis of industry and trade.

The description of the landscape of Alsace, which is criss-crossed by a network of holiday routes, is accompanied by detailed maps of those areas which we have chosen as being particularly rewarding to the visitor. We show travel routes through the north of the region, through central Alsace and finally through the south.

A great many visitor to Alsace makes use of a long weekend for a restful excursion, interspersed with culinary high points. Take a drive along one of the routes recommended, and you will most certainly get your money's worth. However, don't be entirely bound by our suggestions. There are still many other small surprises in store for visitors to Alsace.

Whether you are a gourmet, a nature lover, a really fit mountain hiker, an art lover or a pilgrim following the trail of history, you are assured of an enjoyable holiday. Certainly, even those people who want nothing more than a nice summer holiday in Alsace and who dislike ambitious travel guides will find some interesting suggestions in this book. Alsace is suitable for a family holiday and also for a trip to some important cultural event in Strasbourg or Colmar for instance. Imagine yourself sitting at some time or other in a Strasbourg bistro, leafing through this book, gearing yourself for a visit to the splendid cathedral and for an experience with the following amusing anecdote dating from the 18th century.

In those days there were tradesmen's booths between the buttresses of the cathedral, and it is said that the boards of the booths were piled high with bottles of spirits, soap, tobacco, herrings, stinking cheese, fat and "other repulsive items". In 1722 the booths were torn down and replaced by shops, which were then taken over by ladies of the oldest profession in the world who were affectionately known as the "Cathedral swallows". A contemporary prelate remarked: "The ladies and gentlemen only have to take two or three steps to go to confession."

Preceding pages: early morning mist veiling the rich and varied Alsatian landscape; Riquewihr, the wine lover's paradise; proud farmers show off a lorry load of *Choucroute*, world-famous sauerkraut from Alsace; an idyllic village setting, with local girl in traditional costume and in the background, tourists find their way around.

STRASBOURG

The history and character of the city of Strasbourg are closely linked with its geographical situation. Because of its position, midway between Prague and Paris, its people were not only citizens of the Holy Roman Empire, but, later on, also of Germany and France. Recently the city fathers wrote the slogan *Carrefour de l'Europe* (the crossroads of Europe). This can be visualised on a map of Europe with no national borders and with Strasbourg at the centre.

The Alsatian dialects may become ever more rare on the streets or in the schools, but there is an unmistakable flair about Strasbourg that distinguishes it from other French cities. The half-timbered houses of the old city, the bakeries, breweries and wine taverns are all reminiscent of buildings from the same period to be seen on the other bank of the Rhine. The Germanic and Alemmanic influence is even reflected in the faces of the people of Strasbourg and in their taste for certain styles of ornament.

The Monument aux Morts in the centre of the **Place de la République**, built in 1936 in honour of the dead of World War I, shows a sorrowing mother holding two dead sons in her arms, one German and one French; a moving symbol of the fate of many thousands in this border country.

The "crisis of indentity" undergone by the capital of the Department Bas-Rhin has, if anything, become greater over the last few years. Its situation and its atmosphere made it an ideal choice for the "capital of Europe", the Europe of the European Community, intended as the realisation of the dream of international co-operation among the European nations. At present, "European unity" is confined to regular meetings of the European Parliament and the Council of Europe in the imposing Palais de l'Europe. The people of Stras-bourg complain from time to time about the arrival of the "Eurocrats" in their city, because their high expense allowances caused rents and restaurant prices to hit the ceiling. When Parliament meets, hotels and restaurants in Strasbourg are full. The shops do well, particularly in the peak season, and Europe is certainly profitable for business people in Strasbourg. Many "average" tourists feel their hearts ache when faced with the prices of the first-class "European" accommodation and restaurants. A few miles away you will find the peaceful countryside, pleasant villages and hotels and restaurants with friendly service; that is precisely the beauty of Alsace.

Visitors to Strasbourg will have the pleasure of getting to know a living, modern European city that still keeps its traditions. The inimitable architecture of the medieval houses, the famous Cathedral, the excellent local cuisine,

the local wines and beers, and also the many art galleries and historical museums, the boat trips on the Ill, the cafes, decorated with geraniums, which serve such delicious cakes...there are indeed many reasons for visiting Strasbourg.

Two thousand years of Strasbourg: The history of Strasbourg goes back 2,000 years. In A.D. 12 the Roman proconsul Drusus built a fortress in the marshy area between the rivers Ill and Bruche, close to the Rhine. This place was called Argentoratum. The city grew in regular stages, proclaimed its independence from its Bishop in 1262, and became an Imperial City. Despite the difficult times which the city and its people had to live through, Strasbourg flourished in the Middle Ages. Many remains dating from this period survived the ravages of time and are worth seeing. They give Strasbourg its character.

The modern name for the city is also of medieval origin: Strateburgum (the Place of Roads). It shows what an important nodal point Strasbourg was at that time, situated between Germany, France, Switzerland and Holland. Many merchants became rich in those days. The city grew and became the pride of its inhabitants. In the 11th century the city fathers decided to build a cathedral which became the symbol of the city. They set up a civil body, *L'Oeuvre Notre Dame*, to carry out the work of the building, which should, according to tradition, have been done by the church. In the 15th century, Strasbourg grew more independently of the Catholic church and became a centre of Humanism. The seeds of the Reformation began to grow in the early 16th century: the writings of Luther were easily distributed with the help of Gutenberg's printing press. At the height of the movement, the Cathedral even became Protestant. The University, at which Goethe, among others, once studied, was founded in 1621.

In 1681 Louis XIV added Alsace to France. The people demanded the status of a "Free City", freedom of religion and self-determination, but their demands did not stand up for long to the pressures of history and the persecution of the Protestants by Louis XIV, and it was not long before Catholic masses were heard once more in the Cathedral.

Gradually the people of Strasbourg got used to being under French rule, and the city flourished once more. There are traces of the period too, such as the **Classical Château des Rohans**, the second most famous building in the city on the left bank of the Ill.

As with so many churches, the Cathedral was turned into a "Temple of Reason" at the time of the Revolution, and the city lost its freedom. A ridiculous construction, known among the people of Strasbourg as the "coffee pot", was placed on top of the 466 foot (142 metre) high cathedral tower.

Later, the Cathedral received an even

The symbol of the city, amid the roofs of the old town.

more depressing addition: on 19 June 1940, when the German troops marched in, the swastika flag of Nazi Germany was flown from the tower. The Führer was fond of the idyllic old city (possibly because a good part of its population had left before his arrival), but no more masses were permitted in the Cathedral. One is reminded of the rhetorical question which he asked the troops, as they occupied Strasbourg: "Shall we leave this jewel in the hands of the French?" At the end of the war, Alsace was back in French hands, and the Cathedral back in the hands of the Catholics.

A substantial part of the Cathedral is hidden by scaffolding. The Cathedral may no longer be the plaything of politicians, but acid rain and the pollution of the Strasbourg atmosphere are even more damaging. The deep pink sandstone has been seriously damaged by environmental influences such as jet fighter planes breaking the sound bar-

rier. The building work is a race against time and the weather. You can get a clear view of the front facade of the Cathedral from the Cathedral Square and from the pedestrian precinct.

If you approach the Cathedral from the Rue Mercière, it seems to consist solely of one huge wall which rears up at the end of the street. The **West Facade** with its three portals (in honour of the Trinity) is richly decorated. Near the left portal are the statues of Virtue, victorious in the struggle with Sin. On the right are figures of the wise virgins and the foolish ones who were tempted. At the main entrance, above which is the great rose window with its diameter of about 49 feet (15 metres), the twelve lions symbolise the twelve tribes of Israel. The gallery of the apostles, the figures of the prophets and the scenes from the Old and New Testaments are worth scrutinising. Nearly all these sculptures have been replaced or re-

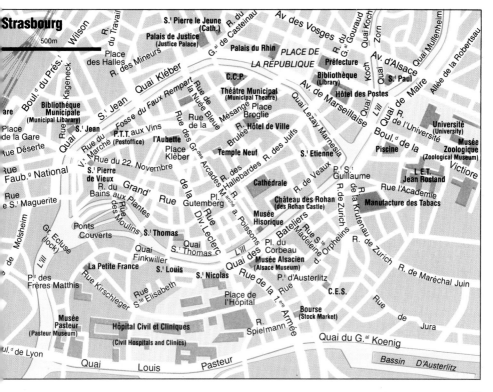

stored over the years, but there are some intact originals dating from 1300, such as the first three rows of sculptures.

A side entrance to the right of the facade leads to the steep spiral staircase up the **tower**. The climb is worthwhile, not only because of the magnificent view but also because of the giant works of the clock. It is fascinating to watch the gigantic cog wheels interlock and put the whole works into movement in one short stroke. However, if you feel you can't cope with the 330 steps to the viewing platform, stay at the bottom; there is much to see at ground level.

If you enter the Cathedral through the main entrance (south portal) or through the 125 foot (38 metre) high porch of the west facade, you will not be struck by the dull and often unnerving silence of some great cathedrals. There is constant movement, scraping of chairs and general restlessness, so that it is easy for a visitor to forget that this is a place of worship. On the other hand, you will get a good impression of how it must have been when churches were once centres of urban life. A little, sunlight-filled chapel on the left side of the choir is reserved for those visitors who want a quiet place to pray in.

One of the oldest monuments is the famous **Angel Pillar**, also known as the *Last Judgement*. This central structural pillar is covered with high reliefs dating from the 13th century. They depict the apostles Mark, John, Matthew and Luke and their symbols (lion, eagle, angel and ox). Next to it is the statue of the "little man" in his hat, leaning on a balustrade. He seems to be taking a sceptical look at the pillar. Some say that the statue is a self-portrait of the architect, Nicholas von Hagenau, but others claim that the figure is that of an ordinary visitor, overcome with doubts regarding the structural strength of the pillar, and was turned into a statue be-

A view of Strasbourg yesterday **(right)** and today **(below)**.

cause of his lack of faith: "Here you shall stay until it all falls down!"

The **astronomical clock** is a magnet for tourists. Arrive at 12.30 on the dot, if you want to see the midday show. The clock (its works were made in 1842 by the Strasbourg clockmaker Schwilgué) is half an hour slow. At 12.30 the twelve apostles on their turntable start to move and bow before the figure of Christ. A cock crows three times and flaps its wings. After this, an angel upends an hourglass for the next "countdown". The seven days of the week, starting with Sunday, are represented by the divinities Apollo, Diana, Mars, Mercury, Jupiter, Venus and Saturn, who appear one after the other in a window above the clock. When the quarters are struck, angels appear and represent the four ages of human life. A figure symbolising death strikes on the hour.

The **stained glass windows** mostly date from the 14th and 15th centuries.

The central rose window has been restored, but has kept its original appearance. The 500,000 glass pieces of the giant mosaic of colours were taken out during World War II. Some parts were later discovered in a salt mine in Württemberg in Germany.

The finely chiselled octagonal **chancel** dates from 1485. One of the two organs was also built at this time. The paintings and the glass windows of the choir are modern. The *Window of Europe* was installed in 1956 when the European institutions settled in Strasbourg. "Politics" still finds its way into church life.

The *son-et-lumière* productions take place from mid-April till the end of September. Beautiful works of art are floodlit, and enable visitors to explore the Cathedral's history. The events are held almost daily at 8 pm (in German) and at 9 pm (in French). Tickets are sold at the entrance from 6.30 pm onwards.

THE OLD CITY

The Cathedral is the centre of Strasbourg's Old City, which takes up an island framed by two branches of the river Ill. This part of Strasbourg is rich in traditions and should be worthwhile visiting, with its narrow medieval streets, its houses built close together, with their high gabled roofs even nowadays still covered with the famous "beaver's tail" tiles.

The **Cathedral Square** lies in front of the north facade of the Cathedral and opens out from the **Rue Mercière**. Two of the buildings in this square are symbols of the city and attract tourists and streets musicians (and also pickpockets, so beware!). They are the **Kammerzell House** and the **Pharmacie du Cerf**. There is a restaurant in the Kammerzell House (closed on Wednesdays and from mid-February to mid-March),

which offers good home cooking from the local cuisine on the ground floor, *nouvelle cuisine* and traditional French dishes on the first. There is an enchanting view, plus memorable surroundings and good food, but such attractions don't exactly come cheap. You will notice the Kammerzell House at once. The dark, foursquare corner house is lightened by the floral decorations (geraniums) and by the window panes, which sparkle in the sun. The white tables and white umbrellas also do their bit to brighten up the sombre walls with their dark, richly carved beams, at least in the summer time. This house dates from 1589 and was completely restored in 1954. A skilfully worked door has survived from the Renaissance period.

Well, did you treat yourself to a large and rich meal? Are you now in need of *Alka-Seltzer*? You can buy it in the Pharmacie du Cerf, in the building right opposite the Cathedral. It dates from the 13th century, and its owners have just recently discovered previously unknown frescoes on the inner walls. They are unlikely to show them to you, but at least you can take a look around the pharmacy, which the present owner has restored according to his own taste.

On your tour of sights around the Cathedral, be sure to include a visit to the **Musée de l'Œuvre Notre Dame**, in the Maison de l'Œuvre. This consists of two houses; the left-hand part dates from the 14th century, the right-hand part was built in a Renaissance style in the 16th century. From the outside, you can see a pretty medieval garden in one of the inner courtyards. The Maison de l'Œuvre was originally built for the labours of the architects and sculptors who worked on the Cathedral. Here you can follow the impressive history of the growth of the Cathedral, which many local craftsmen and artists, and also ordinary citizens, saw as their work of a lifetime. You can get an impression of the lengthy history of the building

Preceding pages, the famou᷄ west port﹐ of Strasb﹒ Cathedral Left, rooftops ᷄ the old ci᷄

process, of the secrets of the builders working here, which were handed down from father to son. Even today, the *Fondation* is responsible for the upkeep of the building's structure and for restoration work to the Cathedral. The museum houses beautiful and ancient sculptures and glass windows from the Cathedral—the latter are considered to be the oldest that have remained intact. One particularly valuable piece is a bust of Christ dating from the second half of the 11th century. In the museum you can also see the plans of the building and the original statues, which have been replaced in the Cathedral itself by copies. Also part of the exhibition is a collection of naive Alsatian art, which blends very well with the medieval items in the rooms. There are wall hangings on the staircases leading to the exhibition rooms, where you can see gold and silver handicrafts dating from the 15th to the 17th century, glittering witnesses

Petite
ce" at
t.

to the wealth of Alsace at the time. Finally, view the collection of Renaissance art. Here you can also see works by Hans Baldung Grien (a pupil of Dürer's). You can also see Alsatian decorative art: furnishings and pictures with fashions and interiors dating from the 17th century.

Majestic and mysterious: The **Rohan Palace** right next door is worth a lengthy visit, as it houses some important museums. Once known as the "Versailles of the east", it was built for the Prince-Bishop Louis de Rohan, the "black sheep" of the family, a lover of luxury, whose part in the infamous diamond necklace affair among Marie Antoinette's circle brought the Rohan family its scandalous reputation. You can read more about them in the section on Saverne (Route des châteaux).

If you're very lucky, you can watch the performance of a traditional music group in costume in the inner courtyard

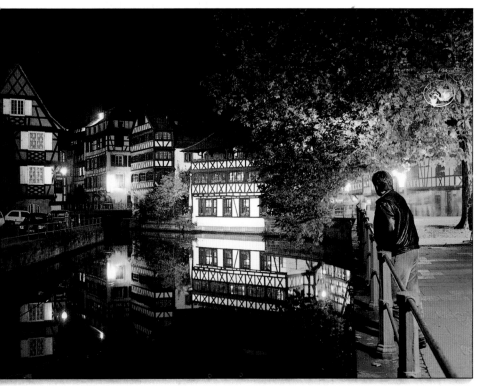

of the Rohan palace. They may look a bit strange amidst the 18th century architecture, but the atmosphere of the bare courtyard is enlightened by the lively, inviting display.

The first part of the tour will lead you through the Rohan apartments, which are completely furnished with wall hangings, furniture, carvings and richly painted ceilings. The **Grands Appartements** on the ground floor were once inhabited by Louis XV and Marie Antoinette. The bedroom was used solely to provide the appropriate setting for the ceremony of awakening, the *lever du roi* (like the rising of the sun), and the bed was certainly not intended for sleeping, but was used only when the king received subjects who had to take part in the various complicated ceremonies. Flower motifs were symbolic of sleep, like little cherubs of dreams. The four corners of the ceiling represented the various times of the day: sunrise, noon, evening and night. The sun in the centre—what else could it be?—is a symbol of the king.

Some rooms have only recently been renovated. Among them is the **Salon d'Assemblée**, with its four corners representing the four "corners" of the world and with the emblems of the Rohan family in the centre. In the **Cardinal's Library** there are fragments of a series of tapestries with scenes from the life of the Roman emperor Constantine. But the palace has more to offer than opulent aristocratic rooms. It also contains the Musée des Beaux Arts. Here you can take a close look at *La Belle Strasbourgeoise*. This unknown beauty whose name no-one knows was painted in 1703 by Nicolas de Largillière. Doubts have been voiced as to whether she was really from Strasbourg. Some claimed that she was a Parisienne in fancy dress. However, Strasbourg women from wealthy fami-

Memorial the dead two world wars in th Place de République

lies wore large fancy hats around 1700 and had no use for umbrellas.

Apart from *La Belle Strasbourgeoise* you will find paintings from the Middle Ages up to the end of the 18th century. Awaiting your examination are works of the Italian school by Giotto, Lippi, Botticelli and Fra Angelo, pictures by El Greco, Murillo and Goya, Dutch and Flemish masters such as van Dyck, de Hooch and Rubens.

Another museum not to be missed is the **Archaeological Museum**. Apart from a valuable collection of Alsatian finds, you can see a replica of a Gallo-Roman tavern here, together with many other interesting items from the history of Strasbourg.

Finally, focus your attention to the **Musée des Arts Décoratifs**, which has *objets d'art* and pieces of craft work such as those made in and around Strasbourg from the 17th to the 19th century. Among the porcelain collection, the works of the Hannong family are bound to attract you. A dispute about monopoly rights drove the Hannongs to ruin, but their works from 1721 to 1782 had a great influence on European ceramics manufacturers. Scrutinise the pieces from their blue period. Then study the multicoloured ceramics, often in animal form, which were created using their own individual technique.

At the bridge of **Pont du Corbeau** (Raven Bridge), don't let your good mood be spoiled when you hear that this was the bridge where criminals were drowned and their bodies then left for the ravens. Go on to the **Musée Historique** or the **Musée d'Art Moderne** next door in the old Customs House. By now your head may be spinning from all these museums. If it's not, and if the weather is not suitable for walking, go visit the **Musée Alsacien** (on the opposite bank of the Ill) and its collection of folk art, which is worth seeing.

Rohan
ace:
irs in the
rtyard.

The museum is dedicated to Jean-Frédéric Oberlin, the Alsatian pioneer in the social and educational field.

La Petite France: If you go for a walk here, the oldest part of the city, on the western tip of the island, you may perhaps ask yourself if you haven't walked into a film set or an oversize doll house. With some justification, *La Petite France* is so picturesque that it seems a little unreal. The tourists strolling through the pretty little streets and the boat-loads of visitors with their clicking cameras only add to the impression of having stepped into a dream world. It would be a shame to miss out on this little commercialised but medieval village, which has been completely restored. It now looks as if it had been created solely as a picturesque backdrop for amateur photographers.

Four mighty towers, dating from the 14th century, rise along the main road, the **Rue du Bain des Plantes**. The name of the street is a reminder of the public bath houses which once stood here long ago. In those days fishermen, tanners and millers lived in this quarter. Apart from the street names and the broad mansard roofs of the houses, where hides were once hung to dry, you will find few reminders of the times when craftsmen and traders went about their daily tasks in these streets. You may visit La Petite France at the crack of dawn, when the rays of the morning sun are reflected on the still water of the canal and the facades of the houses are bathed in pink light...

Walk up as far as the **Ponts Couverts** (covered bridges). These are neither covered nor built upon, but their names, like those of the streets, date from the Middle Ages. The three bridges are linked by watchtowers which formed part of the city's fortifications. There is a pretty little park on the quayside which invites you to take a rest.

Place Brog in Strasbo

Downriver you will see the **Vauban lock**, also known as the Great Lock, because it is the largest "water gate" within the city. **The lock terrace** is open from nine am until midnight. From here you can get a beautiful view of La Petite France, "little France". There are two churches well worth visiting in this quarter: **St Thomas** and **St Pierre-le-Vieux**. The former is a Protestant church, a typical example of local Gothic architecture. The tomb of the Maréchal de Saxe is the pride of Strasbourg. Louis XI had commissioned the monument from the famous artist Jean-Baptiste Pigalle. It depicts the brave warrior de Saxe, calmy stepping into his grave, while Death holds the coffin lid up for him in a friendly manner.

St Pierre-le-Vieux has changed its denomination several times since it was built, and is today used by both Christian churches. Of interest are the panels depicting Christ's passion, painted in 15th century Flemish style. Each panel bears the portrait and the coat of arms of the donor who gave it to the church.

Place Kléber: You will certainly see this square more than once, as it is one of the main crossroads of the city. In the centre of the square is the monumental statue of the hero General Kléber, who died during Napoleon's Egyptian campaign. You will be drawn to the large, red building, **l'Aubette**. Its name is a reminder of its former military role as the place where the guard was changed at dawn (*aube*). In 1870 both it and its collection of art were destroyed by Prussian troops. After its restoration in the 1920s, the Dadaist Hans Arp and his wife Sophie Taeuber created murals inside the building, which later aroused the displeasure of the Nazis during the most recent German occupation. The murals, like all other works of Arp and Taeuber, were declared "decadent" and destroyed. Close by, towards Place Gutenberg, is the **Rue des Arcades**, which was built on top of old Roman fortifications. Here there are no reminders of the "postcard village" scenes of La Petite France.

In **Place Gutenberg**, carved in stone, was the inventor of the printing press who developed and refined his revolutionary discovery in Strasbourg. Thoughtfully, he inspects his unrolled work with its letters *Et la lumière fut* (And there was Light), for the first large-scale work to be printed in Europe was of course the Bible. In this rather bare square, the statue keeps the Hôtel du Commerce company. The latter, a Renaissance building, has unusually large windows with three sections. These are decorated above the window frames. An original touch is given by the identical but much smaller windows under the roof, which give the building its charm. In this building you will find, apart from the Chamber of Commerce, the Tourist Information Office, where all your questions can be answered.

e
rasbourg
era
use.

THE OTHER STRASBOURG

If you have the time and want to look at other less famous parts of the city (which won't, however, be so full of tourists), leave La Petite France, the Cathedral and the Place Kléber behind you and go to the eastern part of the island, and to the canal banks of the artificial **Fossé du Faux Rempart** (False Walls Canal). The Protestant church of St-Pierre-le-Jeune has been rebuilt here on old foundations; the original building goes back to the 7th century. The four-aisled pillared basilica which you can see today dates from the 13th and 14th centuries. The building was restored around the year 1900. Notable is the Gothic crucifix with its figure of Christ, with paintings dating from the the year 1620.

Now stroll through the Rue de la Nuée-Bleu, whose strange name is a reminder of the blue haze that hung over the street when bleach was still being manufactured here. Turn off into the **Rue de la Mésange**, one of the most popular streets in Strasbourg, which leads into the **Place Broglie**. This square, set with several rows of trees, was laid out in 1742 and named after the Maréchal de Broglie, who came from an old Piedmontese family. The square was once a busy horse-trading market, but now is one of the quietest squares in the city. It awakens to new life every year at the time of the Christmas market. Just follow the groups of children making their way here, and you won't miss it! The 18th century **Hôtel de Ville** (Town Hall) is the most important building in the square and also one of the most impressive town halls in France. However, it has to share its fame with the **Opéra du Rhin** and the statue of General Leclerc, who liberated Strasbourg in World War II.

Incidentally, this square is also famous because the French national anthem was composed in what is now the Banque de France. In 1792, Rouget de l'Isle composed a stirring march, which he called *Chant de guerre de l'armée du Rhin* (Battle Song of the Rhine Army). The song received its present title *La Marseillaise*, when it was sung by revolutionaries from the south of France marching into Paris on their way to storm the Tuileries.

On the other side of the canal lies the broad **Place de la République**, with a park at its centre. The sculptor Drivier created the **Monument aux morts** here in 1936. At the edge of the square is the Palais du Rhin, the former Imperial Palace and opposite it are the National Theatre and the National Library.

The Avenue de la Paix leads in a northerly direction to the **Synagogue de la Paix** and to an 18th century park, known simply as **Les Contades**. Free concerts by the *Strasbourg Music Soci-*

ses along
river III
Petite
ce).
t,
estrian
inct in
sbourg.

ety are held here every week (from May to September).

The University: Outside the ring of water encircling the old city is the **University** with its broad sprawl of lecture halls, student halls of residence, administrative buildings, the medical faculty and the hospital. The University was founded in 1621 and started life as a theological college, which was later expanded. Famous professors have taught here. Johann Daniel Schöpflin, professor of History and Rhetoric, was the founder of the Brussels Academy. Christoph Wilhelm von Koch, Professor of Law at Strasbourg, was a member of the executive legal body and campaigned for the introduction of constitutional principles. He spent several months in prison because of his activities. An older, central building, the **Palais Universitaire**, is reminiscent of Italian Renaissance buildings, although it was not built until 1880.

A walk through the Botanical Gardens at the other end of the broad lawns is a pleasant experience. The Observatory and the Planetarium lie beyond the gardens. You can take a mid-afternoon trip to other stars and to the moon, but you should first enquire about the opening hours (tel. 88 36 12 50). The Planetarium, by the way, is closed during the holiday month of August.

The **Avenue du Général de Gaulle**, the **Esplanade Quarter**, is an example of successful modern city architecture. Here, three statues by Hans Arp have survived the ups and downs of history unharmed. Only the pigeons won't leave them alone.

Would you like to mix with the students? If the weather permits, go to the **Citadelle**, a park by the waterside, laid out in the ruins of the Vauban fortress, which like many other fortresses was built during the rule of Louis XIV in the 17th century.

Shopping i the Christm Market.

To the northeast of the city centre is the **European Quarter**. Here, the most beautiful spot is surely the **Orangerie**, a delightful park, also known as Le Nôtre after the architect who also designed the park of Versailles. It dates from 1692 and was restored when Josephine Bonaparte travelled through the area and showed her appreciation of the park. On Wednesdays, Saturdays and Sundays there are brief *son et lumière* performances (evenings, after 9 pm).

Visitors to the park can view the ongoing exhibitions and stroll in the park. Rowing boats are moored, rocking gently on the water, in a small romantic lake, which also has the obligatory ducks and geese. Quiet promenades and shady walks lead along the banks of the canal as far as the Rhine.

The **Palais d'Europe** opened its doors to the "Eurocrats" in 1977. Guided tours are possible if the European parliament isn't in session. It meets alternately here and in Brussels. The Council of Europe meets only in Strasbourg.

Strasbourg Port: The city's situation near the Rhine naturally led to the development of a large and important inland port. The Rhine rises from two springs in the Swiss Alps, flows through Lake Constance and the Jura Mountains as far as Basle, and then flows majestically northwards between Germany and France till it reaches Rotterdam and the North Sea. It is the longest stretch of navigable river in Western Europe and one of the busiest. Its economic importance is unquestioned.

The port of Strasbourg stretches along the Rhine for some six miles (10 km). You can take a boat trip around the port and watch the busy activities around the docks and warehouses. The boat tour goes under the "Pont d'Europe" bridge, which leads across the river to Germany. You will also see the canal lock, part of a system being built to link the Rhine with the Danube.

The impressive size of some of the barges which travel the waterways amazes all the visitors. You can't help thinking of it as "Little France": 20,000 ships a year moor here.

You disembark from the tour on the **Promenade Dauphin**. From late June to early September you can take a three-hour tour during the week, a four-hour one at weekends. A snack bar and a restaurant on board provide the opportunity for refreshments.

You can take a one-hour boat trip around the city itself. The tour passes all the sights and includes the Palais d'Europe. The boats depart regularly between March and the first week in September, and during the warm weather, from May to September, they even make night trips. The boats moor right next to the Palais de Rohan.

But that's not all that Strasbourg has to offer, of course. There are numerous festivals, exhibitions, sporting and cul-

ad of
us, near
Opera
use.

tural events, all of which take place throughout the year. You can find up-to-date details of what's on offer from your hotel or the tourist office.

There is jousting along the banks of the Ill, next to the Rohan Palace. This makes a spectacle which fascinates observers (Mondays and Fridays during July and August, at 8.30 pm).

If you want to find out more about the annual international music festival, the jazz festival in the Citadelle park or other musical events, ring the *Societé des Amis de la Musique de Strasbourg*, tel: 88 32 43 10. In the autumn, around mid-September, you can take part in the German-French festival which is held on both banks of the Rhine—a party on a gigantic scale!

At the time of the summer solstice or the *Fête de St Jean*, there is a fleamarket from the end of June to early July in the *Parc Municipal des Expositions* (in the exhibition area).

You will be sure to see some folk dance groups during your holiday, as the dancers appear on every possible occasion during the high season. Of course, you must not forget 14 July, which is celebrated here as everywhere else in France with marching bands, fireworks, dance and music, as well as a light show at the Cathedral. Have fun!

The Strasbourg cuisine: Strasbourg is the centre of the Alsatian art of cooking. In this city, which guards its traditions, the care of the kitchen and the cellar is accorded great importance. There is no way you will avoid tasting some local specialties. Try a Winstub (wine tavern), for instance, where you can eat at affordable prices. The big restaurants, such as *Buerehiesel* or *Au Crocodile*, offer the more exquisite dishes, but the prices are also out of this world! In the Winstubs, you can order a single dish, a *hors d'oeuvre* on its own (not usually possible elsewhere in France), a side

Guild sign: an invitation to sumptuous meals.

dish, a measure of beer, or you can order a whole five-course menu with the finest of wines, just as you wish. However, make sure that your "gourmet day" doesn't fall on a Sunday, as almost all the chefs have that day off.

The city itself has its own specialties to offer, such as Strasbourg sausages or Strasbourg *foie gras*. An Alsatian wine will go down well with any dish.

If you are in Alsace in the autumn, you simply must try the new, fruity, fresh white wine which runs down your throat like water. At this time of the year the wine lovers can be seen sitting with their green-stemmed glasses and cracking fresh nuts, dropping the nutshells onto the floor. Since everyone does so here, there is no need for you to use a litter bin in this case.

If you feel chilly in the evenings, try an *eau de vie*, a cherry or plum brandy. It is said that these are the only drinks that can make the devil himself drunk.

Everything you see or experience in Strasbourg will bring you face to face with the city's traditions. The local people love their music, their museums and their famous sights. The only thing that Strasbourg doesn't want to be is a mere meeting place of European politicians and a tourist centre.

One day, this city may really become the focal point of a true European Community, as the city fathers once imagined. But even without this new role, Strasbourg will always remain an important and interesting trading city on the banks of the Rhine.

In addition, Strasbourg is a good starting point for your journey through Alsace. Here you will find, in concentration, something of the essence of all the other Alsatian cities. You will find out much about its inhabitants, their history and traditions in the well-organised museums. The city extends a hearty welcome to all its visitors.

tempting display of nes.

COLMAR

Colmar is not only the capital of Upper Alsace, but has for years been known as the "capital of Alsatian wine". The city's own coat of arms takes this fact into account. According to legend, Hercules, driving the cattle of Geryoneus towards Greece, is believed to have stopped off in Colmar and, after a few jugs of Alsatian wine, fallen into a deep sleep. Once awakened from his tipsy dreams, claims the legend, he forgot his club, which was then incorporated into the city's coat of arms as proof that even the strength of Hercules was no match for the wines of Alsace.

The wine and the excellent well-run restaurants, which pamper their guests with the culinary delights of Alsatian cuisine, are, however, not the only reasons for stopping in Colmar.

The city is in a strategic position on the north-south route from Strasbourg to Basle, and is set among a network of little rivers, which used to be navigable in earlier times and have contributed much to the city's economic growth. It was not so long ago that the farmers and market gardeners from the surrounding country rowed their loaded barges along the Thur, the Lauch and the Ill and moored by the market halls along the banks of the Lauch. Today Colmar is the centre of a major industrial area, and the Canal d'Alsace, only eight miles (13 km) away, is of economic significance.

A stroll through the picturesque old town with its narrow streets curling around St. Martin's Cathedral gives the visitor the impression of walking through a medieval stage set. The little crooked half-timbered houses, the proud, richly adorned houses of the wealthy merchants, and the former guild quarters which follow the banks of the Lauch are eloquent witnesses to the past and make the city's history come alive most impressively.

Colmar in the Middle Ages: The origins of the name "Colmar" are not quite clear. Some believe the name came from *Colis Maris* (Hill of Mars). Others, because of the famous cabbage fields in the vicinity, take it as a form of *Kohlmarkt* (German for cabbage market). The widespread theory is that the name comes from *Columbarum* (Dovecote), as there was, near the Roman camp of Argentovario (Horbourg), a villa with a large dovecote (which, however, was just as likely to have been a funeral parlour with niches for urns).

In any case, it is definitely established that there was a Franconian royal court to the west of the former Roman camp of Horbourg. It was first mentioned in 823 in a charter of Louis the Pious. It is from this settlement that the sons of Louis, who were conspiring against their father because of the division of their inheritance, are believed to have set out to take their father prisoner on

eceding ges, left d right, e Isenheim tar in Imar.

the Field of Red to the west of Colmar. Ever since then the Field of Red has been known as the *Field of Lies*. In the 10th century, Otto the Great arranged for the cathedral chapter of Constance and the monastery of Peterlingen (now Payerne) to share the former royal lands of Columbarum. The city of Colmar developed from the Lower Court (belonging to Constance) and the Upper Court (belonging to Peterlingen).

Colmar first flourished during the Hohenstaufen dynasty. In 1220 the imperial governor had a wall built around the city, and in 1226 Colmar was promoted to Free Imperial City by the Hohenstaufen emperor Frederick II. Imperial favour towards the city was expressed by several visits. Once Frederick entered Colmar at the head of an unusual procession, which included camels, veiled women and Ethiopian eunuchs, to the surprise of the citizens.

Rudolf of Habsburg also showed favour to the city; in 1278 he presented Colmar, which had joined the Rhine League of Cities, with the right to its own jurisprudence with city privileges.

From 1230 onwards several mendicant orders settled in the city. In later years, they left their mark on the spiritual life of Colmar, and also on its architecture and art. (For instance, in 1389 Colmar was the birthplace of a reform movement within the Dominican order. The movement campaigned for strict observation of the law of poverty and was intended to spread across Europe.)

The **Dominican church**, whose foundation stone was laid by Rudolf of Habsburg, was built in 1283. Its architecture reflects the order's claims to poverty. Wide spaces and simplicity are characteristics of this church hall of reddish-yellow sandstone, its central aisle supported by a number of slender pillars. The stained glass windows, by members of the Colmar School of the

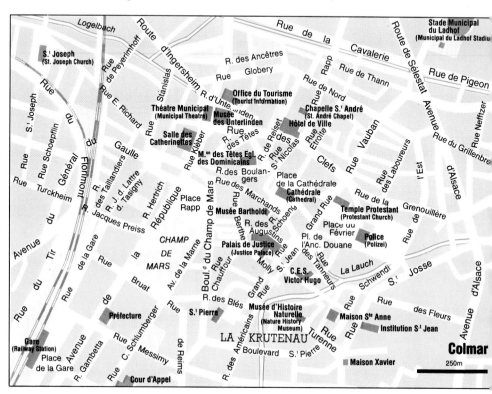

14th century, portray scenes from the New Testament.

Today you can see the *Madonna among the Roses* hanging above the altar in the choir. The picture was painted in 1473 by Schongauer for St. Martin's Cathedral. A copy of the work can be seen only in the Boston Museum. In 1720 the central part of the original triptych (the side panels were lost) was shortened by 1.65 ft (50 cm) all round to fit into a curved frame. Still, the mutilated masterpiece is impressive. In the figure of Mary, Schongauer has left the early German conventions of portraying the Madonna behind him, and has indeed stepped into a new creative realm. The expressive nature of the figure has often given rise to comparisons with the Sistine Madonna.

Martin Schongauer was born in 1445 in Colmar, studied under the Colmar painter Kaspar Isenmann and with a copper engraver in Strasbourg, and later

founded his own school in Colmar. Apart from *Madonna among the Roses*, he also created the panels of the altar of the Antonite monastery in Isenheim and the frescoes in the church at Breisach.

A few years after the Dominican monks, Dominican nuns settled in Colmar, in a convent with the symbol of St. John under the linden tree. In later years, the **Unterlindenkloster** (Linden Tree Convent) became a spiritual and intellectual centre. It was one of the main centres of mysticism in the Rhine valley and had close contacts with Meister Eckhardt and Jean Tauler.

During the Revolution, the order was dissolved, and since 1850 the convent came under the care of the Schongauer Society and was turned into a museum. Today it is one of the most beautiful and most frequently visited in France. Above all, it is the *Isenheimer Altar* of the artist Matthias Neithart that has made the museum world-famous, and

Petit vre or erlinden seum in mar.

yet the *Petit Louvre* holds a few other treasures. In the old convent cellar is an archaic collection of Gallo-Roman and Merovingian-Frankish items. There are also two halls with works from the Impressionist to the abstract modern periods (with paintings by Picasso, Leger, Vasarely and Braque, etc). The first floor is devoted to works of Alsatian folk art. The eastern wing holds a collection of Alsatian primitive paintings, with great works by Cranach (the Elder), Holbein (the Elder), Urbain Huter and Kaspar Isenmann.

A walk through these halls prepares you for the visit to the convent chapel, which contains important treasures of the museum. From the gallery you can view the altars, which come from the former Antonite monastery in neighbouring Isenheim. There, in the late 13th century, the Antonites founded a monastery to care for the sick who suffered from the so-called *St. Anthony's*

Fire, i.e. smallpox. The altar was believed to have healing powers for the sick who came and today it forms the heart of the collection in the choir of the convent chapel. In 1510 Matthias Neithart, known as Grünewald, was commissioned to paint the altar shrine carved by the Strasbourg woodcarver Nikolaus Hagenau. Nowadays the altar panels have been repositioned to make the sequence of pictures clearer.

Originally, the panels, painted on both sides, depicted the passing of the church year. Then, on ordinary working days, the panels were closed and the altar showed the Crucifixion. During Christian festivals, the outer pair of panels, depicting the Annunciation, Mary and the infant Christ, and the Resurrection, were opened. The inner pair of panels was opened only on significant Christian feast days and showed scenes of the work of St. Anthony.

Even nowadays, much is unclear

The Koifhu symbol of economic prosperity in the city.

about the life of the artist who made this inimitable masterpiece. His life story inspired Paul Hindemith to write his opera *Mathis der Maler*. Matthias Grünewald was a much respected court painter in the service of Albrecht of Brandenburg. Later, during the troubled times of the Reformation and the Peasants' War, Grünewald stood on the side of the people and fell into disgrace.

In the nave you can see the *Annunciation*, painted by Martin Schongauer and intended for the Antonite monastery, and the altar of the Passion with its 16 panels, commissioned by the Dominican church, which shows the life of Mary in eight panels on the back.

The economic and cultural rise of the city of Colmar was not totally untroubled, and the people often had to fight for their freedom. The Bishop of Strasbourg twice tried to take the city. The first attempt failed, due to the intervention of Rudolf of Habsburg. How-

ever, in 1266 the bishop's troops invaded the city, under the guise of Habsburg followers. But they were driven out again, thanks to the efforts of the mayor, Rösselmann, who died at the head of the civil militia. Twenty years later, Colmar was besieged again by the once helpful Rudolf of Habsburg, as the city refused to pay taxes owed to him.

In 1630 the city voted itself a democratic constitution, which gave the guilds a prominent position and thus took into account the economic development of the city. Evidence of the economic rise of Colmar is the **Koifhus** (Ancienne Douane), of 1480. Goods subject to excise duty were kept on the ground floor of this building, with its roof made of coloured glazed tiles and its balustrade about the eaves. Loaded carts could drive with ease through the great Gothic gates, crowned by the Habsburg double-headed eagle. The council of the Decapolis met on the first

icacies
he
tival of
e and folk
ditions.

floor. Today, the glass windows of the meeting hall are still adorned with the coats of arms of the ten member cities. The staircase tower and the roofed open-air staircase were built in the 16th and 17th centuries.

A few well-preserved medieval houses can still be seen today, such as the Adolph House (1350) on the south side of the square in front of St Martin's Cathedral, the *Huselin zum Swan* (Little Swan House, 1480) in the Gothic style as well as the Gihe House (1385), in which the Schongauer family lived for a time. However, no mention can be made of Colmar's medieval architecture without including St. Martin's Cathedral. With its colourful tiled roof and the south tower with its Renaissance top, it has become a symbol of the city. First of all, Maître Humbert was commissioned in 1250 to build a new church on top of the Ottonian pillared basilica dating from the year 1000. In the years

that followed, Meister Wilhelm of Marburg, from the Rhineland, and later Meister Henselin from the Swabian Parler school took over the building project. Changes over the project architect led to the church being a combination of Rhineland, French, Gothic and Romanesque elements. Despite attempts to finance the building by a sort of inheritance tax (every citizen had to donate the best piece of his inheritance, whether it was a pig, a cow, or a jacket) you realise by looking at the church that money was tight when it was built. Only the south tower, 236 ft (72 m) high, was completed, and the building is quite plain, except for the south side.

The St. Nicholas portal on the southern transept is spectacular. The lower part is Romanesque and shows the legend of St. Nicholas, the Gothic upper part shows the Last Judgement. The wall above the portal is decorated with a tracery rampart. In the lower part of

The coloure glazed tiles are a speci feature of t cathedral o St. Martin.

the ornamented section, Maître Humbert left his portrait for posterity.

Unfortunately the interior is not very interesting any more, as this church too was turned into a "Temple of Reason" during the French Revolution. Only a few 14th century stained glass windows have survived and some wall paintings, unfortunately in poor condition. The valuable pieces, such as the *Altar of the Passion* made in 1556 by Gaspard Isenmann and Martin Schongauer's *Madonna among the Roses*, have been housed in other churches in Colmar, as St. Martin's does not have the necessary security facilities.

Religious divisions: The Reformation arrived a little late in Colmar. In 1522 the printer Armandus Farckell printed the works of Luther, and in 1575 the majority of the Council expressed their support for the reformed faith. Although the new Protestants filled the important economic positions in town,

the troubles of the Reformation and the Peasants' War only brushed the fringes of life in Colmar, and did not hinder the economic development of the city.

In the years that followed, the city flourished and its burgesses became wealthy, as is shown by many buildings, particularly those in the Rue des Marchands and in the Grande Rue. The **Koifhus** was expanded to meet demand and the old **Wachthof** (*Coups de Garde*) was built anew, in the style of the Italian Renaissance. Originally, this building with its beautiful Renaissance entrance supported by Tuscan pillars served as city armoury and guardroom. A few years later, the built-on, loggia-like judicial court annexe, adorned with five arches, masks and coats of arms, was torn down again. Next door is the Pfister house, built in 1573 for a hatter from Besancon. One of the most beautiful burgess' houses in the city, it has a painted facade and a wooden balcony.

ere you
sip on
famous
ot wines.

Culturally speaking, Colmar's role was modest compared to previous years. The famous poet Jörg Wickram and Colmar's school of Meistersinger kept folk culture and the theatre alive.

Life in Colmar was fairly placid until the turbulent Thirty Years' War. Even nowadays, the appearance of the city is still due mainly to the decorated Renaissance buildings. In 1609 the Maison des Têtes, with its facade adorned with about 100 masks, was built. The **Arcade house** and the so-called St John's house date from the same period.

Peace was shattered, however, when Colmar, together with a large portion of Alsace, was leased to Charles le Téméraire. Charles' steward, Pierre of Hagebach, extorted so much from the country that the Alsatians stood by their Duke Sigismund, who had leased the province from financial necessity, and helped to pay his debts. Despite the paid-up debts, however, Hagebach re-

fused to release Alsace, and had to be driven out by force. You can still see the sword which was used to behead this enemy after the victorious campaign; it's in the Petit Louvre.

More troubles was to come later, when the Swedes occupied Colmar during the Thirty Years' War. The Swedes brought the Protestant faith back to Colmar: Ferdinand II had proscribed it in 1628 and Protestants were forced to leave the city. The fact that the city was not razed at that time is said to be due to the Pinot wine, which is still considered one of the best wines. The Swedes were believed to have got drunk that they forgot to destroy the city.

The Tokay grapes had been brought to Alsace by the poet and gourmet, General Field Marshal Lazarus of Schwendi from his victorious campaigns in Hungary. The episode with the Swedes would alone have been reason enough to set up a memorial to the brave Alsa-

Left, the Schwendi fountain in front of the Koifhus. Right, the Maison des Têtes.

tian, and there is one in front of the Koifhus, showing the Generalissimo holding a bunch of Tokay grapes instead of a sword.

To rid the Swedes, Colmar, together with other cities of the Decapolis, placed itself under Richelieu's protection. But instead of providing the hoped-for protection and freedom, the Sun King demolished the walls of the city in 1673. He also had the city occupied by troops and forced its population to pledge loyalty to France. However, as compensation, the city was made the highest judicial authority in Alsace. Catholicism, the French state religion, was re-introduced. The Jesuits and the Capuchin monks attempted to gather the lost sheep and show them the right path once more.

Although relations with the French authorities improved in the years that followed, the religious split still remained unhealed until the 18th century.

The people, mainly Protestant, remained true to the German language, and the Catholic elite used French.

Colmar in the Age of Enlightenment: Many important buildings were put up in Colmar in the late 18th century, such as the Jesuit chapel and library, with paintings by Hans Melling, built in 1742; the Classical building of the Sovereign Council of Alsace, which moved to Colmar in 1698; the old hospital in the Place du Février; and many elegant town houses.

From an intellectual and economic point of view, Colmar in the Age of Enlightenment was a city open to all innovations. Many schools were opened and new journals published. The first manufacturing industries settled outside the gates of the city. It was thus not surprising that the Revolution evoked a positive response in Colmar, especially as one of the members of the Directorate, Reubell, was born in

'etite
ise along
river
ch.

Colmar. In 1793 Catholic church services were proscribed. An altar to the Goddess of Reason was erected in the choir of St. Martin's; a gigantic structure crowned by a blazing fire in an urn. Revolutionary speeches were made before this altar and subversive songs were sung. Once, a great feast for the elderly was held. A worthy citizen of Colmar, nearly 100 years old, was made the hero of the evening. Pressed to make a speech, the honoured gentleman could manage only "Long live the King!"

During the era of the Empire, the Emperor Napoleon Bonaparte also honoured Colmar with a visit, but was not impressed: as far as he was concerned, Colmar was nothing but *un trou* (a hole). However, Voltaire showed more enthusiasm. He spent some time in the city and declared his wish to become an Alsatian. It was probably the creature comforts offered by the city that led him to make this remark. Later, however, he complained that Colmar was a "capital of Hottentots, ruled by Jesuits". It was, after all, the latter order that had initiated and supervised the book-burnings.

Colmar never again achieved the importance in the artistic field that it had held in the late Middle Ages, yet there were some talented artists among its citizens in the 19th century. Among them was the graphic artist and lithographer Jacques Rothemüller, who recorded the beauty of his homeland in many fine detailed prints.

Another talented citizen of Colmar was the sculptor Frédéric Auguste Bartholdi. The house where he was born, now the **Bartholdi Museum**, is in the Rue des Marchands. Bartholdi not only created a number of monuments for his hometown (the Schongauer memorial, the Rosselman memorial, the Schwendi fountain among others), but also the Lion of Belfort, a symbol of resistance to German occupation, the Helvetia monument in Basle, the Vercingetorix monument in Clermont-Ferrand and his most famous work, the Statue of Liberty, a present from France to the United States of America.

Bartholdi, who was in sympathy with the ideas of the Enlightenment, was commissioned to make the Statue of Liberty by the *American-French Friendship Society*, which saw in the founding of the United States the "perfection of the French Revolution", which appeared to have been betrayed in the France of Napoleon III. After a test assembly of the statue in Paris in 1876 (for which Gustave Eiffel built the scaffolding), the weighty lady, costing 600,000 francs, was to be shipped to America. However, technical and financial problems delayed the transporting of the statue, dismembered and packed in 200 boxes, to New York by rail and by sea until 1885.

The delight of the Americans was not exactly boundless, as they had failed to raise enough money to build a suitable base. However, there was no limit to the American spirit of invention. Joseph Pulitzer held a sponsorship campaign which not only helped Miss Liberty gain her base, but also made his journal *The World* a successful advertising media with a wide circulation. During the repair work undertaken for the USA bicentenary celebrations, the old formula was used: repairs were financed by the granting of advertising licences.

In 1870, despite bitter opposition among the populace, Colmar was occupied by German troops once more and became the capital of Upper Alsace. Even though the buildings put up during the annexation, such as the post office, the railway station and the new law courts, were of late 19th century German design, the Alsatians still considered themselves French. Committed individuals such as the priest Wetterle, the member of parliament Charles Gard and the cartoonist Hansi (Jean Jacques Waltz) waged a bitter struggle against all things German. On 18 November

1918 Colmar was liberated and a year later was ceded back to France.

Colmar in the 20th century: Between the two world wars, no drastic changes took place in Colmar. Although the city suffered from the global economic crisis, some new industries did settle in the vicinity, and apart from the wine trade the tourist industry offered new opportunities for employment and business.

In 1940 Colmar was once again occupied by German troops, but despite the hard battles around the "Colmar pocket" the city suffered little damage until its liberation in 1945.

Where the centuries and two world wars had failed, progress-obsessed city planners almost succeeded in the 1950s. A wave of modernisation swept across France, and the demolition of a large part of the old city was earmarked. However, the Malreaux law, which protected old town centres and provided funds for modernisation and restoration, ended this fury of development.

First of all, the tanner's quarter with its old craftsmen's houses was restored. To meet modern standards, the buildings were often demolished. The pressure of a rapidly increasing population forced the houses built up as high as the attic. Where restoration was impossible, new buildings filled the gaps, but they had to fit in with the traditional architecture of the old city. Projecting upper stories, bay and oriel windows brightened up the dull facades; long streets were adorned with annexes, courtyards and gardens.

Similar work was done in the Fishermen's Quarter and in Little Venice. The whole outlook of the old city was to be preserved, but the accommodation had to meet modern standards. The outcome was a success. Colmar was awarded the gold medal of the *European Foundation for Historical Preservation and Quality of Life*.

MULHOUSE

If you visit Mulhouse, especially if you are on holiday, you will at first be surprised by the plainness, the modernity and the busy life of this city (the second largest in Alsace, with a population of 120,000), which is in marked contrast to the other towns and cities, equipped as they are with historic and artistic riches. However, visitors should not allow themselves to be frightened away, for they will have plenty of opportunity to learn about the beginnings and the development of our modern industrial age, and they will find evidence of the past no less exciting and magnificent because it is tucked away behind unassuming facades.

There may be a dearth of architectural "highlights" in the city, but the local authorities have tried to overcome this lack with museums, which can un-

doubtedly claim to be unique. The city itself, with its workers' housing estates (not all of them dull, by any means) and grey industrial architecture does actually confirm that development in Alsace did not stop in the 18th or 19th century.

It all started, just as it did in many other places, with a mill on the banks of the Ill. To be sure, the convenient position on the Rhine and the proximity to Basle played a part, and it was not long before the city began to develop. In the early Middle Ages there were two settlements—one belonging to Strasbourg, the other to the monastery of Masmünster—which grew together. Under the Hohenstaufen dynasty, the former town of Mülhausen was given its first set of fortifications. It was not long, though, before the secular powers came into conflict with the spiritual. But the people of Mulhouse knew how to look after their economic and political interests. The city reached its high-

Preceding pages, Schutzenberger bee has been around sin 1740—the noblesse oblige of tradition.

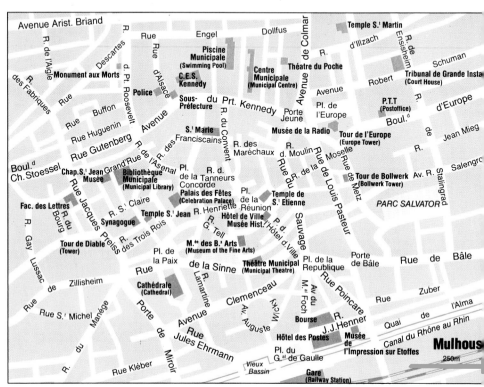

est point of prosperity during the Industrial Revolution.

As early as the 13th century, the Hohenstaufen dynasty took away the bishop's right of governorship. The people of Mulhouse allied themselves with Rudolf of Habsburg and drove their spiritual overlord from the city. In 1293 Adolf of Nassau granted them civic rights. In 1354 they joined the Alsatian league of cities (the Decapolis) and, after a long struggle, they drove the aristocracy out of the city. However, a civil war fought over next to nothing, the so-called Six Plappert (a coin of small value) War, showed how tense the situation was even within the middle classes. The war brought the city to the edge of ruin.

The miller's journeyman Hermann Klee had been dismissed from his service, and his master owed him the infamous six coins in wages. However, servitude had not robbed Hermann Klee

of his wits, and he turned to the urban aristocracy, already infuriated because they had been thrown out of the city council by the middle classes. In Peter of Eguisheim he found a willing ally. Eguisheim immediately kidnapped a couple of burgesses of Mulhouse as hostages, and was only prepared to release them for a considerable ransom. Long drawn-out negotiations were unsuccessful, and so the city took up arms against him. Finally, the knight had to flee to his castle, which was by now commanded by none other than Klee. In 1466, the castle was stormed. Peter and the miller's journeyman were hanged, and the building was burned down. Only three towers remained standing. The people of Mulhouse ignored these towers for a long time, until some farmers discovered by accident that they could tell the time of day from the shadows thrown by the towers.

The much weakened city now faced

:urator of easure chapel Jean, ouse.

new threats from the nobility, this time from Burgundy. The Decapolis declined to protect them, so they sought help from the Swiss. Berne and Solothurn were among the first sworn allies. In 1506 a treaty of protection was signed with Basle, and in 1515 the city was granted membership in the Swiss Confederation. This connection lasted until 1528, when the city's *Confessio Mulhusina* made a radical decision in favour of the non-Lutheran Reformed church and thus split off from the Catholic Swiss. This development can be better understood if one takes into consideration that Calvinist thought appealed more to business ethics of the burgesses than Catholicism.

In 1789 the city council decided to join the young French Republic. This, too, was primarily an economically motivated decision, for the customs barriers for trade with France would have been an insurmountable obstacle for the growing businesses of the city. The production of printed calico, begun by the citizens Koechlin, Schmaltzer and Dollfus in 1746, had initiated a considerable boom in the city's prosperity. This was the birth of Mulhouse's Industrial Revolution.

The city soon became the second most important in Alsace and could certainly stand comparison with Manchester, for calico printing also brought in other industries. Accommodation for workers was built, and the population grew from 6,000 in 1798 to 70,000 in 1870. Social problems of course increased with the growth of the population. The industrial processes required skilled employees, and the workforce had to be accommodated. In 1832, 22 industrial companies joined forces to form the *Société Industrielle* and founded technical colleges and the first business college in France, further proof of the farsightedness and business

Mulhouse Place de l Réunion.

acumen of the people of Mulhouse. There was more: it was recognised that a prosperous textile industry needed a workforce which could live in decent surroundings. A successor to the aged Dollfus, who also held the post of mayor, had work begun in 1851 on a workers' new town in Dornach, the so-called *Cité ouvrière*. With its pretty front gardens the development was a model for its times and is still of interest to architects today. Mulhouse has remained the French production centre of printed fabrics to this day. However, other industries also grew significantly, in particular potash mining and multi-national companies such as Peugeot, Rhône-Poulenc etc.

The city suffered much from both world wars and lost almost all its historic buildings. In 1945, it saw the start of a new boom as an economic centre after the construction of the Grand Canal d'Alsace.

Nevertheless, you should not, on your way to the textile, art, railway and automobile museums, miss out on the architectural treasures. Go through the pedestrian precinct, which leads you past more or less exclusive shops, and you will come to the Place de la Réunion and to the one truly beautiful building in the city, the **Town Hall** dating from 1552. The painted outer facade, in the Swiss style, acts like a *trompe l' oeil* painting. The facade depicts allegories of the virtues and figures from the Bible. The meeting hall in the Town Hall still has windows with medallion panes dating from the 16th and 17th centuries. Apart from these, the building contains the **Musée Historique**, which is well worth a look. It has departments of local archaeology, the history of Mulhouse and the folk traditions and arts of Sundgau. The greatest attraction, however, is the clapper stone. It was hung around the necks of scandal-mongers

and false witnesses who then had to parade through the city in shame.

The **Place de la Réunion** forms the purely Alsatian part of the city centre of Mulhouse, thanks not least to the Temple St. Etienne (a Protestant church) which has been restored to its original appearance. Inside, substantial portions of the stained glass windows, gifts of the counts of Ferrette in 1340, have survived. They depict scenes from the Old and New Testaments.

The **Chapelle St. Jean** has an idyllic location right in the middle of the busy city, surrounded by a park. This is a former chapel of the Knights of Malta. The beautiful frescoes were painted in the 16th century, partly by the Hans Herbster workshop, which included the artist Hans Holbein the Younger. The chapel now houses a rock collection.

The **New Quarter** near the Jardin de la Bourse gives an impression of upper middle-class life in post-Napoleonic times, with its Classical theatre and the synagogue for the Jewish community, which once had 300 members.

Once past the **Place de la République**, you can either turn left to the Museum of Fine Arts (well worth it if you're interested in the local artists Henner and Lehmann, and Fauvistes), or, passing the ramparts, go to the **Place de l'Europe** with the coats of arms of European cities set into the paving. The square is probably intended to demonstrate the broad scale of the city, but the multi-storey car park and the high-rise block, constructed like the tangent of a circle, give it the atmosphere of a lifeless suburb.

The main attractions of Mulhouse are the technical museums. The **Museum of Printed Fabrics** is a must for visitors, even for those who aren't *that* interested in cloth and textiles.

The **Musée National de l'Automobile**, one of the most important and

The Botanic Gardens of Mulhouse considered the most beautiful in France.

valuable collections of cars in the world, owes its origins to circumstances which belong to the less acceptable face of Mulhouse capitalism. The Schlumpf brothers, with the help of their profitable textile factories, built up a manufacturing empire employing several thousands of people. The somewhat extraordinary passion of Franz Schlumpf, who was then among the six wealthiest men in France in 1972, led to the sudden bankruptcy of the business in 1976. The two brothers had grown up near Milan, the hometown of the car designer Ettore Bugatti, who became their nemesis. With an almost fanatical obsession they bought anything made by Bugatti, even electric models for children. Prototypes and special models, even the most famous car in the world, Ettore Bugatti's personal La Royale, a coupé, came into their hands. There are 464 cars and 98 brand names in the collection today, among them cars which

belonged to Charlie Chaplin, President Poincaré, the Emperor Bao Dai and Maurice Trintignant.

Such an exotic hobby cost money, of course—the value of the collection is estimated at 80 million francs today—and Franz Schlumpf froze the wages in his textile factory in order to spend every available franc on his private collection, which was open only to connoisseurs and a select circle. In October 1976 the workforce went on strike, and besieged the Schlumpf villa in Malmersbach. The elitist dream world of the Schlumpfs collapsed and the brothers fled to Basle. The collection, under the name *Worker's Museum*, was open to the public.

Old factory buildings in the Avenue Colmar on the opposite bank of the Ill have been turned into exhibition halls. However, these are also on the near side of the motorway, so it is advisable to go by car. The exhibition area covers

214,780 sq ft (20,000 sq m) and is lit by 500 replicas of old street lanterns. You should allow at least two hours for the distance of about one and a quarter miles (2 km) involved. In this extensive museum complex there are also restaurants and a sales stand where you can buy models of the exhibited cars for your mantelpiece at home.

A little further out, in Dornach, on the road to Thann, is the railway museum, the **Musée Francais du Chemin de Fer**, which has its rightful place in this industrial city. Businessmen in Mulhouse invested early in this technological development which was at first regarded with much scepticism elsewhere. The first railway line in Alsace, after all, was opened in the mid-19th century. SNCF, French state railways, have made every effort to present the exhibition attractively. One of the many locomotives is sited above a trench, another has been cut in half lengthways,

so that you can see the insides of these monsters. The engine in yet another locomotive can be set in motion by visitors. Right in the entrance hall is the famous Eagle (*l'Aigle*), built in 1864 by Stephenson in Newcastle. The fire brigade museum is in the hall next door. The pride of the exhibits must surely be the old telephone switchboard of the former Mulhouse fire station.

The city fathers have developed an entire new museum concept in the **Maison de la Céramique** (Ceramics Museum) and proved that they are open to new developments and influences, in cultural as in other fields. Here, in contrast to the classic ceramics villages of Betschdorf and Souflenheim, which keep to their old traditions, the modern potter's craft and ceramic art are displayed individually, although old techniques are certainly taken into account as well. A former brick works, with an area of 19,375 sq ft (1,800 sq m), pro-

A must for train lover Musée Français du Chemin de Fer.

vides space for an exhibition of old ceramics, mostly from the building industry, as well as a department for over 40 ceramic artists from eastern France. The continually-changing display of their work provides a refreshing picture of this craft, which has long been part of life in Alsace. The house is not actually a museum, but a meeting place of industry and craft, and also of the ceramic craftsmen and the general public. A workshop built for this purpose is permanently open to all visitors and trained potters here give advice to interested amateurs. The house will be extended to include a department showing mass-produced products of Alsace.

Although—or perhaps because—Mulhouse is a city of smoking chimneys, it is nonetheless equipped with many parks and gardens, and among them the **Zoological and Botanical Gardens** are worth a visit. These gardens are the product of the innovative spirit of the 19th century and, with their extraordinary landscaping, are considered the most beautiful in France. Not far away is the Parc à la Française, a garden in the French style presented to the city by the arts patron Alfred Wallach. If you want more of nature, drive to the **Rhine Forest**, which will soon be declared a nature reserve, or to the area near the airport between the Rhine and the Rhine Canal, known as the **Petite Camargue Alsacienne** because of the many migrant birds and the rare water birds which settle here. ARIENA, a society for the preservation of nature, organises guided tours.

Finally, in Mulhouse you cannot do entirely without the old architecture that has left its indelible mark on all of Alsace. The **church of Ottmarsheim** is in fact one of the crowning glories of Ottonian architecture. It is modelled on the Palace Chapel in Aachen and does indeed show an exceptional clarity and

sée
tional de
utomobile:
Schlumpf
thers'
ection
now open
the public.

originality in its form, which is not the least due to the fact that all the important measures are in multiples of three (if you use the Benedictine foot as a standard). First of all, try looking at this well-planned yet plain-looking octagonal space without any preconceived ideas of art history. You will be amazed to discover that the medieval architects with their simple techniques were able to make use of space in a way that modern, hi-tech architecture rarely succeeds in doing.

If, after seeing Mulhouse and its urban bourgeois culture, you feel the need for some peasant and rural atmosphere, you don't have to drive very far, as the *Maisons Paysannes d'Alsace*, a society founded in 1971, has had a new "old" village built in Ungersheim. The village, the **Eco-Musée**, consists of a great variety of half-timbered houses from all over Alsace. The tradition of building timber-framed houses died out in the 19th century, and many excellent examples of this ancient building craft were left to decay. It was then that the society went into action. Hundreds of houses have been catalogued; whenever an owner wanted to demolish an old building, *Maisons Paysannes* intervened, stripped the old house beam by beam (often discovering potsherds or coins in the walls, put in for ritual or magical reasons) and rebuilt it here in the marsh, where the ground subsided because of potash mining. Of course, not every single house could be saved. The society have restricted themselves to characteristic examples and attempted to reflect the great variety of half-timbered buildings. In the Eco-Musée, therefore, you can find houses from the Sundgau, from the Upper Alsatian plain, or from the wine-growing areas. The museum is constantly being expanded. After all, there are some 30 different areas in Alsace with

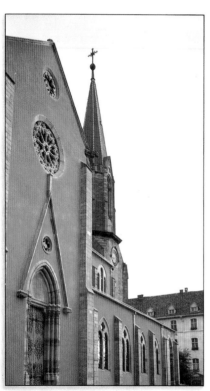

each boasting a particular building style. While here, you can watch craftsmen at work, using the old techniques in their restoration work. A section of the museum houses a bakery and a restaurant. If you would like to know more about the creation and work of the museum, the techniques of timber-frame building and the other regional styles, you should get the excellent and detailed handbook (which can be obtained at the ticket office).

On the way back to Mulhouse, you can make a short diversion to **Ensisheim**, the former capital of the county of Upper Alsace and the residence of the governor who looked after the Habsburg interests. In the Grand Rue you can still see the residence of the Austrian government, which later went to the *Conseil d'Alsace*. Today this space is taken up by the Town Hall with its beautiful hall of Gothic arcades and the interesting wooden ceiling in the

Salle du Conseil. In 492, a meteorite fell on the town and aroused worldwide interest. Its remains are displayed at the small museum in the building.

Certainly Mulhouse and its immediate environs do not have a wealth of art treasures, idyllic landscapes and recreational places that other districts of Alsace boast of. However, this comparatively dull city helps to secure the quality of life for the entire region, and not only via the tourist industry. In this city, you learn to understand that the industrial world forms an important part of our culture.

Textile and Wallpaper Museum: Mulhouse and its museums shock visitors out of any dreams of "romantic" Alsace and push them, in a manner not exactly gentle, back into the 20th century. However, none of these museums demonstrates the links between European industry and colonialism as well as the **Textile and Wallpaper Museum.**

ew
p-sign
dst old
roundings.

Cotton fabric, in colours previously unknown, was extremely popular in Europe during the late 16th century. The sailors of Christendom brought home not only spices, but also the colourful and colourfast Indiennes. A brisk trade developed in the 17th century, after the founding of the East India Company, which soon set up bases in the colonies and which was no longer contented with local designs, but had European patterns produced. Soon the production of printed calico was copied in Europe. France was an exception. The local silk and wool industries could not compete with their cotton rivals, so in 1686 Louis XIV made a proclamation: "His Majesty in his wisdom has commanded that all factories in the kingdom which print on white cotton shall cease to exist on the day of the said proclamation and the printing patterns for the same shall be made unserviceable and destroyed."

This prohibition was nonetheless

broken from the beginning, and nothing held back the victory of calico. In 1759 the prohibition had to be rescinded. Thirteen years before, the gentlemen Dollfus, Koechlin, Schmalzer and Feer had opened a small calico printing works in Mulhouse, *Schmalzer & Cie.* Its success was overwhelming, so much so that the partners split up and founded their own businesses. By 1787 there were 19 calico printing works. In the 19th century, the textile industry in Mulhouse reached its peak. In 1856, 52 million yards (48 million metres) of textiles were produced.

The French market expanded within Europe. Women wore summer dresses from Mulhouse. When Latin America, the Middle East and the Far East had been opened up, French firms began producing textile goods aimed at these markets. For instance, they printed materials in Turkish red for the Ottoman Empire. Today there are still six textile printing works in Alsace, and they account for about 40 per cent of French production.

Apart from a collection of cloth samples, the museum has a department of documentation and an extensive library. From June to September there are demonstrations of textile printing every Monday.

Just outside Mulhouse, in **Rixheim**, you can visit the **Wallpaper Museum**, which is part of the Textile Museum. Wallpaper as such was, for a long time, a wall decoration reserved for poorer houses. By the early 18th century, however, wallpaper had become so popular that no house in Paris was without some. The prohibition on printing cloth caused many Indienne manufacturers to change over to this new branch of production. Once English velvet paper and hand-painted Chinese paper had come on the market, no upper class house was without its papered walls.

Wallpaper manufacture became industrialised with Jean Baptiste Reveil-

Machine fo printing on wallpaper.

lon who had his workers glue the individual strips of paper together, before they were coloured. In 1790 the Indienne manufacturer J. J. Dollfus opened a wallpaper printing works in Mulhouse. Jean Zuber, major shareholder in the business in 1802, gave the company his name, which still has close ties with the company to this day. Next to the museum is a showroom where you can admire grandiose wallpaper patterns from the 19th century.

In 1804 Zuber brought his landscape printed papers onto the market. They were intended to transport the buyer into a dream landscape, an idealised America, perhaps, or Greece. With the sale of the wallpaper series *Les combats des Grecs*, Zuber supported the Greek struggle for independence from the Turks. However, most of the walls of the prosperous middle classes reflected colonial times. The exotic representations provide information on the current view of the conquered peoples held by the upper middle classes.

From 1870 on, the price of paper went down and the market expanded. The motifs became less elaborate, and there was a tendency towards imitations of leather, cloth, prints. A change came about with the work of William Morris and Art Nouveau. Now, wallpaper no longer imitated other materials, but was itself the basis for experiments with colour and shapes. The "Wallpaper Crisis" began with Le Corbusier. He represented the opinion that wallpaper was outmoded and should be replaced by chalk-coloured oil paint.

Before leaving the museum, you should strike up a chat with the lady at the ticket office. She seems to have some personal connection with the house of Zuber and apparently knows all about the factory's rich and famous customers who obviously do not believe that the "Wallpaper Crisis" exists.

THE NORTH

The holiday routes which we are about to describe lie to the north of Strasbourg or on the same level.

The circular route through the picturesque villages leads to northern Alsace. On your journey, you will see the occasional sign pointing out that you are on the *Circuit des villages pittoresques*.

However, you need not have to stick to the succession of villages that rigidly. We would rather you develop an interest for the sights of Alsace than to systematically tick off one place after another as stopovers. Please remember that you are in charge of conducting your very own personal tour. You may opt out of the recommended routes and follow your own itinerary whenever you fancy.

Up in the north, in Wissembourg, you can change to the **Castle Route** and then onto the **Northern Wine Route**. The Castle Route, *Route des châteaux*, leads you right across the nature reserve of the northern Vosges, a popular place for excursions, with many interesting sights. Here, too, you don't need to follow the routes exactly. From Saverne, you can head straight for the Kochersberg region and then back to Strasbourg, or travel further up via Marmoutier as far as Schirmeck and then follow the ridge of the Vosges *Route des crêtes* if you want to pass Strasbourg by.

In the **Kochersberg** region you will often see signs with the inscription *Route du tabac*, though it isn't only tobacco that flourishes around here. This area has always been regarded as Strasbourg's larder and as a result is "rich" and inviting to famished visitors.

We hope you will have a pleasant and adventurous trip through the northern region of Alsace.

Preceding pages, lush green meadows in Kochersberg.

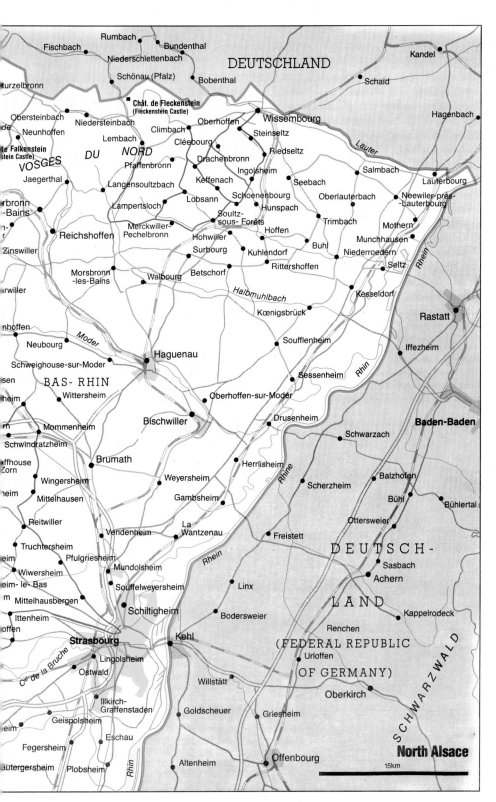

North Alsace

15km

125

THE PICTURESQUE VILLAGES

Travelling through the northern border region, you will come across signs saying *Circuit des Villages Pittoresques*. The half-timbered houses here are among the most beautiful and best-preserved in Alsace. This is true of **Seebach** and **Hunspach**, where you find curved panes in some of the windows, and for **Hohwiller**, the potters' village with its winding lanes. The houses here face the street at an angle, and one can get a view of village life from the side windows. In **Hoffen** and in **Soultz-sous-Forêts** are streets full of these friendly houses. **Kuhlendorf** has the only half-timbered church in Alsace.

Schoenenburg, however, does not live up to its name, for connected to it, slightly hidden in the woods, is a hideous monument to more recent history, a concrete bunker of the **Maginot Line**, the defences dating from the two world wars. A notable contrast to the rather sinister bunker is formed by one of the beautiful, almost prehistoric-looking stone benches, of which there are still some 450 in Alsace. The first was built in honour of the birth of the King of Rome, the son of Napoleon. Further benches were set up in honour of the marriage of Napoleon II in 1854.

Haguenau and the sacred forest: The imperial palace of **Haguenau** was once a favourite stopover for the Hohenstaufens. There is now a Jesuit college on the site of the former palace which once sheltered Frederick Barbarossa and hid the imperial jewels. The Emperor Henry VI, Richard Lionheart, Philippe August, Rudolf of Habsburg, Adolf of Nassau and Louis of Bavaria also stayed here, as did Reinmar the Old and Bernhard of Clairvaux. In 1164 Haguenau received town privileges and became a Free Imperial City in 1260. The town has, however, kept little of its former glory as the capital of the Decapolis and cultural centre. Bombing raids, new supermarkets and modern urban architecture have robbed the town (also a centre of the Alsatian beer industry) of its face. The rebuilding of the facade of the former Governor's Hall has not been very successful either.

The Governor's Hall houses the **Musée d'Alsace**, which is well worth visiting, especially on account of the traditional costumes from the region between Zorn and Moder, of the pottery workshop, the naive glass painting and the exhibition of tools used in viniculture. Worth seeing also is the **parish church of St George**, with its three-aisled pillared nave modelled on Hohenstaufen church buildings. From 1250 on the transept and the choir were built in the tradition of the builders of Strasbourg Cathedral. A real treasure, though, is the sacristy, which dates back to 1523. It is one of the best pieces of

stonemasons' work in Alsace. Here is also where the two oldest bells in the country are hung. Unfortunately, the church is not always open.

If you arrive in Haguenau in early September, you can attend the popular hop festival. Haguenau may not fulfil all the expectations you may associate with a former imperial palace, but the forest, where there are many footpaths and cycle tracks, and the monasteries more than make up for them. The only sacred building in the forest itself is the **chapel of St. Arbogastes**. Arbogastes was the first Bishop of Strasbourg and is honoured as the patron saint of the struggle against tiredness! He founded the Benedictine monastery of **Surbourg** at the edge of the forest.

The abbey church, a cruciform basilica in the early Romanesque style, was built in the 11th century. The choir, with its Gothic cruciform vaulting, was added later in the 15th century. Even so, the building shows an extraordinary clarity, unity and simplicity of line, not the least due to the rhythmic pattern of square pillars and round columns.

Seltz, an army camp in Roman times, became a Benedictine monastery some 1,000 years later. The Empress Adelaide, widow of Otto I, who was regent of the empire up until her death in 999, felt at home in this monastery. The abbey church was destroyed in World War I and was replaced by a new building in 1960. The best-preserved monastery of the Haguenau Forest is **Walbourg**. Building began on the abbey church in the 11th century. The church also comprises, despite destruction during the Peasants' War, a sacristy dating from the 16th century, sculptures and frescoes from the 15th, and church windows by Pierre d'Andlau dating from 1461. Frederick Barbarossa's father was buried in the abbey in 1147.

On the way to Strasbourg, you can

Lining the streets of t village are narrow str of gardens with colou flowers.

make a stop in **Brumath**. Here barrows were discovered containing items from the Hallstätt culture, which have found a home in the beautiful museum together with Gallo-Roman stone steles and votive inscriptions, as well as boxes of items in bronze, iron, bone and earthenware. In **Weyersheim** one of the greatest of German artists was born in 1484 or 1486. This was Hans Baldung, who received his nickname Grien during his apprenticeship in Strasbourg. The village can also be counted among the *villages pittoresques* on account of its many old half-timbered houses, some of which still have beams with the date of their construction inscribed.

The German poet Goethe also studied law as a young man in Strasbourg. His studies were to have far-reaching consequences, for it was then that he met and was very much impressed by the author Herder, and other literati such as Jung-Stilling, the *Sturm und Drang*

dramatist H. Leopold Wagner, and also J.M.R. Lenz, who followed in Goethe's footsteps. Goethe also met Alsatians such as Weyland, Engelbach Lerse and the placid J.D. Salzmann.

It was Weyland who proposed to Goethe that they should undertake the six-hour ride to see a vicar's family whom he knew, the Brions. Goethe quickly agreed and was pleased, but he wanted to travel incognito, just to allow himself some fun. He slipped into the role of a poor theology student, wearing a well-worn suit that was far too small for him. On their arrival in Sessenheim, Weyland apologised, saying that the Brion house was not in a very good condition and rather poor in appearance, but promised Goethe that the family was a very lively one.

Goethe was 21 then, and everything simple and rustic attracted him. For him, the house had "the very quality which is called picturesque, and which exercised such a magical attraction on me when I met it in Dutch art." In fact, the reception was very lively and free of constraint. Father and Mother Brion made a very tolerant and open-minded impression. However, it was their daughter Friederike, "on the borderline between a country and a city girl", who impressed Goethe so much the next morning that he was angry with himself because of his deception and his unprecedented exit. He had wanted to go back to Strasbourg, change his clothes and to return that same evening.

On the way, he remembered an innkeeper's son from Drusenheim, who had worn quite presentable clothes and who was as tall as himself. Goethe exchanged clothes with him, then styled his hair in similar fashion, and went back, once more not himself. However, this time he revealed himself, and was welcomed as a member of the family. There grew between him and Friederike the famous, much-quoted love affair, which was to end tragically for Frie-

se
dings
ne past
lly ever
; lifeless.

derike after only six months, and which the poet in his old age described in an entertaining style. The interested traveller should refer to the relevant passages from *Dichtung und Wahrheit*.

It is certain that Goethe dedicated many poems to his beloved and gave them to her in return for her ability to plan something entertaining for each of his visits. It can also be taken as certain that Goethe fell into a deep depression after their parting, and his friend Salzmann stood by him. Goethe apparently soon managed to pull himself out of it: "But human beings want to live; so I took a genuine interest in other people, I tried to disentangle them from embarrassment, and to reunite what was on the verge of parting, as I did not want them to suffer as I had."

One may argue about how decisive the influence of the Friederike episode was on Goethe's subsequent work, but the people of Sessenheim at least are of the opinion that part of his poetic work is due to a daughter of their village. They have furnished a small Goethe museum in the old guardhouse, which contains a collection of documents. The old barn behind the vicarage has been rebuilt in the original style, and recently a "Goethe tree" was even planted in the garden of the vicarage. The landlord of the Ox Inn has spent years of painstaking work in collecting everything that might have had some connection with the famous poet, even down to the weathercock which would have greeted Goethe on his rides to Sessenheim. This compensates for the fact that you can search for the idyllic atmosphere and the "fairy garden" which Goethe found in vain. Nothing here really adds to your knowledge of the famous poet. Whatever did happen between the two young people will probably remain a matter for speculation, as almost nothing survived of their exchange of letters. Frie-

Signboard at the old Goethe ba

derike's sister, who continued to take an interest in Goethe's work until her death, was believed to have burned all the letters; she claimed they annoyed her. Even Friederike's date of birth remains unknown.

The North Marsh: One of the most beautiful landscapes of northern Alsace is in the North Marsh region between **La Wantzenau** and **Münchhausen**. Here you can find a protected environment with a rich variety of plants and animals. Nowadays you're even supposed to feel pleased when the wretched and infamous midges turn up again every summer, proof that the wetlands with their marshy, reed-grown shores of little water courses are still alive. However, the young Goethe considered the creatures a plague. They pestered him so much that he assured Pastor Brion, the father of Friederike, "that these midges alone made me doubt the idea that a good and wise God created the world." The landscape right in the north, around Münchhausen, is a real treasure. Here the frutiful flood waters of the Rhine, the "Cherry Rhine", overflow the banks every June. You may be able to observe fishermen working along the banks. Even now you have to hunt for an idyllic spot, as a hydroelectric power station threatens to destroy the last of this special ecology.

In **Mothern**, whose inhabitants once had an infamous reputation for wild freebooters, there are still many boatmen's families. The village square has a memorial to this craft. The Rhine, of course, is no longer inviting to swimmers. The gravel pits are however suitable for swimming, as the water is changed regularly through the filter of Rhine sand and gravel, and many fishes from the Rhine have now settled here. Even the peaceful, sometimes melancholy landscape of the **Bas-Rhin** is not safe from the invasion of civilisation.

ple of
senheim
rded
derike,
ghter of
village,
Goethe's
sonal
e.

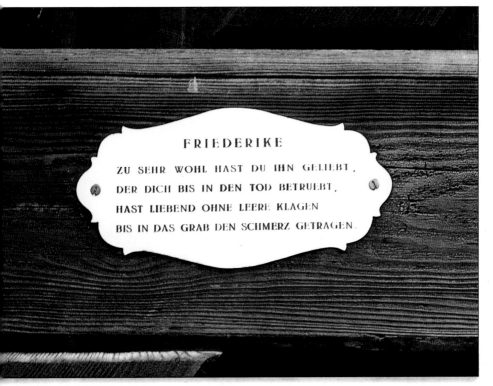

FRIEDERIKE

ZU SEHR WOHL HAST DU IHN GELIEBT,
DER DICH BIS IN DEN TOD BETRUEBT,
HAST LIEBEND OHNE LEERE KLAGEN
BIS IN DAS GRAB DEN SCHMERZ GETRAGEN.

STONEWARE AND POTTER'S WARE

If you visit the two famous potters' villages of **Soufflenheim** and **Betschdorf**, you will immediately notice that both villages produce quite different wares: Betschdorf produces a blue-grey stoneware, which is fired at particularly high temperatures, and Soufflenheim produces colourful pottery in warm natural shades ranging from white via golden yellow to rusty red and brown. An investigation carried out by the Freiburg-based *Institut für Volkskunde* in 1975 showed that the potters in each village knew very little about the techniques of their respective counterparts.

In Betschdorf, there were potters making ordinary earthenware long before the stoneware makers. The new process is believed to have arisen in the second half of the 13th century, yet the first stoneware producer was not documented until 1717. He came from Miehlen in the Taunus forest and was followed by Jean Dietrich Stolzer, also from Miehlen, who stayed in Betschdorf for only two years. During the 19th century many families came to Betschdorf from the Palatinate, the Westerwald and the Trier area—probably drawn by the wealth of clay in the forest of Haguenau. However, it was the Westerwald style of ceramics that had a definitive influence on Betschdorf production. Even nowadays, fine earthy clay is imported from that area and mixed with the less rich local material.

The status of the immigrant potters was at first not highly respectable among the villagers. They were foreigners, and despised as such. They were accused of "sneaking in" with cartloads of "garbage" from Germany. It is said that the first families sold everything and returned to their homelands. The potters who had remained at home discovered crumbs of Alsatian clay sticking to the clogs of those who returned, and asked them where it came from. Thereupon some families from the Westerwald moved permanently to Upper Betschdorf. The potters are fairly influential, with some sitting on the local council. Stoneware is hard earthenware which cannot be scratched even with steel, and which unlike earthenware will hold water without a glaze.

Most of the potteries are family concerns. For generations, the craft was passed from father to son. The men are responsible for getting the clay, preparing it for turning and firing, while the women attach the handles and work at ornamenting and painting the vessels.

From 1922 to 1968 the companies formed a co-operative, which fixed the prices for ordinary ware, but not for engraved and painted fancy products. They dug out the clay together. The clay pit in the forest belonged to the town of Haguenau, which had previously as-

Betschdorf salt glaze (blue firing

signed a small section to each potter. Later a factory for earthenware pipes created such a high demand that the town's section of the clay pits was soon used up, and the townsfolk asked if they could use the potters' sections. This was granted, and in return the the factory, with its mechanical diggers, now provides material for the potters.

The decorative patterns (because of the high temperatures, only cobalt colours are used) and the shapes of the jugs, pots and bowls have remained consistent for generations. This trend also applies to the Soufflenheim wares. The potters here trace back their rights for digging clay in the Haguenau forest to the times of Barbarossa. The legend says that the latter was once attacked by a wild boar while hunting. A potter rescued him, and since then the potters have been permitted to dig the clay without paying taxes for it. Soufflenheim pottery is more often mass-pro-

ily-
ed
s in
flenheim
use
tional
gns.

duced, using stencils. It is very soft and easily scratched, but the variety of shapes is greater than that of the Betschdorf ceramics. Here they make objects of daily use, the most famous being the *crinoline* (a milk jug), small figurines and whistling water pipes. Decorations are done with engraving tools, rods and brushes. Earth from the surrounding area are used to make up the colours.

Mass production and the use of gas-fired kilns have robbed most of the wares of their hand-crafted originality. One exception is Loys Ruhlmann in Betschdorf, who uses his own new designs on his wares. He works mostly with reductive firing, in which oxygen is gradually removed from the glaze and a brownish, irregular colour results. Ruhlmann still uses a wood-fired kiln. However, neither his rivals nor the tourists have much time for his original pieces, so he occasionally travels to the Westerwald to promote his wares.

ROUTE DES CHÂTEAUX

This route of castles and palaces runs from Wissembourg through the north of Alsace down to Schirmeck in the Bruche valley. It is not a tourist route, which is quite the reverse. There are many cultural and historical attractions to see, but if you set out to see the sights one after another, you will soon discover the limits of your receptive faculties. In other words, the holiday route of castles and palaces needs either rigorous planning before you set out or—and this is the more enjoyable course to take—a talent for improvisation.

Romance for individualists: Before setting out on this journey, you should be clear in your own mind that the delights of a tour of castles in Alsace do not consist only of viewing ancient monuments. The journey will only become a really interesting experience if repeatedly looked at the combination of culture and nature—and not only because a great part of the route runs through the *Parc Naturel Regional des Vosges du Nord* (Northern Vosges Nature Park). If you can spend a few days on the Route des châteaux, it is best to pick out first a few points along the route which may be of personal interest to you, and then leave the rest of your itinerary up to snap decisions according to personal inclination and the weather. Our suggestions have been made with such a travel plan in mind. They are not fixed points on an itinerary, but rather pointers to individual places and sights which are worthy diversions. Speaking of diversions, most of the old castles and castle ruins which are mentioned in this chapter lie along the Route des châteaux but cannot be reached directly by car. You will therefore have to walk, or to phrase it better, you will have the opportunity to walk, five minutes here, a quarter of an hour there, and occasionally even a full hour. These circumstances do have their advantages. On the one hand, they mean that consumer culture of mass tourism doesn't stand a chance here. On the other hand these forest walks mean that visitors not only get to see the castle in question, they also get to experience the atmosphere which surrounds these walls. The atmosphere, by the way, is "Romantic" in the true sense of the word. If you want to get away from all the clichés and find out what the term "Romance" really means, you should follow the Route des châteaux.

Incidentally, you should not try to follow the exact course of the castle route on the map or by the signs. The official information is partly full of gaps and partly contradictory. Take this as a positive appeal to your individuality. In the end, everybody has the chance to work out his or her very own personal Route des châteaux within the described area. For this chapter, we will

ceding
les,
vest time
he
hersberg
ion.
t and
t,
ned
tles are
ommon
ht in
ace.

stick to the route which begins in the north near Wissembourg, proceed south-west to La-Petite-Pierre and then on to southern Alsace.

Wissembourg: At first glance, this town in the Lauter valley does not reveal that it possesses a long and famous history. On this eastern edge of the northern Vosges the Romans built a settlement. However, Wissembourg really flourished around the time when the Benedictine monastery in the town became a Free Imperial Abbey. **St. Pierre-et-St. Paul**, the church of the former abbey, is incidentally the largest Gothic church in Alsace after Strasbourg cathedral. A special discovery awaits experts on the Gothic—the notably deeply set stone trellised window frames of the nave. The stained glass is for the most part in very good condition. The most beautiful features of the church are the cloisters (you reach them via a small door from the northern side of the nave). The ingenious simplicity of their stone trellis work is said to be exemplary Gothic architecture.

When you return from the cloisters into the church, look in the choir for the statue of King Dagobert. There is a special story attached to this statue. For a long time, Dagobert was considered to be the founder of the monastery, until one day it was discovered that the monks had simply forged the charter of the foundation, supposedly dating from 632, some 500 years later. This was a popular method during the Middle Ages of securing oneself and one's property—whether it was monastic land or a small county—from the greedy intentions displayed by surrounding landowners to incorporate. Only when one's chartered rights showed well-established judicial and economic independence could one at least lay a claim to being left in peace by wicked and probably stronger neighbours.

**Left,
town hall in
Wissembou
Below,
typical
landscape
of northern
Alsace.**

Only a few dozen steps will take you from the church to the bridge over the Lauter, from which you can get a good view of the **Bruch Quarter**. At first sight this is a confusing and highly picturesque tangle of medieval homes and business premises, partly built in the half-timbered style, partly adorned with gables and roof beams dating from the early Renaissance.

The way from the river Lauter to the Town Hall is worth taking, not because of the official building itself (the old Town Hall was burned down by the French in 1677, and the new building dates from the 18th century) but more for its proximity to the old Dominican monastery and the little restaurant *Au Petit Dominicain* (on the corner of the Rue nationale and the Rue des Dominicains). Eat a pike-perch here, and taste the Riesling from nearby Cleebourg twice over—in the sauce that comes with the fish and, of course, in the wine

that goes with the meal. The rule is to take the wine that was used in the preparation of the dish. The Alsatian cooks have managed to turn culinary customs around. Not only is the Riesling very popular as a drinking wine, it also serves as an aromatic ingredient by the cooks as well.

Another useful tip for those who like beer, though not only for them: the inn *Au Saumon* in the Place Poincaré between the Town Hall and the church is a little piece of Bavaria in the middle of Alsace. It has a real beer garden with shady chestnut trees.

Col du Pfaffenschlick: If, coming from Wissembourg, you don't make for the Route des châteaux via the worthwhile diversion of the northern Alsatian wine route, you shouldn't miss at least part of this stretch. So don't take the direct route from Wissembourg via Col du Pigeon, but rather the road to Merckwiller-Pechelbronn as far as Drach-

ssembourg:
Pierre-et-
Paul.

THE NORTHERN WINE ROUTE

As unassuming as it appears, the northern *Route du vin* between Wissembourg and Soultz-sous-Forêts should be taken seriously as an alternative to its big sister (the actual *Route du vin*) through central and southern Alsace. While the latter, particularly along the main route, is overrun with tourists and coaches, the former has unspoilt quiet villages along the northern wine route which the occasional adventurous traveller makes an attempt to visit. Here, you will notice that a number of villages make themselves especially attractive during the holiday season.

However, traditions are still bound within the hilly wine-growing area around Cleebourg that this mini-region has not lost any of its original charm. If you want to, you can easily complete the entire northern wine route within two hours—but if you take a day or even two over it, you will find it much more rewarding.

The route itself is circular, and Wissembourg forms its starting and finishing point. Because of the gradual increase in the effect of the sights (and the delights of various degustations), it is advisable to follow the route in a clockwise direction.

First of all, leave Wissembourg in a southerly direction and drive to Oberhofen. Then turn left and go via **Steinselzt** (nearby lies the **Geisberg**, where on 4 August 1870 the Franco-Prussian War began with the Battle of Wissembourg) to Riedseltz. Carry on through the little wine village of **Ingolsheim** to **Schoenenburg** (incidentally, it is worthwhile taking a ten-minute diversion to Hunspach, which is considered one of the most beautiful and complete half-timbered villages in Alsace).

While in Schoenenburg, you should make an attempt to visit another reminder of the wars and conflicts between Germany and France: the narrow, endlessly long barracks, where the troops of the Maginot Line were quartered at the beginning of World War II. The Maginot Line was strongly fortified near Schoenenburg. However, this area is not just a reminder of war; it bears also the signs of reconciliation. A row of vineyards to the west of Schoenenburg belongs to families of German descent, from the Palatinate, which has led to the well-known German saying that the best Palatinate wine grows in Alsace.

Keep travelling south to the little town of Soultz-sous-Forêts with its picturesque old town, and then turn off in a westerly direction towards Merckwiller-Pechelbronn. This town is not actually on the Route du vin, but still it is worth seeing for another reason. Until thirty years ago, it was the oil metropolis of Alsace! Doubters may go and take a look round the **Oil Museum**, which is also open on Sunday afternoons in the main season in July and August. As early as the Middle Ages, peasants here were using crude oil to grease their wagon wheels. They then went on to refine the oil (hence the name Pechelbronn, from German Pech=tar) and use it for medicinal purposes. The oil boom of Merckwiller is gone for good, and the little town has gone back to its medicinal traditions and has become a spa. Treatment is not carried out with oil products, but with the medicinal waters of the hot springs which were discovered in the neighbourhood of Merckwiller.

From this point on the route turns north once more. Via Lobsann and Drachenbronn you will reach **Cleebourg**, the northernmost wine-growing community in Alsace and also the place which has given its name to this wine-growing region. The Pinot of Cleebourg, and especially the Cleebourg Riesling, are more highly regarded by many connoisseurs for their exquisite dryness than the rival southern wines.

As far as the wine is concerned, it is better to pay little attention to the opinions of others and to rely on your own tastebuds. There is an excellent opportunity to try that out next to the central Cleebourg wine cellar, in the restaurant **A la Cavêde Cleebourg** (67160 Wissembourg, Tel. 88 94 52 18). However, if you pass through at midday or in the evening, don't just enjoy the wine on its own, but order pheasant on a bed of sauerkraut, an Alsatian specialty.

The restaurant is situated only half a mile past the turn-off to Cleebourg, but don't let that tempt you to pass by the wine village on the other side, so to speak. A stroll through the main street, lined by beautiful half-timbered houses and barns, is highly recommended. Perhaps, it would seem distinctly odd to the modern traveller to think that this village actually once (in the 17th century) belonged to the Swedish (!) crown.

They store only the best wines.

enbronn, then turn right over the small Col du Pfaffenschlick to Climbach.

Your reward for this diversion awaits you at the highest point of the pass of Col du Pfaffenschlick. Here, at a wonderful sleepy crossroads, the tables of the **Restaurant du Pfaffenschlick** invite the traveller to stay a while. The friendly landlady will serve all kinds of dishes to accompany the good, strong Cleebourg wine. However, they will only actually cook for you if you order beforehand. So, if you want to enjoy a genuine Baeckoffa or an excellent roast pheasant, chat with the landlady...

Continue via Climbach to **Lembach**. Before you give in to the charms of gastronomy, go for a meal to Fernand Mischler's **Auberge du Cheval Blanc**, you should do something to earn this unparalleled culinary pleasure. After all, the first real castle of the long Route des châteaux is so close you could almost touch it.

Burg Fleckenstein: If you feel you could manage two and a half miles (4 km) of walking, leave your car two and a half miles behind Lembach, where the road divides towards Birche and Schönau, and set off along the circular route, which leads for the most part through shady woods of mixed conifers and broadleaved trees, but which goes quite steeply downhill in the first stages. You will come first to the Riegelsberg and the Litschhof saddle, from there to the ruins of **Hohenburg** (with its splendid view), the ruins of **Löwenstein** and finally, already on your way down, to **Fleckenstein**.

Fleckenstein castle has become famous because of a marvellous engraving by Matthäus Merian: in a fashion usually reserved for depicting the Tower of Babel, a narrow, vertiginous rock rises out of the mountainous forest, and on this rock rises the mighty castle. Of course such a castle was considered unconquerable, and for exactly that reason it must have been a real thorn in the side not only of the enemies of the Fleckenstein family, but of their various overlords as well.

For a long time it was said that the castle, which indeed remained untouched from the 12th to the 17th centuries because of its strategic position on the road from Haguenau to Kaiserslautern, was destroyed in 1674 by French troops under Maréchal Vaubaun. It was the country vicar and passionate local historian Ihme from Bärenthal who was able to prove that the Maréchal himself obviously failed to take Fleckenstein–the castle was not destroyed until six years afterwards, by order of the French king Louis XIV, who accorded the castles of his vassals sufficient respect to order the whole lot of them levelled in 1680.

As far as Fleckenstein was concerned, this move was a failure. Even the ruins of the two fortified towers that remain on the high castle rock are still

A walk to Fleckenste castle.

imposing enough today. Many of the halls and passages within the rock are still well preserved and can be seen.

It will take you three-quarters of an hour to get back to the fork in the road where you left your car. Those who hate walking can of course drive right up to the car park under the castle, and the very clever drivers and walkers will easily find the little lake down by the roadside, where you can take a refreshing swim to wind up your expedition in the summer. If you feel like a good meal at this point, you have two excellent choices. Decisions, decisions.

You can either drive back into Lembach to the **Auberge du Cheval Blanc**, where Ferdinand Mischler (whose family inn has existed for 80 years) combines the good old Alsatian traditions with the higher, indeed exclusive demands of modern gourmet cuisine–sometimes even in the same dish, for instance in his home-made terrines. You can't go wrong in the Cheval Blanc if you order fish or poultry (try the duck breast), and try the iced *Guglhupf* for dessert. The fame of Mischlers has in the meantime made its way across the Rhine to Germany, with the result that the "White Horse" is, especially at weekends, full of *Schwobe* (Swabians– as the Alsatians still call all Germans). This has two disadvantages: first of all, the prices have gone up (as you can tell from the over-expensive wine list), and secondly, you can hardly get a table without booking first. The exact address is: Auberge du Cheval Blanc, 4, Rue de Wissembourg, 67510 Lembach, Tel. 88 94 41 86.

Much plainer, but no less a gourmet's delight, is the **Restaurant Anthon** in nearby **Obersteinbach**, which fits unobtrusively into this village of 300 people. Here it would be best to stick to the regional dishes, which are usually prepared and served in the Anthon with remarkable elegance. In the autumn you can order game from the surrounding

forests. Only a few know that the restaurant has a small hotel attached to it. In order to obtain one of the seven countrified and very comfortably furnished rooms, it is essential to make a reservation beforehand: Hotel-Restaurant Anthon, 40, Rue Principale, 67510 Obersteinbach, Tel. 88 09 25 01.

Obersteinbach is also a good place to stay overnight because close by there are no less than ten castle ruins to be visited. Apart from the ruins of **Hohenfels**, **Lützelhardt**, **Schöneck**, **Old and New Windstein** (the two are three miles–5 km–apart), **Wittschlössel** and **Wineck**, the most important are the ruins of **Little Arnsbeck** (right up on the wooded slope above Obersteinbach). **Frönsburg** and finally **Wasigenstein**.

The last two castle ruins were once twin castles; for each of them, their fortified walls arose on two neighbouring rocks. In particular, the beautifully situ-

ated ruins of Wasigenstein are still impressive enough to give the visitor a glimpse of the former greatness and importance of the castle. According to the middle-high German Waltharilied, it was in the ravine between the two castle rocks of Wasigenstein that the bloody duel took place between the Nibelung King Gunther of Worms and Walther of Aquitaine. The duel ended indecisively, but only because Gunther's vassal Hagen of Tronje (the one who later killed Siegfried) came to his lord's assistance at the last minute. Whether the story is truth or legend, at any rate the forests and ruins of Wasigenstein are enough to take the visitor back into the world of fairy tales and legends without any difficulty. You can get to the ruins using either of two footpaths: 45 minutes from Obersteinbach or about 30 minutes from Klingenfels, which you will come to if you drive from Obersteinbach to Niedersteinbach

and turn left just before Niedersteinbach onto the D 190.

No end to castles: There are four more ruins worth visiting, if you come from Obersteinbach to Niederbronn, taking not the direct southern route through the attractive Schwarzbach valley, but going west first for a couple of miles to Sturzelbronn, turn left in the direction of Neuhoffen when you come to the village, and then follow this road to the right again in the direction of Philippsbourg once you are out of the village. After two and a half miles (4 km) along this route you will come to the ruins of **Rothenburg**. From here, a little road through the forest leads you in a westerly direction to the Lake Hanau, above which rises **Waldeck Castle**. You can leave the castle with a view from below, and, as far as the weather allows or commands, pay attention to the well-patronised bathing possibilities along Lake Hanau.

At the side of the road from here to Niederbronn lie the **Falkenstein**, the ruins of **Ramstein** (take a diversion from Philippsbourg, turning right in the direction of Baerenthal), and finally **Wasenburg**, which is interesting because it was built on the site of a Roman temple of Mercury, still visible today.

Niederbronn is above all famous for its thermal springs. Wherever people come to take the waters, the gastromonic industry makes a special effort, as it does here, as a visit to the Hôtel Bristol (4, Place de l'Hôtel de Ville, 67110 Niederbronn-les-Bains, Tel. 88 09 61 44) will convince you.

Architecturally speaking, the town of Niederbronn has little to offer. The two churches are 19th century replicas, and it is uncertain whether the Celts really celebrated bloody rituals in the Camp Celtique (a huge block of rock with chiselled runnels in the surface).

From Niederbronn, travel along the German-French tourist route and on to **Ingwiller**–but first look up....

Cave dwellings Graufthal.

Castle Lichtenberg is worth a visit only because it is the only Alsatian ruins of which large parts have survived, despite being fired at by German artillery in 1870. It is true that the French force occupying the castle gave in fairly quickly, with fortunate results for posterity, which can now admire the two massive round towers from the 13th century, the Renaissance tombs in the choir of the castle chapel and the walls, tombs and barracks designed by Vauban, the greatest architect of fortifications in all France. Castle Lichtenberg and the village of the same name can be reached by turning right at Rothbach on the road from Niederbronn to Ingwiller. Another road leads directly from Lichtenberg through the romantic Moder valley and on to…

Bouxwiller: Some travel guides describe this little town as "cosy and attractive", but don't be put off by that. On the contrary, here as so often in northern

Alsace the unspectacular contains the true idyllic charm. If you have an hour's time or only half an hour's, stroll through the old town with its jumble of oriels and balconies, gables and half-timbered work, evidence of ancient civic pride, and you will be fascinated by its very attractive nature. And as for cosiness, a quick glance at the past will convince you that the people of Bouxwiller were not short of cunning, particularly the women. The local hill, the nearby **Bastberg**, was after all always considered to be the place where witches from all over Europe met on 30 April, to fly off together the following day to an orgiastic witches' sabbath on the Brocken in the Harz mountains. Goethe made the preliminary studies for his Walpurgisnight scenes in *Faust* here. It comes as no surprise that there were always a few witches living in Bouxwiller itself.

Probably the most prominent of them

elhardt:
castle
ved from
ther.

145

was Barbara of Ottenheim, the mistress of the Count of Lichtenberg, who played such tricks on her lover that he was unable to express his fury other than by oppressing his subjects. The men, once again, could not see the connection, and willingly went off to forced labour, but the women had no trouble in seeing the beautiful Barbara as the source of all their misfortunes. So they gathered together and set off with pitchforks, roasting spits and ladles to Castle Lichtenstein to demand the punishment of the cruel beauty. They managed to get Barbara accused of witchcraft and banished, and she died in exile in 1462 in mysterious circumstances (officially recorded as suicide). This occasion has gone down in history as the Women's War of Bouxwiller.

It also comes as no surprise, after all these dreadful goings-on, that the uncle of Heinrich Heine whose activities as a confidence trickster, quack healer and womaniser are described by the poet (the uncle appears in the role of the Chevalier de Geldern) chose Bouxwiller, of all places, for his retirement!

The journey goes on to **La-Petite-Pierre**. The direct route via Wieterwiller is recommended especially for those travelling in groups of at least five people. Bookings can be made preferably three days in advance, into the farmhouse **Zuem Dorfwappe** (3, Rue Principale, 67340 Weiterswiller, Tel. 88 89 48 19), whereupon Ferdinand and Simone Bloch will serve an ample Alsatian meal equal to none. If you belong to the greedy kind, it would be your own fault if you then cannot manage the best bits, such as the *Fernkäse* (a young, plate-shaped cheese sprinkled with ground peppercorns), or Madame Bloch's very special home-made *fromage blanc*. But if you are genuinely more interested in culture than in gastronomy, drive a couple of miles to the west of Bouxwiller, and you will soon come to...

Neuwiller: Here stands yet another castle which you could visit (the ruins of Herrenstein to the west of the town), but for once this need not be the main reason for coming to **Neuwiller**. The cultural and historic experience here is provided by the **Benedictine abbey**, with its abbey church, begun in Carolingian times and completed in the high Gothic period, the church of **St. Adelphus**. From Neuwiller, following a beautiful road through the forest, you come to...

La-Petite-Pierre: In German, or more accurately in middle-high German, the name of this place is Lützelstein. The town and the castle lie on a long outcrop of limestone. The castle itself is in very good condition, mainly because it has been rebuilt twice: in 1566, after the medieval fortress had fallen victim to several sieges, and in 1680, as the Maréchal Vauban destroyed once again, then rebuilt it as a garrison point. **La-Petite-Pierre** is a suitable starting point for excursions into the...

North Vosges Nature Park (*Parc Régional des Vosges du Nord*): This huge nature reserve adjoins the German Naturpark Pfälzerwald. As agriculture in the forest, which had formed the landscape for centuries in this area, became more and more of an economic failure, the French government turned to an exemplary programme to preserve this mountainous and wooded area.

The protection and re-introduction of endangered animals and plants (such as the re-introduction of chamois and beavers) played an important, but not decisive, part. At the same time the administrators of the park were concerned that those particular economic activities should be encouraged which would best guarantee the preservation of the natural environment: tourism for one, and industries (such as woodworking crafts) related to the environment for another. The protection of buildings is an integral part of the natural protection. Whoever owns and wants to renovate a historic building will have an architect's services provided free by the administration of the nature park. You can get information about walking and accommodation in the North Vosges Nature Park in the castle of La-Petite-Pierre, which houses the Maison du Parc Régional des Vosges du Nord, Château de la Petite Pierre, 67290 Wingen-sur-Moder, Tel. 88 70 46 55.

By the way, La-Petite-Pierre also offers good cuisine, for instance in the Trois Roses restaurant or in the Lion d'Or. However, if you have a knack for the quaint and the exceptional, you can drive a little further on and come to the lonely village of…

Graufthal: This place is worth mentioning and visiting because of the cave dwellings above the river valley, which were inhabited right up till the middle of this century. In addition, you will find some smugglers' caves in the rocky ground of the forest near Bonne

well-served tle of Petite-rre (or elstein).

Fontaine–a few miles to the south of Graufthal and to the left of the road from Oberhof to Phalsbourg. Worth mentioning, among others, is the hotel and restaurant **Au Vieux Moulin** (Graufthal–67320 Drulingen, Tel. 88 70 17 28), which provides local cuisine and pleasant accommodation at very civilised prices. Carry on via Phalsbourg (the ruins of Phalsbourg castle can be seen) and you will come to…

Lutzelbourg: Instead of more castles, you can admire one of the wonders of technology here. A little to the west of the village is the canal lift, which saves the Rhine-Marne Canal at least two dozen locks by lifting the boats plus the water in an oversized diagonal lift which rises more than 330 ft (100 m). To complete the attraction, a few hundred yards on the boats travel through a tunnel 8,786 ft (2,678 m) long. You can experience this interesting trip through the tunnel on a boat.

SAVERNE

The name of the Roman to whom Saverne owes its founding is not recorded. At any rate, he must have been a man with a considerable nose for profit. His idea of building a waystation for travellers on the road between Argentorum (better known as Strasbourg) and Divodorum (Metz) showed a far-sighted business sense. The position of his waystation was about as perfect as it could be: in the valley of the Zorn river, on the eastern edge of the Vosges, at the point where the road over the pass—the only one in the northern part of the range—leads over the hills. It is thus not surprising that the *Itinerarium Antonii*, a travel guide dating from late Roman times, recommended that its readers stay here. The place was then known as *Tres Tabernae* which means three taverns with food and lodging. The French version of the name (Saverne) and the German (Zabern) both come from the Latin word *tabernae*.

The three former taverns have developed into a busy town of about 11,000 inhabitants. In western Alsace, Saverne is considered a centre of industry and trade. Several metalworking industries were established in this town, which is also a major market for the produce of the agriculture and forestry of the Alsatian plain. Wine, tobacco, timber and grain are the main products traded here.

The economic position of Saverne, however, does no damage to its attraction to tourists. The town offers everything which a traveller's heart could desire, from the archaeological museum to the gourmet restaurants and the various leisure and sports activities. Even if there was nothing else for the town to show than the famous **Rohan palace** and the unique **house of** the magistrate's clerk **Katz**, it would be worth visiting Saverne just to see them. So you can trust in the judgement of a well-known traveller in Alsace, named Goethe, who particularly liked Saverne: "With two worthy friends and table partners, Engelbach and Weyland, both born in Lower Alsace, I went on horseback to Saverne, where in fine weather the little friendly place seemed to smile at us most charmingly."

Goethe was delighted by the prince-bishop's palace, built for Bishop Eugene of Fürstenbach between 1666 and 1670, which dominated the town with its magnificence. "The sight of the Bishop's Palace aroused our admiration; the breadth, size and splendour of new stables were evidence of the comforts of the owner. The magnificence of the staircase surprised us. We entered the rooms and halls with awe; the only contrast was the person of the Cardinal himself, a little shrunken man, whom we saw at the table."

The building which the famous poet admired unfortunately no longer exists.

It was burned down to its foundations on 7 September 1779. The palace is a new building today, designed by Salins de Montfort, architect of Versailles. It remained unfinished for a long time and was only completed towards the end of the last century. Goethe showed himself no less impressed than by the architectural masterpiece of the Saverne palace when he saw a wonder of road-building, which had cost the citizens of the town a lot of money. This was the road over the Saverne Pass, the gap through the Vosges that had always formed the shortest route from Alsace to central France. By 1740 the road through this pass, some 2.5 miles (4 km) long, had been built up into a fairly convenient route for travellers, according to the standards then. The whole project, if anecdotes can be believed, goes back to the Sun King Louis XIV. He is supposed to have looked down on the town and exclaimed *"Quel beau jardin!"*

("What a beautiful garden!"). He had reason enough to feel pleased, for Alsace had just become part of France after a long period of wars and conflict. This was in 1681.

The pleasure of the monarch was clouded by the poor condition of the road over the crest of the Vosges. Hardly had he arrived back in Versailles, the king commanded "that the roads shall be properly surfaced, otherwise there will be a fine of 150 livres."

The threat certainly worked, and Goethe recorded in his diary in 1770: "In the light of the rising sun we saw before us the famous Saverne Pass road, created by unthinkable labour. Built in snaking curves over the most dreadful rocks, the hard-surfaced road, wide enough for three wagons to drive abreast, rises so gently up the hill that one hardly feels it."

Saverne's position, excellent from a trade and military or strategic point of

The Rohan palace in Saverne.

view, was not always to the advantage of the town. Ever since it was built, the town has been in the midst of campaigns and wars. The settlement of *Tres Tabernae* had hardly been founded before it was burned down by the Alemanni. Saverne's misfortunes continued for centuries. On countless occasions the town was besieged, plundered, destroyed and ravaged by enemy troops.

In the 12th century the English invaded Saverne several times; in 1444 it was the Armagnacs, wandering mercenaries. The Thirty Years' War meant an unending succession of woe and misery for Saverne. The besiegers—at times French, at times Imperial troops—succeeded one after the other with depressing regularity. Because of its strong fortifications (it was said that they were built according to the calendar, as the walls had 52 towers with seven battlements between every two towers) the town provoked repeated attacks.

The bloodiest chapter in the history of the town was the murder of the Bundschuh peasants. In the confusion that existed during the Reformation period the Alsatian farmers joined together in the *Bundschuh* league (the name came from the wood-soled thonged shoes that they wore) to defend themselves against the brutal exploitation and oppression by their feudal lords. There was armed insurgence against the clergy and the authorities. In the end, the Austrian governor in Alsace could no longer control the situation and called in Duke Antoine of Lorraine. In the spring of 1525, a peasant army of more than 30,000, led by Erasmus Gerber, had barricaded themselves in Saverne and set up their headquarters here. The people of the town supported the rebels. After a siege by the troops of the Duke, which lasted many weeks, the food supplies began to run out. The peasants decided to capitulate. They were offered safe conduct out of the town if they laid down their weapons first. The

gates of the town had barely been opened when the mercenaries of Lorraine attacked the unarmed peasants and butchered them in a most bestial fashion. More than 20,000 peasants are believed to have been murdered on this day, 17 May 1525. The chronicles claimed that the soil was dyed red with blood as far as Lupstein, some six miles (10 km) away.

There are hardly any traces of those warlike times in the town nowadays, but many of the opulent period when Saverne was the residence of the Bishops of Strasbourg, after they had been driven out of a Strasbourg which turned Protestant during the Reformation.

There was no lack of colourful characters among the Prince-Bishops who ruled from Strasbourg. One of them was Wilhelm Eugen of Fürstenbach, who became bishop in 1682, even though his greatest abilities seemed to lie in the spreading of the scandals of various

151

European courts. It was no obstacle to his election to the post of cardinal to have been imprisoned in Vienna for four years as a spy and escaped execution only because the French king put pressure on the German emperor.

After the Fürstenbach family, the position went to the Rohan dynasty. Saverne had four bishops from this line. The last of them, Louis-René de Rohan-Guémé (who had the present palace built), exceeded all his predecessors in pomp, court luxury and sheer extravagance. The *Necklace Affair*, which he instigated and which finally tripped him up, was responsible for the entry of Saverne and its bishops into the more scandalous chapters of history.

The story sounded like the plot of a bad novel. The suspicious and ambitious Cardinal and Prince-Bishop had fallen into disgrace in Versailles and was banished to Strasbourg and Saverne. There he led a life which suited his

erotic inclinations actively encouraged by the adventurer, occultist and alchemist Giuseppe Balsamo, better known as Count Cagliostro. The Prince-Bishop, whose chosen motto was "I cannot be king, I will not be duke—I am Rohan", had higher ambitions, however. One of his former mistresses, a fake countess, whispered to him that Queen Marie-Antoinette longed for a necklace which the King did not want to give her, as it was too expensive—it was rumoured to cost 1.6 million livres.

Cardinal Rohan, either because of an undying passion for the Queen or because he saw the chance to make himself popular again at court, was prepared to advance the sum to the jewellers Boehmer and Bassenge. A *tête-à-tête* with the Queen by night was to be his reward. Indeed it came about, except that the Queen was no queen, but a Parisian prostitute. Rohan allowed himself to be deceived, and the "countess" vanished to England with the necklace.

In the summer of 1785, the deception was uncovered, and the Cardinal was lucky not to be treated too harshly—after a short stay in the Bastille, he was permanently banished to Alsace. More serious were the political consequences: the people's anger was rightly inflamed when they heard of this corruption and decadence in court society. If visitors to Saverne can admire the Rohan palace today, this at any rate is due to the great love of the Cardinal.

The building, somewhat too pompous for the small town, has given the Saverne the slightly tongue-in-cheek title of "the Versailles of Alsace". You should on no account miss out on a visit to the **Château de Rohan**, which is centrally situated in the Place du Général de Gaulle. It has been used for various purposes—under Napoleon I it was a home for war widows and civil servants, from 1870 to 1918 it was the barracks of the German occupying forces—and it now houses official

Notre-Dame de-la-Nativ

departments. It also contains the interesting **Town Museum**, which exhibits prehistoric finds, artifacts from the Roman period and objects which belonged to the Rohan family. The impressive splendour of the palace is not obvious to the visitor on the street side, but from the park side, where you can see the Classical facade. The park is bordered on two sides by the Rhine-Marne Canal, built from 1828-53.

From the palace square, we recommend a tour of the other sights of Saverne. Just a few yards to the right of the palace lies the Romanesque-Gothic parish church, **Notre-Dame-de-la-Nativité**, with its five-storeyed tower. Worth looking at are the well-preserved remains of the Haguenauer Brothers' *Ascension*, the chancel dating from 1495 and made by Hammer, the architect of Strasbourg Cathedral, and the bishops' tombs in the choir. A few steps to the right, next to the church, is the Little Palace, **Petit Château**, with its Renaissance entrance, which was once used as a bishop's residence.

You can get to know the old town of the Saverne bourgeoisie best by taking a walk along the **Grand'Rue**. This main road of the town has a number of interesting Renaissance houses, among them the world-famous **Maison Katz**, an ornate half-timbered house with a two-storeyed oriel, built in 1605. Many connoisseurs consider it one of the most beautiful houses in Alsace. The **Town Hall**, a building in the style of the Italian Renaissance and dating from the turn of the century, is also interesting. Behind it rises the former Franciscan church. This 14th century building has some impressive tombs and artistically skilful 17th century Gothic cloisters.

Saverne likes being called "Ville des Rose"—the Rose Town. Proof that it has earned this name can be found in the **Rose Garden**, which is worth a look and which has more than 1,400 different varieties of the flower. It is some 500 metres away to the west of the town centre. Plant lovers should also visit the beautifully laid out **Botanical Gardens** along the Saverne Pass Road.

Saverne countryside is full of variety and is an ideal base for excursions. Among many other possibilities, we recommend as worthwhile trips into the immediate neighbourhood to the castles and to the little village of **St. Jean-Saverne**. The Romanesque 12th century church is worth a visit. Its entrance, designed by Baroque master architect Michael Mengs from Vorarlberg with a tower and an antechamber, is unique.

From St. Jean-Saverne you can climb up to the **Michaelsberg**, where you can enjoy the view, and see the pilgrims' chapel and remains of a pagan cult site. According to legend, the witches set out from here for the Bastberg, a waystation on their flight to the Brocken.

All too soon, it's time to continue your trip along the Route des châteaux.

king out
ards
ded hills.

MORE OF ROUTE DES CHÂTEAUX

Dabo: Go south along the course of the river Zorn and you will come to a rock which can be seen from a distance. At the point where the castle of Dagsburg once stood a chapel was built in the last century in honour of the first (and only) Pope to come from Alsace: Leo IX, who had been Bruno of Dagsburg before his election. The hill and the chapel are popular places for pilgrimages and excursions from all over Alsace, and on days with fine weather, you will find a corresponding crowd here. If you like to visit ancient monuments, travel on to Wangenbourg and Engelthal (where you can, apart from the ruins of Wangenbourg, also see Freudeneck castle), or, even better, go on to...

Burg Nideck: You can reach the castle from the car park for ramblers (7.5 miles/12 km—beyond Wangenbourg, towards Oberhaslach). From here, it takes 30 minutes to get to the ruins of this impressive castle. There are other routes to the castle from Oberhas-lach (passing three other ruins, Hohenstein, the larger and the smaller Ringelstein— takes four hours) or from the Auberge Cascades du Nideck (takes 50 minutes).

Whichever way you take, you have to walk to get to **Nideck**, and this is why there are no great floods of tourists which prevent you from surrendering yourself to the magic of the ruins. You can best do this by climbing the well-preserved massive tower in the lower half of the castle—first on the inside, and then in the open air up some stone steps on the side (take care if you have children with you!) to the highest platform. There you can stretch out on a fine summer's day, looking either up to the blue sky or to the faraway hills and forested valleys below the castle.

Where the Route des Châteaux takes you.

155

Once giants lived in Nideck Castle—such is the popular legend, which Albert von Chamisso used in his ballad of *Giant's Toy*. In actual fact, Nideck was held by lieges of the Bishop of Strasbourg, who lived in this castle built in the 13th century and destroyed by fire in 1636. A little below the ruin a waterfall cascades down porphyry rocks more than 82 feet (25 metres) high. The circular route back to the ramblers' car park leads past the waterfall and takes three-quarters of an hour.

Nideck is the final and the high point of the Route des châteaux. If you have the inclination and the time to stay a few more days in Alsace, you have two possibilities. You may drive via **Niederhaslach** (the High Gothic **church of St. Florentius** is remarkable not so much for its exterior but for the interior with its beautiful glass windows), through the Bruche valley to **Schirmeck** (a quiet holiday town with a number of good restaurants and hotels); from here it is worth making a diversion to the peak of the 3,310 ft (1,009 m) high Donon, below which an impressive pagan site dating from Celtic times can be found. From Schirmeck, after 20 minutes drive, you will come to the connection with the Route des Crêtes.

Or, to take the other alternative, drive back to Wangenbourg-Engelthal from the ramblers' car park by the roadside and from there follow the small link road via Birkenwald and Dimsthal to...

Marmoutier: This is the end of the Route des châteaux. It is not only the castle that is worth looking at here (although there is another ruin that can be visited: Ochsenstein castle above the nearby Reinhard Minster), but the church, belonging to the famous **Benedictine abbey of Marmoutier**. You should not miss the visual introduction to art history which this church offers.

This introduction is at its most effec-

Left, the church of St. Afre. Below, pillar capit. of the Marmoutie minster.

156

tive if you visit the church in the afternoon, when the beams of sunlight make the reddish sandstone of the western walls glow. Here you can see the militant theology behind the architectural concept "western walls". In a medieval church, the tower and the altar faced east, towards the light—in one sense, towards the rising sun, and in another, towards Jerusalem and Nazareth. The opposite side, the western walls, was the border between the church and the world. It was at the same time the entrance and the defensive wall. The west facades of Gothic cathedrals rarely have any sense of the defensive but the design of the Romanesque period is often the opposite. The Romanesque west walls are imposing and hostile—the church as fortress.

The nave of the church is not Romanesque, but Gothic, and so the hostile impression of the outside is lost in the lightness with which the skilfully

carved pillars seem to rise above.

The course in building styles has not ended yet. The space around the altar dates in its present form from the Baroque period and the ornate decorations of the choir are in a style for which the description "Neo-Gothic" is inadequate. These are (even if this stylistic term is not uusually applied to sacred buildings) pure "Louis Quinze".

Incidentally, Albert Schweitzer occasionally played the **organ** of Marmoutier, which was built by Silbermann. If you want to especially listen to its musical sounds, come to the daylong concert on the last Sunday in September. It is only seven and a half miles (12 km) from Marmoutier to Marlenheim—and to the starting point of the great Alsatian wine route. To put it another way, if you travel the Route du vin from south to north, make it a must to visit the **abbey church** of Marmoutier at the end of the route.

itional
ume for
youth of
ice?

THE KOCHERSBERG REGION

If you're looking for the land that flows with milk and honey, you would do well to travel to the area around the Kochersberg. It's no land of Cockaigne—you won't find roast pigeons on your dinner plate—but there is hardly another area for miles around that has been so favoured by nature as the one between Strasbourg, Molsheim, Saverne and Haguenau. For centuries this area has been known as the "granary of Alsace". Today, whatever crop that grows—or flourishes—on this highly fertile soil can claim its place among the top produces of French agriculture.

Of course, chief among these products is the wine, especially the sparkling white kind. However, the asparagus of the area is also famous, as are the hops, from which the strong, bitter Alsatian beer is brewed. Also, every imaginable kind of fruit is grown around the Kochersberg, partly for the table and partly to be distilled into very strong spirits such as the famous cherry brandy or the *Quetsche* (plum brandy). Finally, the basis of Alsatian *choucroute*, the sauerkraut cabbages, should not be forgotten. In some villages, festivals are held in their honour. Geological oddities led to the Kochersberg region becoming the larder of Alsace. In prehistoric times, before anyone could imagine that the land between the rivers Bruche and Moder became an Eldorado for the cultivation of culinary delights, the Vosges and the Black Forest formed one range, the Variscan Mountains, as geologists named the central European range of the Carboniferous age. Once the central section had sunk, in the Tertiary period, it formed the Upper Rhine Valley and the huge lake between the eastern and western wings of the range.

Geological ages passed until the Rhine found its way through to the north. Once the lake could drain, it left a bed of limestone sediments, gravel which let water through and dry sand. After the Ice Age, the winds brought loess to settle on these layers, which mixed with clay formed an extrmely fertile soil, the basis of the present-day flourishing cultivation of grain, fruit and vegetables in Alsace. In addition, the climate is particularly favourable in the Kochersberg region. It lies in the rain and wind shadow of the Vosges, which is why the summers are warm and the winters mild and there are usually no extremes of temperature.

This makes the Alsatian plain a perfect place to grow tobacco, which has been cultivated here for more than 300 years. In 1620, so they say, a certain Robert Koenigsmann is supposed to have planted the first seedlings to the north of Strasbourg. Today, tobacco cultivation covers an area of 593 acres (240 hectares), which makes it the sec-ond largest tobacco-growing area in France after the Dordogne. The varieties most often cultivated are *Paraguay*, which has been grown in Alsace since 1860 and which grows nowhere else in France, *Virginie*, which has been grown in Alsace since 1878, and *Gendertheimer*, a variety which originates in Germany. The latest variety added to the list is *Variété-Alsace*, which was grown since 1982.

Passionate smokers, for whom life has become increasingly difficult of late, will probably find balm for their souls in the knowledge that there are tobacco festivals in some Alsatian villages during the summer months. In **Fessenheim-le-Bas**, for instance, there is a spectacle, where you could demonstrate your smoking skills in the "Great Pipe Smoking Competition" in **Benfeld** at the end of August, when much acrid smoke rises.

Alsace, which really has no lack of

Preceding pages, village festival of old time Below, the Kochersberg region is the granar of Alsace.

holiday and tourist routes, has lately created a *Route du tabac*, initiated by a society which has taken the appropriate name of *Confrèrie Jean Nicot*. In order to get to know the region around Kochersberg, however, it is not necessary to to follow the marked holiday routes. This inviting countryside of gardens and parks with its lush vegetation and pretty, well-kept villages makes it worthwhile to go on your own journeys of discovery. Driving north from Strasbourg, you can explore the area in a series of one-day excursions.

To choose a small number of destinations from those on offer: Just outside Strasbourg on the D41 road is **Mittelhausbergen**. This former imperial town now has a mere 850 inhabitants, and it also has a row of pretty, well-preserved half-timbered houses. The Lutheran church is a curiosity. It is a wooden building which has an onion-domed tower. If you travel a few miles

northeast of Mittelhausbergen onto the high plateau of Kochersberg, you will find yourself in the middle of the green, luxuriant landscape of the vineyards, and the asparagus and tobacco fields. The little town of Pfuhlgriesheim was once an imperial town, or more precisely, half of it belonged to the emperor and half to the bishops of Strasbourg.

In the church of **Pfuhlgriesheim**, in which Catholic and Protestant services are held alternately, you can admire frescoes from the 14th century and Baroque sculptures. If you have no liking for sacred art, but are more interested in history or archaeology, your visit will still be rewarded. Here, burial grounds and remains of Neolithic housing have been discovered.

Mittelhausen lies on the D 32 and is worth a visit because of its palace, which was built between 1300 and 1400 and is surrounded by a rectangular fortification with four towers. In the neigh-

bouring town of **Wingersheim**, which belonged to the governorship of Haguenau in the Middle Ages, there are tombs dating from the Hallstatt period, including grave goods, which can be seen. The church in Wingersheim is an exemplary model for the mix of building styles and architecture so frequently found in Alsace. The bell tower is Romanesque, the nave is in the Baroque style (18th century), the three altars and confessionals are also Baroque, while the chancel and the organ housing are Neo-Gothic.

Schwindratzheim on the banks of the Zorn has some very fine half-timbered houses, and—of interest once again to prehistory buffs—it has tombs on display dating from the New Stone Age and the Bronze Age. It's only a stone's throw from Schwindratzheim to **Hochfelden**, the centre of the agricultural area around the Kochersberg, on the Canal de la Marne au Rhin (Rhine-Marne-Canal). The town was once a gift from the Emperor Otto I to his wife Adelaide. In 1388 the town was conquered by the Count Palatinate Robert and destroyed. However, some items have survived since Roman times: tombs, weapons, jewellery and coins.

From Hochfelden you come to **Schaffhouse-sur-Zorn**, a village of 250 inhabitants, which has some precious Merovingian sarcophagi worth a look. For those with a romantic inclination, a visit to the **Old Watermill** on the Zorn is recommended.

Carry on via **Gougenheim**, which went down in history because Conrad, Duke of Swabia and Alsace, was defeated here by the Bishop of Strasbourg in 1130, and you will eventually come to **Woellenheim, Willgottheim** and **Schnersheim**. These three communities depend entirely on agriculture and lie at the foot of the highest hill of the region, which also gives it its name: the

Scarecrow are still in fashion.

988 ft (301 m) high Kochersberg. In the midst of the broad fields lie the large and picturesque Alsatian farmhouses. This is also a centre of tobacco cultivation. In many farms the plants are hung up to dry in large sheds. When the tobacco is dry except for a residue of 10 per cent damp, the leaves are tied in bundles and sent on to be processed further.

In **Avenheim**, part of the Schnersheim community, there is a spring containing sulphate which reportedly never fails. In earlier years the water from this spring was often used for medicinal purposes, but progress in the field of pharmaceutics led to this "natural medicine" being forgotten. However, people still drink the water for health reasons and vouch for its healing powers. It is a treatment for anaemia and consumption, or so the local claims run. No-one who regularly drank the waters ever suffered from these complaints, the local people will assure you.

Wasselonne, the town on the Mossig river, lies 15.5 miles (25 km) to the west of Strasbourg, and with its population of 4,200 it is one of the largest and most individual towns in the Kochersberg region. The town is a regional centre of trade and industry and has a long history. The town was first mentioned in 754; in those days it was still known as *Villa Wazzeleneheim*. During the Reformation, Wasselonne was one of the centres of Protestantism.

There are a few stone monuments to the currents of history, among them for example the Gothic gate tower and the two smaller round towers, all parts of the former town fortifications. From the point of view of art history, the Protestant church is interesting. It was built from 1755-57 and has an organ by J.A. Silbermann, which was brought here in time of war in 1792 from the Dominican church in Guebwiller between Colmar and Mulhouse. Also among the interest-

ditional gs still e some eal.

ing sights of Wasselonne are the fine, stately half-timbered houses.

Only three miles (5 km) to the south of Wasselonne, on the N4, lies **Marlenheim**, a picturesque old wine village, which is covered in flowers from spring through to autumn. Marlenheim was raised to the status of royal estate by the Merovingians. The royal court resided here up until Carolingian times. It is claimed that Louis the Pious was forced to spend some years around A.D. 830 here, after his three sons from his first marriage had imprisoned him because they were dissatisfied with his division of the inheritance of the Frankish empire and wanted to prevent their stepbrother, later King Charles the Bald, from getting too big a piece of the cake.

From a tourist's point of view Marlenheim has become famous for a folk festival which is celebrated annually in August: the wedding of *Ami Fritz* (from the novel of the same name by Emile

Erckmann and Aléxandre Chatrian), which is staged with the help of 20 folk music groups from the area.

Marlenheim has another specialty to offer, though. This is where the *Red Vorlauf* comes from, a wine of special excellence, which—so it is said—surpasses many Burgundies. The *Vorlauf* is also special because there are hardly any red wines produced in Alsace any more—in contrast to 60 years ago. Incidentally, it was this same red wine which once saved Marlenheim from destruction. During the Thirty Years' War, the Swedes, infamous for their destruction and plundering, fell upon the village. The people of Marlenheim immediately offered them their *Vorlauf*. Apparently, the Swedes liked the wine very much. They decided that a village where such good things grow should on no account be burned. Marlenheim was thus spared, and the Swedes marched off again, laden with war booty of a particular kind, namely several barrels of excellent wine.

Travelling through the Kochersberg region, you should not miss out on a trip to **Avolsheim**. Not far from the little village, in the middle of a fertile field, lonely in its old churchyard, is the Dompeter, the oldest church in Alsace. Next to it in weighty dignity stands a 1,000-year-old lime tree. This picture fascinates every observer, who will feel as if he/she has gone back through time to a forgotten age. The Dompeter (the name probably comes from *Domus Petri*—House of St. Peter) is documented as being consecrated in 1049 by Pope Leo IX, who came from Alsace. The foundations of the little three-aisled basilica, which was altered many times over the centuries, rest on the remains of a still older building. The Dompeter was the parish church of a village which was destroyed during the Thirty Years' War and never rebuilt. This dignified church in its abandoned graveyard is a witness to a sad chapter in the history of Alsace.

Left, one who fancies curious pipes. Right, profile of an old farmhouse. Following pages, demarcati what's pri *property.*

ACCES

AUX PRES

INTERDIT

Abschneider zerstören die Vegetation

Bitte auf den Wegen bleiben

Alpenverein

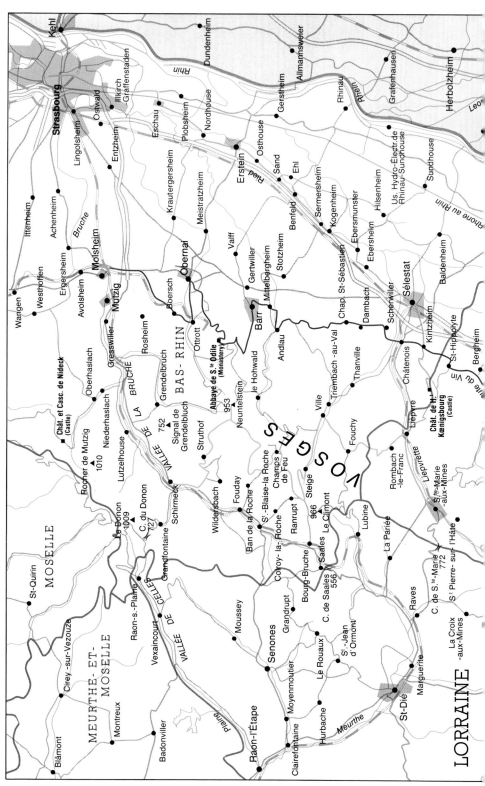

168

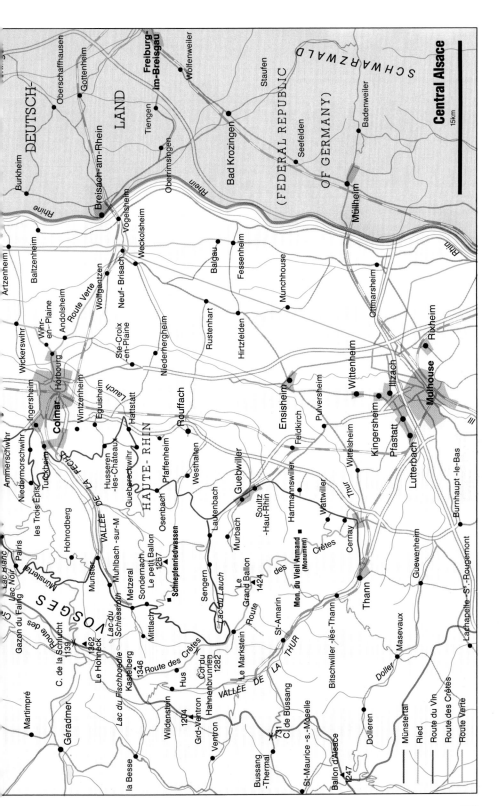

Central Alsace

15km

DEUTSCH-

Oberschaffhausen

Gottenheim

Freiburg-im-Breisgau

Wolfenweiler

LAND

Burkheim

Staufen

Breisach-am-Rhein

Tiengen

Oberrimsingen

Seefelden

Bad Krozingen

Badenweiler

Vogelsheim

Rhein

(FEDERAL REPUBLIC

Weckolsheim

SCHWARZWALD

OF GERMANY)

Mülheim

Artzenheim

Baltzenheim

Rhein

Wickerswihr

Wihr-en-Plaine

Andolsheim

Route Verte

Balgau

Fessenheim

Rhin

Wintzenheim

Ste-Croix-en-Plaine

Niederhergheim

Rustenhart

Munchhouse

Ingersheim

Horbourg

Wolfgantzen

Neuf-Brisach

Hirtzfelden

Ottmarsheim

Ammerschwihr

Colmar

Eguisheim

Hattstatt

Rouffach

Ensisheim

Wittenheim

Illzach

Rixheim

Niedermorschwihr

Lauch

Pulversheim

Mulhouse

les Trois Epis

Turckheim

Husseren-les-Châteaux

Pfaffenheim

Westhalten

HAUTE- RHIN

Feldkirch

Wittelsheim

Kingersheim

Pfastatt

Hohrodberg

Gueberschwihr

Osenbach

Pairis

Lac Blanc

Lac Noir

VALLÉE DE LA FECHT

Muhlbach -sur-M

Schnepfenriedwassen 1267

Laubach

Murbach

Guebwiller

Soultz -Haut-Rhin

Hartmannswiller

Wattwiller

Thur

Lutterbach

Burnhaupt -le-Bas

Martimpré

Munster

Sondernach

Le petit Ballon

des Crêtes

Cernay

Gazon du Faing

Route des Crêtes

Metzeral

Sengern

Le Grand Ballon 1424

Mon. du Vieil Armand (Monument)

Guewenheim

Géradmer

C. de la Schlucht 1139

Le Hohneck 1362

Lac du Schiessroth

Lac de Fischboedle

Mittlach

VOSGES

Kastelberg 1346

Lac du Lauch

St-Amarin

Thann

Lachapelle -Sⁱ-Rougemont

la Besse

Col du Hahnenbrunnen 1282

Hus

Le Markstein

Route des Crêtes

Route des Crêtes

VALLÉE DE LA THUR

Bitschwiller -lès-Thann

Masevaux

Doller

Dolleren

Wildenstein

Grd-Ventron 1204

Ventron

Münsterthal

Ried

Route du Vin

Route des Crêtes

Route Verte

Bussang -Thermal

731 C. de Bussang

St-Maurice -s.-Moselle

Ballon d'Alsace 1247

169

IN CENTRAL ALSACE

After having travelled through the north, you should preferably spend some time now getting to know the popular and much-visited centre of Alsace. It lies along the wine route, which you may want to head next after your visit to the Kochersberg region. The main part of the article on the wine route, which begins on page 187, gives emphasis on good eating and drinking, not on listing all the places which lie along the famed wine route.

From Strasbourg, you can reach the typically Alsatian marsh country between the Rhine and the Ill, as well as the interesting and fortunately not-too-crowded stretch from Strasbourg to Haut-Koenigsbourg. Both actually lie on the wine route, but have less to offer by way of the delights of glass and table.

After you have visited the sights and have been momentarily wedged in the crowd of information-hungry tourists, your stomach might just begin to rumble. Therefore, it's time you make your way in a westerly direction and follow the Route du vin to the Munster Valley. In the article about this valley (page 201), with its high pastures and green hills, the "joys of the table" are also in the foreground.

Parallel to the wine route, on the west of Alsace is the Route des crêtes, which runs through the mountains. Nature lovers will certainly find what they are looking for in this area!

One stretch crosses nearly all those listed above, and that is why we have intentionally missed out its western section. This is the Route verte, which trails from Neuf-Brisach to Colmar. This route is perhaps not a picturesque stretch, but at least it will give you an impression of the many contrasts that Alsace has to offer.

A river snakes its way through green fields

THE ALSATIAN MARSHES

The country between Strasbourg and Sélestat is one of the least known regions of Alsace. One reason for this may be that the area is somewhat overshadowed by the main tourist attractions: the "European" city of Strasbourg to the north, the cities of Cólmar and Mulhouse in the south, and in the west, the nonplus ultra of mass tourism, the wine route, all put the rest of Alsace in the shade. It is surely not to the detriment of the country between the Rhine and the Ill that it is often overlooked by the hordes of visitors to Alsace. The villages seem more authentic and are not as crowded as the others along the Route du vin. The sights and the natural beauty of the marsh of this area is comparable with any other region in Alsace.

The quickest and most comfortable route for your journey between Strasbourg and Sélestat is the motorway-like Route nationale N 83. However, you will see and learn more about the countryside if you use the country roads parallel to the N 83, which often have little traffic. In good weather they are excellent for bicycle tours.

From the Alsatian capital your way leads first to **Illkirch-Graffenstaden**, a community with a population of around 20,000, which however is so closely linked to Strasbourg that it can almost be counted as a suburb. More than 300 years ago, on 30 September 1681, the the treaty was signed in Illkirch-Graffenstaden in which Strasbourg, surrounded by French troops, recognised the authority of France under Louis XIV and by which the city, for the first time in its history, became French.

Travelling along the Ill, the "most noble river" in the country, as Sebastian Münster wrote in 1541, you reach **Eschau**, where the remains of one of the oldest abbeys in Alsace can be seen.

Here the bishop of Strasbourg, Remigius, had a Benedictine convent built in 770. In 926 it was destroyed by the Magyars and a few decades later it was rebuilt. In 1822 the weakened ancient walls of the early medieval building were finally demolished. However, an early Romanesque pillared basilica, dating from 1050, has survived.

Hipsheim, three miles (5 km) further on to the south, has entered into the history of the saints. On a bitter cold winter's night, to be precise on the night of 12 February 1202, St. Ludo, son of a Scottish duke, is believed to have frozen to death under a tree where the village now stands. In memory of "Lodde", as he is known to the Alsatians, a Baroque-style chapel was built. It may seem somewhat macabre to many outsiders, but it is proof of the practical nature of the Alsatians that they chose St. Ludo as the saint to be invoked in cases of aching limbs and frostbite.

aic
tivity
he wall.

Drive on along the D 288 via **Nord-house** to **Erstein**. This town, which is decorated with flowers throughout the summer months, has a long history behind it. It was founded by the Romans. From the 10th to the 12th centuries Erstein was the residence of the Saxon emperors. The chroniclers recorded that Louis the Pious once gave the town to his son, the future Emperor Lothar I, as a gift.

Lothar's wife Irmingard founded a Benedictine abbey in Erstein in 840, although nothing has remained of the building. Worth seeing is the palace of the Zorn von Bulach family and the beautiful old half-timbered farmhouses. Loyal Gaullists among the population of Erstein still speak proudly of the fact that General Charles de Gaulle celebrated his first Christmas after the liberation from the German occupying forces in 1945 here in the church of Erstein.

A mile and a half from Erstein is the old imperial town of **Osthouse**. The town has belonged to the Zorn von Bulach family since the 14th century. They built a **moated castle**, which is considered one of the finest examples of this type of architecture in Alsace. If you are interested in buildings by the water, however, you should also look at the old mill on the river Ill, which can be seen in the village of **Sand**, not far to the south of Osthouse.

Here stands a 19th century chapel in memory of St. Maternus, the first apostle of Alsace. The saint is believed to have died and been buried at **Ehl**, previously known as Ellelum or Helvetum, once a strategically important Roman settlement on the right bank of the Ill. Today Ehl comprises only a few houses. The church of St. Maternus, lying off the road in the open fields, is the only building that has survived from the long-destroyed monastery in which

By the waters of Ebersmuns

St. Maternus is supposed to have carried out his work of converting Alsace.

In **Sermersheim**, to the south of Ehl on the N83, you are already right in the middle of the flood plains of the Ill and the Rhine, in the wetlands of the Alsatian Marshes. If you look at pictures of an earlier time, you can see how far the destruction of nature through human interference has progressed. Ever since the course of the Rhine was regulated and the Rhine Canal was completed, the water table has sunk lower and lower, so that experts fear that in a few years the wetlands with their unique ecology will have disappeared and turned into park-like meadowland. This has already happened in some places in the region between Colmar and Benfeld. There are still 250 species of birds living in the marshes. There are also many rare plants, and you can still see marsh iris on the banks of the Ill, but if the destruction of the natural environment contin-

ues as it has done, these habitats will soon belong to the past.

The three onion-domed towers of the Benedictine church of **Ebersmunster** can be seen from far off across the plain. The monastery which belonged to the church and was dissolved during the French Revolution owes its foundation—according to legend—to a great miracle. We are told that Siegebert, a son of King Dagobert II, was attacked by a wild boar while hunting and mortally wounded by its tusks. Preparations were already being made to lower him into his grave when Bishop Arbogastes came running from Strasbourg and, no-one knows how, restored the corpse to new life.

In gratitude King Dagobert gave the miracle-working cleric what are now the communities of Ebersmunster and Ebersheim. It is not legend, but historical fact that the abbey of Ebersmunster was founded in the 7th century by Duke

Aldaric and was one of the most important in Alsace.

During the Thirty Years' War the abbey and its church were razed to the ground. The new church was not completed until 1715, and was destroyed again after only two years, having been struck by lightning. Two years later building began again, this time under the careful direction of the most famous architect of Baroque times, Pater Thumb from Vorarlberg. Work was completed when the interior was finished in 1759.

During those years the most perfect and certainly the most beautiful Baroque church in Alsace was created, something quite unexpected in this country famous for its Gothic and Romanesque sacred buildings. This church, which has survived in perfect condition, possesses a joyous architectural harmony of proportion and a colourful interior, and glows with the kind of charm that one usually only sees in South German Baroque churches.

It is worthwhile visiting the church if only to see the opulent painted ceiling, created in part by the Tirolean master Joseph Magnes, or the the magnificent carvings, of which the most impressive is the mighty figure of Samson supporting the chancel with his hands.

Lovers of organ music will be delighted by the sound of the Silbermann organ, which performs in concerts on Sundays in May, during the *heures musicales*. Three generations of the Silbermann family, who had emigrated to Alsace from the Ore Mountains (now in East Germany), built many admirable organs between 1700 and the end of the Ancient régime. Only two organs considered authentic works by the famous masters are left: the organs of Marmoutier and Ebersmunster, built by Andreas Silbermann, the oldest of the family, between 1730 and 1732.

Sainte Foy
or Sancta
Fides—on
of the fine
Romanesq
churches i
Alsace.

Sélestat on the Ill: You should allow some time to visit the friendly provincial town of **Sélestat** (population 16,000), especially for the well-kept old city centre with its narrow alleys, half-timbered houses and famous historical buildings, which deserve a detailed tour. The sights are concentrated in the old town. Drive along the road from Châtenois into the town centre and follow the main through road N 59/D 424 into the old town centre.

Sélestat is on the border of the two Departements which make up Alsace, and is therefore almost in the geographical centre of the province. In the late Middle Ages, at the time of the Reformation, Sélestat was also something of a spiritual and intellectual centre of Alsace, for since the early 15th century there had been a Latin school here, which was famous and respected throughout Europe, and where world-famous scholars came to teach.

Among them was Erasmus of Rotterdam, the greatest thinker of his time, who praised *nobile Selestadium* (noble Sélestat) the centre of Humanism and scholarship, in his works.

Today Sélestat is one of the country's economic centres; some thriving textile and metal working companies have settled in the town, but this has not done any damage to the pleasant and peaceful character of Sélestat.

The town, especially the old town which is surrounded by boulevards, has its origins in a Roman settlement on the Ill, which probably already existed at the beginning of the first century A.D. The name of the settlement is not recorded. There are, however, two versions, one fanciful and the other matter-of-fact, as to how the town got its old German name of Schlettstein. Legend claims that once upon a time, a giant named Schletto lived here and that he was the actual founder of the town and

gave its name to it. Evidence of Schletto's existence is presented in the form of an enormous bone, which was found on the banks of the Ill, and which is on show to the public in the museum. Palaeontologists, who as representatives of science and of course renowned for their lack of imagination, are quite unimpressed by this popular explanation and firmly insist that the bone belonged to a dinosaur which must have terrorised the area millions of years ago. If you follow this theory, then the sober and logical explanation is that the name comes from old-high German *slâte*, which means nothing more than swamp, marsh or wetland and describes the situation of the town in the flood plain of the Ill.

Sélestat was an early choice for a residence of the great and powerful, possibly because of its favourable position on the Ill. In 728 the royal palace of the Merovingians was first documented as "Selastatt". In 775 Charlemagne celebrated Christmas here; he was on his way from Thonville to Italy.

The two Hohenstaufen emperors, Frederick Barbarossa and Frederick II, showed the town many examples in their favour. Sélestat received many privileges, and Frederick II even gave the town imperial freedom in 1254. Sélestat joined the Decapolis, the union of ten Alsatian towns, in 1354 as a Free Imperial City. The Peasant's War, the troubles of the Reformation and the Thirty Years' War caused extensive damage, and when France annexed Alsace in 1673 Sélestat was so loyal to the Empire that the Sun King Louis XIV refused as a matter of principle to receive its representatives.

During World War II, the town remained largely undamaged, although the front line did run through the whole town in 1944-45.

The centre of German Humanism: The

The church St. George in Sélestat one of the largest Gothic churches in the region.

most important epoch in the town's history lies a long way back, in the age of Humanism. In 1441 the Westfalian Ludwig Dringenberg, the head of the Latin school, which was run along wholly conventional lines up till that time, took up the currents of Humanist thought which came mainly from Flanders and Italy, and began to put the curriculum, which was overloaded with church dogma, on a new basis. The centre of the new teaching and thinking was formed by the study of Greek and Roman antiquity, ancient languages, the skills of rhetoric and poetry.

From this university-like school, which soon gained a reputation as a centre of early Humanist learning, came a series of famous men, among them the theologian and lawyer Jakob Wimpfeling (1450-1518), who became rector of Heidelberg University and received the honorific title *Praeceptor Germaniae*. Among other famous ex-scholars at this

Humanist Latin school were two Humanists born in Sélestat itself, Martin Bucer (1491-1551), a craftsman's son, and Beatus Rhenanus (1485-1547), who came from a butcher's family.

Shortly before his death in 1547 Rhenanus left his private library to the town. It is considered one of the most important cultural treasures of Alsace. The 670 leather-bound volumes of this famous son of Sélestat are the basis of the **Bibliothèque Humaniste**, an extremely precious collection, which can now be seen in the town museum, the former Corn Hall (*Rue de la Bibliothèque*). There is no comparably comprehensive evidence from this period, which was so fruitful for European thought. The glass cases display Merovingian and Carolingian manuscripts, charters of Charlemagne, the Book of the Miracles of St. Fides (*Liber Miracolorum Sanctae Fides*) which was created about 1100 and is richly illustrated

ummer,
ches
part of
scene
wn.

with miniatures, a manuscript by Thomas Murner, Martin Waldseemüllers Cosmographia of 1507—just to name a few of the masterpieces.

However, you will soon realise that it is not only the antiquarian treasures which are fascinating. One of the exhibits in the museum is the famous *Head of Christ*, a magnificent wood carving dating from the 15th century.

On show in the anteroom of the museum is the bust of a young woman, whose noble and earnest features possess a mysterious attraction. This is indeed not a sculpture by some artist, but the actual death mask of an aristocratic lady of Romanesque times, a unique find.

The mask was discovered in 1890 during renovation work in the crypt of the church of **Sainte Foy**. The young woman probably died of the plague, and due to the fear of catching the disease the body was covered with lime. This left the actual image of a person who lived more than 800 years ago for us to see today. The identity of the beautiful woman is not known for certain. Historians believe that she may be Adelheid, the daughter of Hildegard of Büren.

The Countess Hildegard of Büren, the great-grandmother of Barbarossa, brought the Benedictine monks from Conques in southern France to Sélestat, as penance for a murder committed by her son Frederick. Here the monks founded a branch of their parent house and had a church built and dedicated to Saint Fides (St. Foy). The three-aisled basilica is one of the finest Romanesque churches in Alsace, even though over the centuries it has been much altered on the outside as well as within. At the end of last century, attempts were made to restore the church to its original appearance, but with little success.

Only a few yards from Sainte Foy is the second famous church in Sélestat, **St. Georges Minster**, one of the largest Gothic cathedrals in the province. When heating was being laid under the floors, a rotunda, 72 ft (22 m) in diameter, was discovered. This is probably a remnant of the former Carolingian palace chapel, in which Charlemagne celebrated Christmas. Worth taking a look at are the glass windows (1430-60) with scenes from the lives of saints and the stone Renaissance chancel, adorned with sculptures, which is held by a statue of Samson.

Not far from the two churches, in the Rue des Chevaliers, is the Tour d'Horloge, the town gate (14th and 16th centuries), on which a crucifixion scene can be seen. The portcullis is a reminder of the original purpose of the tower: it was part of the town fortifications, built in 1300 under the Hohenstaufen dynasty, and together with the Witches' Tower (to the east of St. Georges) it is one of the two buildings from the town walls which have survived. From the Bibliothèque Humaniste, you go through the

Left, the Witches Tower. Right, the Humanist library of Sélestat.

Rue des Serruriers to the Rue de Verdun with its Renaissance house (No. 18) which once belonged to the former master builder of the town, Stephan Ziegler. The St. Barbare armoury (late Gothic) is in the Place de la Victoire.

Tales of the stork: Various attractions are waiting for you two and a half miles (4 km) to the west of Sélestat on the Alsatian wine route. Since 1972 there has been a stork reserve in this picturesque little town, which as its name **Centre de Réintroduction des Cigognes** (Centre for the Reintroduction of the Stork) points out, is not only intended to delight the visitor but also to promote the very serious purpose of resettling this symbol of Alsace in larger numbers.

For years the storks, which once used to live on the Alsatian plain, have been threatened by extinction. The already much-reduced numbers of wild storks in Alsace are rapidly decreasing. Fewer and fewer birds return from their annual flight from their winter quarters in central Africa. The main reasons for the rapid shrinking of the stork population are the use of pesticides in agriculture, live power cables on which the birds injure themselves fatally, and game-hunting of these beautiful creatures, which is still encouraged and practised in some places. In order to prevent the complete extinction of these charming symbols of good fortune and fertility, the ornithologist Jacques Renaud founded an initiative to resettle the white stork in the late 1960s. Financed entirely by donations from private benefactors, the society imported 60 young storks from North Africa and put them in special reservations in central Alsace. One of these reservations is in Kintzheim, a broad stretch of land with artificial ponds. There are similar stork parks in Hunawihr, in Turkheim and in Molsheim.

In order to suppress the migratory urge of the birds, Monsieur Renaud clips the feathers of one wing, so that they cannot set out on their dangerous journey to the south any more. After two or three years, the feathers grow and the birds can fly again. In the meantime they have "forgotten" their migratory urges and usually stay in the country all the year round.

This simple but successful method of resettling the birds soon proved itself successful. Today there are pairs of storks nesting again on the roofs of nearby villages. The flightless storks are well cared for in the park. The costs of resettlement are paid from the entrance fees. In the open enclosures you can get quite close and admire the beautiful and often very friendly birds, who are often very popular with children. Even though Monsieur Renaud's methods have been seen to be effective and the stork population is beginning to recover, voices have been raised in criticism, particularly among the older inhabitants of Alsace, who claim that it is

Inhabitant Eagle Park in Kinzthei

a shame to deprive the proud heraldic symbol of their country of its freedom—even if it is only for a short time—and to domesticate it.

Above Kintzheim, in the ruins of the castle on its 1083 ft (330 m) high hill, is another attraction: the **Volerie des Aigles**, an eagle reserve. Here, in big avaries, inhabit eagles, vultures, falcons and many other birds of prey. During the summer months, entertaining displays of free-flying, trained birds are held in the great square in front of the castle. These are always popular and attract a number of visitors, who enjoy the excitement of seeing a golden eagle with its 6.5 ft (2 m) of wingspan circling just above their heads.

And, as it's well known that all good things come in threes, go and visit the **Montagne des Singes**, the Monkey Hill, on the road which leads to Haut Koenigsbourg. This is an open enclosure in which a group of Moroccan

Barbary apes was settled in 49 acres (20 hectares) of conferous forest in the early 1970s. The animals soon felt so at home in Alsace that their numbers have now risen to more than 300.

The animals live in complete freedom, but according to those in charge of the project not one has escaped and got lost in the outside world. This might be because their new Alsatian home offers almost the same environment as the region in the North African Atlas Mountains, where the Barbary apes originated. Some animals have been re-exported to Morocco, because of the decimation of the local population by illness.

These three animal parks have certainly not been sited near Kintzheim by accident. They are quite near to Haut-Koenigsbourg castle, the essence of all medieval romanticism, which is visited daily by crowds of tourists.

A massive castle: Going by car from

tlight
a wine-
wing
ion.

Kintzheim, you can get to the castle of Haut-Koenigsbourg, 2,491 ft (755 m) above sea level, by following a winding road for some 15 minutes. On foot, using the marked footpath, you will need a good hour and a half. After Guirbaden near Mollkirch, Haut-Koenigsbourg is the second largest and at the same time the only completely restored castle in Alsace. It lies on a long ridge, about 1,815 ft (550 m) high, and in clear weather the view reaches from the Kaiserstuhl in the east to the Grand Ballon d'Alsace in the south. Just as interesting as its present appearance is the rich and varied history of this towering fortress.

The original castle dates from the 12th and 13th centuries. Around 1147 "Estufin" (the name of the castle in early medieval times, equivalent to the "Staufen" element in Hohenstaufen) was built by the Hohenstaufen family. In the mid-13th century the fortress, already documented as "Königsburg", came into the possession of the Dukes of Lorraine. In 1359 it was bought by the Bishop of Strasbourg.

Over the centuries the owners continued to change, and the castle precincts were expanded several times. At one time it belonged to the Counts of Habsburg, at another to the Counts of Thierstein, and finally—in the 15th century under the Mey brothers from Lambsheim—it was the base of the infamous robber barons.

The castle was often fought over, besieged, destroyed and rebuilt, and was finally demolished by the Swedes in 1635, during the Thirty Years' War. It remained a ruin and was left to decay until the end of the 19th century, as the town of Sélestat, which owned the castle from 1865 on, did not have the money for the upkeep of the ruins.

In order to get rid of this expensive burden once and for all, the town elders of Sélestat had what they thought was a brilliant idea. As Alsace had been part

of the German Empire since 1871, they presented the historic ruin to the highest ruler of the land, Emperor Wilhelm II, in the hope that he would take personal charge of it as a symbol of German history. However, the latter had no thought of keeping and preserving a ruin, but insisted that the castle should be rebuilt. It was not to become an imperial residence, but a memorial and symbol of the re-created empire, and also a symbol of the German history of Alsace. The restoration work, which began in 1899, swallowed up some 2.225 million marks, a massive sum in those days.

It is one of the ironies of history that the Hohenzollern emperor decided to have a large part of the rebuilding costs paid by the imperial state of Alsace-Lorraine, and so the very circumstances that the town council of Sélestat had been trying to avoid came about. Emperor Wilhelm II put the architect Bodo

Haut-Koenigsbou▮ entrance an▮ drawbridge▮

Ebhardt, who had been a complete unknown until then, in charge of the rebuilding. Ebhardt was a self-taught man and he had no experience in restoring or in reconstructing monuments. His lack of formal qualifications was presumably balanced by his imaginative reconstructions of Teutonic chivalry, which seemed to have matched nicely with the Emperor's.

The restoration, therefore, did not have the aim of carefully restoring the old and reconstructing the destroyed sections. Rather, the main object was to reflect the glories of past German greatness. The result was an idealised image in stone and metal of how a medieval castle ought to look.

The result, the present castle of Haut-Koenigsbourg, could not count on meeting with undivided approval. Many contemporary critics made fun of the eclectic styles of building and spoke of a stage set for grand opera or of the undignified plans of a totally insufficiently qualified architect.

Visitors to the huge imposing building of red Vosges sandstone, where nothing much has changed as far as the buildings or the magnificent interior are concerned since the opening ceremony of 1908, should not expect therefore to see a reconstruction of the original castle according to historical and architectural guidelines. The Haut-Koenigsbourg of today is more of a higgeldy-piggeldy collection, influenced by Wilhelmine thought, of all that was considered "Romantic" and "medieval" at the turn of the century.

Incised on the mantlepiece in the Great Hall is the statement "I did not want this." This thought-provoking remark is ascribed to Wilhelm II. Some sarcastic observers claim that he wrote these words in a lucid moment when he realised what had become of Haut-Koenigsburg as a result of his naive ideas.

ut-
enigsbourg
m the
side.

THE WINE ROUTE

Praises of the Upper Alsatian wine route, along which (quoted at random from a travel guide) "the idyllic wine villages are strung like precious pearls on a necklace", can be read and heard in Alsace. For visitors, a trip to Alsace is almost identical with a drive along the Route du vin, only to be disrupted by the tasting of the food and wine.

For this reason, we begin this chapter with a word of caution: the **Route du vin** in the holiday season, and especially its southern section, is hopelessly crowded with tourists. Between June and the autumn months, there are a few villages where locals and visitors have to put up with long traffic jams at the entrances, frustrating delays at restaurants and unnerving crowds in the streets.

Of course, all these villages are festively decorated to attract the tourists, and most of them—you can hardly believe when you look at the hordes of visitors being herded along the well-signposted roads—still grow wine. But that does nothing to change the fact that the idyllic Alsatian life along the wine route has for the most part degenerated into a mere backcloth which disguises rather than displays the individual features and charm of the region.

Unfortunately, the same is true of the much-famed Alsatian cuisine, which we shall consider in the next chapter. Many of the countless restaurants along the Route du vin still take great care and effort over the quality of the food and wine as well as in the service they offer. However, the pressures of mass tourism all too often proved stronger, and the famous Alsatian *choucroute garnie* degenerates into a heap of carelessly pickled and cooked sauerkraut, piled according to the motto *"Quantity not Quality"* with some tinned sausages, a rag of factory-coloured bacon and a few of the less appetising bits of the pig.

There is no better news to be had of some other Alsatian specialties. The goose liver pate is imported from Poland, Israel or heaven knows where, the onion flan is made of frozen pastry, the fresh Munster cheese doesn't come from the farmers in the Munster valley but from the "special offer" shelf of the nearest supermarkets, and the Edelzwicker wine is any old blend, where you have as little chance of finding out where it came from as you have of recognising any of the ingredients.

These warnings are not intended to put you off visiting Alsace. On the contrary, only those who refuse to be fobbed off with the clichés that the skilful advertising campaign of the Department tourist offices has put before them will be able to enjoy the genuine Alsace in the convenient manner which this wine-growing land, still unique in Europe, really deserves.

Even more: we claim that such an

ceding
es,
mn grape
vest under
sun.
,
noisseur
lose.
ht,
-catching
se in the
ketplace
bernai.

enjoyable journey can even be made along the Route du vin, if necessary even in the main holiday season in July or August. All you need is a little imagination and the courage to leave the beaten track, and you will find the true good life—it often lies right next door to the false image.

Our description of the Route du vin is intended to help open the traveller's eyes. For this reason, wherever the general run of travel literature praises the attractions, we often consciously stick to short descriptions (or even warnings). We try instead to break out of the flow of tourists as often as possible and to find stopping places for a journey along the wine route that should be enjoyable in the best sense.

From Molsheim to Obernai: If you follow the wine route faithfully like a tourist from north to south, you will reach **Molsheim** via Marlenheim and Avolsheim. At the end of June the little town looks less like part of the Route du vin and more like a film set of the Wild West. This is the time when the people of Molsheim—and countless cowboy-and-Indian clubs with them—celebrate their Western Festival.

There are also two wine festivals in Molsheim, a small one on 1 May and a major one in mid-October, when you can expect the town to be packed with tourists. Therefore if you want to get to know the real Alsace, you should either avoid Molsheim at this time or make a hasty retreat.

The **Molsheim Jesuit church** is a curiosity. It was built as a Gothic building at the beginning of the Baroque age, which means it was stylistically about 150 years behind the times. Worth seeing is the market square (**Place de la Mairie**) with the medieval butchers' guild house, in which there is a **museum**. Above the open-air staircase there is a beautiful clock showing the

188

phases of the moon, and a wine tavern has settled in the basement. If you like to drink your measure of Riesling at tables where the guests come into very close contact and where the wine acts fast to loosen their tongues, you have come to the right place here.

A pleasant contrast to busy Molsheim is the wine-growing village of **Boersch**, on the road from Niederhaslach to Obernai. It lies only a few miles off the main Route du vin and has withstood the temptation to make too many obvious concessions to the supposed requirements of tourism. It is all the more surprising, because in Boersch there is the **Maison Schaetzel**—the original house of one of the most respected vintner's in Alsace. Before convincing yourself personally with the quality of Schaetzel wines, which is best done during lunch, and informing yourself about viniculture past and present in the exhibition rooms, take a casual half-

hour stroll around the picturesque streets of the village.

They meet at the market square with the **Six-Buckets-Well**—a marvellous example of the typical medieval well form of Alsace. It would be difficult to find a finer example than that of Boersch. Remains of a Romanesque frieze have survived on the choir tower of the church. The picturesque appearance of Boersch is not due only to the impressive family houses of the 17th and 18th centuries, but also to the fortified wall with its upper and lower gate.

Obernai: The former Free Imperial Town is a ten minutes' drive to the east of Boersch. The author René Schickele once lived here. It is one of the great attractions of the Route du vin and therefore, it is very busy. This time there's no help for it. Even if you don't like the hectic crowds of mass tourism, you can't miss out on **Obernai**, because it would mean driving past one of the

Corn
, one of
oldest
dings
bernai,
rs respite
some.

most beautiful towns of Alsace. It is advisable to park your car outside the historic centre and walk through the maze of streets and alleys between the market square and the **Place de l'Etoile**.

In contrast to most towns in Alsace, Obernai was spared destruction in the various wars and also the great fires (which are recorded as occurring regularly throughout the Middle Ages). Visitors can see the undamaged town, unparalled in its completeness as in its lively variety. Each house in the market square has its own characteristics.

In the market square is the corn house of 1554, now a restaurant: **La Halle aux Blés** (Place du Marché, 67210 Obernai, tel. 88 95 56 09), which despite being very busy does not serve mass-produced food but offers excellent traditional Alsatian cuisine.

Try a game dish, venison or wild hare, if they are on the menu, or the excellent pressed meats. In the evening there are

TARTE FLAMBÉE

The Neapolitans have pizza, the Alsatians have Flammenkueche or *tarte flambée*. Eaten as *hors d' oeuvres*, Flammenkueche makes you want to keep on eating—till you find you won't be able to manage the main course.

To make Flammenkueche, you don't need a wood-fired stove (although the Alsatians insist that *tarte flambée* will only succeed if cooked over a real wood-fire). You will have to make a bread dough. In a big bowl, mix 250 cc of lukewarm water with a teaspoon of dried yeast and half a cup of flour. Five minutes later (meanwhile, work on the yeast) add half a teaspoon of salt and more flour (about half a pound) until the dough is firm enough to knead.

Then you must knead the dough on a flour-sprinkled surface for a least ten minutes—it must be well kneaded and not just pushed around a bit! The dough should be smooth and not sticky. If it does stick, add more flour and carry on kneading. Then put the dough back in the bowl, cover it with cloth and leave it for an hour at room temperature. Once it has doubled its volume, start work again; knead it once more and leave it for another hour to double in size. Now cut a large onion into rings and mix it with 125 gms of cottage cheese and 125 gms of crème fraîche, salt and freshly milled pepper. Then let this mixture stand for half an hour to let the onions lose some of their sharp flavour and get a little softer.

The bread dough is rolled out into a thin plate shape and placed on a greased baking tray. Then spread the mixture of onions and cheese over the dough and sprinkle 200 gms of chopped streaky bacon over it. Put the whole in an oven preheated to 230° Celsius and bake for 20 minutes until crunchy. The hotter the *tarte flambée* is served, the better!

Tarte flam being prepared under watchful e

190

Flammenkueche prepared from the wood-fired oven and refreshing Sylvaner or Riesling to drink (in this case, we recommend the vines of the local family vintners, Seilly).

From Ottrott to Kintzheim: It is worth going out of your way to see the pretty wine-growing village of **Ottrott** (just to the south of Boersch and two and a half miles/4 km—to the west of Obernai). Here they serve one of the very few genuine Alsatian red wines (among the non-genuine ones are some of the particularly dark Pinot noirs), the famous **Rouge d'Ottrott**. The best place to try this rarity is the **Restaurant Beau Site** (1, Rue du Général de Gaulle, 67530 Ottrott, tel. 88 95 80 61), where you can also have a very pleasant meal—there are excellent game and fish dishes— and stay overnight.

There are two picturesque castles in the vicinity of Ottrott, **Lützelburg** and **Ratsamhausen**, as well as the hills of

Elsberg and in particular **Mont St. Odile**, which the Alsatians regarded as a sort of national shrine. The 2,503 ft (763 m) high hill is named after St. Odile. The name means "daughter of light" and points to the origins of the legend to which the 7th century convent owes its foundations.

The story begins with an attempt at infanticide. A duke named Eticho once had a blind daughter born to him, and he wanted to have her killed. Her mother, however, fled to Burgundy with the baby and had her baptised there, and by a miracle she received her sight back during her baptism. Eticho then had his daughter brought home. Some years later, like many power-crazy medieval rulers whom fate had denied a male heir, he tried to marry his daughter to a powerful suitor.

Odile escaped from this fate too. She fled from her home through Alsace and to the other side of the Rhine. A second

Mosaic dome in chapel of St. Odile monastery.

miracle saved her from her pursuers—a huge boulder suddenly barred their way. After this event the villainous duke gave up. As a sign of his remorse he founded, among others, the convent on Mont St. Odile—on a site which the Celts had built a shrine more than 1,000 years before. Parts of the Celtic enclosing wall—it runs round the slopes of Mont St. Odile for over six miles (10 km)—can still be seen today. You can get to Barr either from Ottrott or directly from Mont St. Odile. The stream of tourists that flows down the Route du vin does not pass by Barr, but it does rush through the village without robbing too much of its peace. A few yards away from the main road, **Barr** is a sleepy but distinctly charming wine-growing village, and it would be worthwhile to make a brief stop here.

Near the market square is a small museum of furniture and domestic life, which bears the curious name **Musée de**

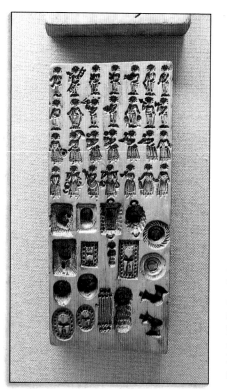

la Folie Marco. In the 18th century a lawyer from Strasbourg named Louis Felix Marco had a magnificent villa built here. The small-town people of Barr obviously thought that the house was a few sizes too big—it was a crazy idea, *une folie*. The museum has valuable furniture of the 18th and 19th centuries on display, splendid examples of Alsatian home life in the old days. We would not really recommend you a visit to the Restaurant-Caveau in the basement of **La Folie**, unless of course you happen to like ice-cold Edelzwicker and warmed-up onion flan.

Continue via the villages of Mittelbergheim, above which rises the ruin of the **castle Hohen-Andlau**, which was inhabited up until the early 19th century, and Eichoffen to…

Andlau: Here is one of the oldest Alsatian abbey churches, which owes its founding, like Mont St. Odile, to the hard-heartedness of a medieval despot. In this case the despot was an emperor—Charles the Fat, who had become tired of his wife Richardis and subsequently banished her to the wild woods. There, the unfortunate Empress met with a good-natured mother bear, who showed her a beautifully situated and well-protected spot in the Andlau valley, which was later chosen as the site for the abbey.

After walking through the town (watch out for the inner courtyards, which are rightly famous), it is a good idea to go into the **Red Ox Inn** (Au Boeuf Rouge: 6, Rue du Docteur Stoltz, tel. 88 08 96 26). Incidentally, if you fancy a good brandy after your meal, you should while you are in Alsace try the *Marc du Gewurztraminer* (known by local people as *Marc du Gewurz* for short). You can stock up with this and other good fruit brandies at the **Distillerie Massnenez** in Dieffenbach (remember: it closes at 5.30 pm!); the little town lies nine miles (15 km) to the southwest of Andlau, near Thanvillé.

Left, a model of baking moulds in the Musée Alsacien. Right, merely tempting the gourme

The Route du vin continues via Epfig to **Dambach**. Even today specialists for timber-framed architecture are inspired by its half-timbered houses. Carry on via Scherwiller and Kintzheim (and possibly go on to make a short diversion to Haut-Koenigsbourg).

St. Hippolyte to Ammerschwihr: The peaceful little town of St. Hippolyte, still completely surrounded by its wall, is the second place where Alsatian red wine originates. Most of the tourists who stop here are gourmets who know exactly where they want to go: to Munsch in the luxurious hotel and restaurant **Aux Ducs de Lorraine** (16, Route du vin, 68590 Sainte-Hippolyte, tel. 89 73 00 09), where, despite sky-high prices, you can always get your money's worth. However, if you like to dine inexpensively (and in a more informal atmosphere), head for the good old inn **The Green Tree** where, in contrast to the Ducs de Lorraine, you can easily

find a table without booking and be able to eat well too.

Bergheim: The town wall with its six towers looks particularly hostile when you come form the north. The medieval lords of Bergheim were indeed not to be taken lightly; their sinister reputation spread as far as Franconia. The town clerk of Nuremberg, Sebald Spreitzer (an early colleague of the famous Hans Sachs) fell in love while on a journey to Alsace with the daughter of a Bergheim innkeeper, who was, however, suspected of heresy and had to answer to the infamous Bergheim Inquisition.

The cunning town clerk saved his beloved and her family from death at the stake by throwing a banquet for some of the Bergheim worthies (including the Inquistor) and having a strolling player appear, disguised for the occasion as fortune teller. Taking a chance, the "fortune teller" claimed to know all about the sinful private lives of those at

The gate to the most-visited tow in Alsace— Riquewihr.

194

the banquet. The Inquisitor was so alarmed on hearing this that he promised to let the entire family at the inn go if only the fortune teller would keep the information to himself. Spreitzer himself recorded this story of successful blackmail for posterity in his carnival play *The Pious Inquisitor*.

No gourmet can avoid taking a trip from Bergheim via **Guémar** (an often underrated and very pretty little wine-growing town) to **Illhaeusern**—that is, assuming that they have booked a table in good time (which, in this case, means at least six weeks in advance) at **Maître Haeberlin's Auberge d l'Ill** (Rue de Collonges, Illhaeusern, 68150 Ribeauvillé, tel. 89 71 83 23).

The praises of Maître Haeberlin (to be precise of the Haeberlins, for surprisingly enough the Auberge d l'Ill still operates as a family concern) have been sung so often that we will content ourselves with a few tips.

Firstly, don't come here on Friday or Saturday evenings (on Monday evenings—in the winter all day Monday—and Tuesday the place is closed anyway). Haeberlin's is always booked, but oddly enough the hustle and bustle is more irritating on these days than on others. This could be because well-heeled would-be gourmets come over from the other (i.e. the German) bank of the Rhine on Fridays and Saturdays.

Secondly, try to avoid the evenings altogether and have lunch here instead—not only because you'll have to spend less money. It is well known that all cats are grey in the dark, and at night all these gourmet temples look more or less festive. However, the really beautifully situated Auberge de l'Ill only unfolds its true charm during the daytime. If you drink your aperitif outdoors on a fine summer's day under the weeping willows on the banks of the Ill (please, nothing other than a glass of

Muscat or Crème d'Alsace, and nothing sweet!)—you will discover why.

Thirdly, Haeberlin offers international cuisine as well as the highly refined regional style of cooking. If you are unlikely to come here more than once or twice a year, try the latter. Other cooks in cuisine-conscious Alsace can prepare lobsters or venison as excellently as Haeberlin, but the regional dishes, such as lentil salad with pork and goose liver, the rabbit salad (*salade de lapereau*), the *Baeckoffe* enriched with truffles or the quail with green wheat can only be found of this quality here, and nowhere else in the world.

The same exclusivity, incidentally, applies to the wine: the highly select wine list (it matches the elevated state of mind, which inevitably overcomes the guest at Haeberlin's) may be ever so tempting with its exquisite Burgundies and Bordeaux—but resist, and stay true to the Alsatian wines.

For the obligatory walk after lunch, you would do best to drive over to **Ribeauvillé** and go on a bit from there to the castle of **Ulrichsburg**. The rocky height, overgrown with all sorts of bushes and with the well-preserved ruins rising on top, is the ideal landscape setting for a pleasant afternoon walk. Ribeauvillé itself is, both from the point of view of the situation and the appearance of the town, not quite as picturesque (and therefore a bit more ordinary) than many other wine-growing towns in the area.

Because of its splendid half-timbered houses and beautiful historical facades it is nonetheless crowded, especially during the main holiday season and particularly on the first Sunday in September. This is when the *Pfifferdaj* takes place, the traditional festival of the pipers and travelling musicians, for whom the judiciary of Rappoltsweiler (the old German name for Ribeauvillé)

Ulrichsburg castle, high above Ribeauvillé

were responsible in the Middle Ages, in a supra-regional sense, so to speak. If, by the way, you want to eat well and have not booked in time at Illhaeusern, you can go to **Joseph Blatter's Restaurant Les Vosges** (2 Grand-Rue, 68150 Ribeauvillé, tel. 89 73 61 39).

You can also have an excellent meal in **Riquewihr** at Francois Kiener's in the **Auberge du Schoenenburg** (2, Rue de la Piscine, 68340 Riquewihr, tel. 89 47 92 28). This is another place where you should keep to the refined version of Alsatian cuisine, such as the escargots with poppy seeds or the rabbit with pickled garlic (robbed of some of its all too overpowering flavour by the pickling process). We have no more to say in praise of Riquewihr here.

The steady flow of tourists which now streams through the unquestionably picturesque old town all the year round, without diminishing in the off-peak season, has turned the former wine-growing village into an open-air museum. Real people, it is claimed, still live in the houses of Riquewihr.

Next to tourism, viniculture is an important source of income, but that doesn't change the fact that the visitor is strongly reminded of Disneyland. Among the hectic crowd, the prettiest of half-timbered houses look like film sets, and if you want to take away only good memories of Alsace, give the hustle and bustle here a wide berth.

Kaysersberg is another popular place for tourists in Alsace and is often visited by those on coach tours. However, this little town is fortunately big enough for the crowds of tourists to disperse. More interesting than the castle, which most of the tourists make tracks for, is the **parish church of Sainte Croix** with its fine Romanesque west portal. The high altar (1518), the work of Master Hans Bongarz from nearby Colmar, depicts among other

ysersberg dicated this seum to famous Schweitzer.

scenes the story of the Passion and is the only surviving carved altar in Alsace.

From the church you can take a relaxing stroll to the Romanesque **White Bridge**, which is a rarity too in this area, with its battlements and arrow slits.

Experts claim that Pierre Immard, the owner of the Kaysersberg restaurant **Chambard** (9, Rue du Géenéral de Gaulle, 68240 Kaysersberg, tel. 89 47 10 17), makes the best *mousse au chocolat* in the world. We were unable to put it to the test, for the simple reason that the *trio des halles* (filet of beef and lamb with veal kidneys and various sauces—delicious, but totally lacking in the restraint practised in modern cuisine) defeated us before we got to the dessert. Nostalgic gourmets, who long for the good old (and often heavy) dishes before nouvelle cuisine, will do well at Immard's, but it's not a closed club—there is a second menu with nouvelle cuisine dishes.

The way from Kaysersberg back to the Route du vin leads through **Kinztheim:** if you want to get to know the best of Alsace without any tourist industry prettification you should definitely make a stop here. Don't be frightened off by the tank at the entrance to the town, which is intended as a memorial to World War II. Instead, walk along the massive, uneven town walls, inspect the well cared-for vegetable gardens in the former moat, and then take a look around the town centre. Here there are no polished-up rows of half-timbered houses, but a friendly mix of various styles and ages of buildings. Only a second glance will tell you that here, close together, there are actually three town palaces.

In one of them, the **Schwendi palace**, is the Alsatian wine museum. It is open mornings and afternoons from early July to late September.

Things get livelier again a few miles on in the former imperial town of **Ammerschwihr**. The town was almost completely destroyed in the last war; apart from the (unremarkable) late Gothic church of St. Martin's, only parts of the old town fortifications have survived, among them the **Fool's Tower**, so-called because of its strange shape (like a jester's cap). However, if you feel that architecture does not only belong in museums, you will not be disappointed by Ammerschwihr. In this little town you can study how even new buildings can fit in to the landscape and the typical historic building styles of their particular environment.

Aux Armes de France (1, Grand-Rue, 68770 Ammerschwihr, tel. 89 47 10 12) has an excellent reputation in the field of Alsatian gastronomy. However, it is probably due to its impressive wine list that makes the place one of the best restaurants in Alsace.

From Turckheim to Thann: In Turckheim, a fairly well-preserved little town, a night watchman makes his

Left,
the fruit of
one's labou
Right,
view of
Rodern
and Haut-
Koenigsbou

rounds between 10 p.m. and 11 p.m. during the summer months—in original costume, of course, with his lantern, horn and halberd. The scene would give a much more medieval and authentic impression if the night watchman wasn't followed on his rounds by tourists, with camera flashlights flickering like summer lightning. By the way, Turckheim produces one of the few Alsatian wines named after its place of origin, *Turckheim Brand*.

Passing near Colmar (see Colmar, page 97) or from Colmar itself the Route du vin continues in the direction of Eguisheim.

Eguisheim is considered one of the places where the genuine (we have to add—just about genuine, nowadays) Alsatian way of life can be seen and admired. It might have something to do with cobbles which cover the streets and squares of Eguisheim and are hardly suitable for cars, but do fit in well with an architecture that seems to consist only of escape routes. There can hardly be a town centre where the buildings make such use of breadth, height and also of depth as in Eguisheim.

Wherever you look, there are protruding roofs and upper storeys, balconies, outside staircases and niches. Particularly well worth seeing are the houses which adjoin the inside of the wall that surrounds Eguisheim. Of no less quality than the town is the interior and the cuisine in the **Caveau d'Eguisheim** (3, Place du Château Saint-Léon, 68420 Eguisheim, tel. 89 41 08 89). The famous (in our opinion much overrated, though) *choucroute d'Alsace* is served here, as genuine as the *Kougelhopf* or *Guglhupf* for dessert.

Eguisheim, incidentally, is also both starting and finishing point for one of the shortest holiday routes in Alsace, the **Route des cinq châteaux**. If you don't know the main Route des châteaux, you can still see what you've missed here, in miniature. A short worthwhile diversion are the ruins of **Pflixburg** castle, situated on a wooded hill, and **Hochlandsburg** castle, towering above the Munster valley.

The further you travel southwards on the Route du vin, the more the floodwaters of tourism ebb away. Because this phenomenon is so pleasant, we really shouldn't tell anyone that the Romanesque church tower of **Gueberschwihr** (built of pink sandstone) is considered the most beautiful in Alsace, and that the town, which history seems to have passed by for the last 400 years, looks like a architectural incarnation of the late Middle Ages.

Those who like half-timbered houses will admittedly not find what they are looking for here. Most of the houses of Gueberschwihr, even the little local palace, look rather unfriendly and sinister with their windowless ground floors. Even so, the town has a rather magical atmosphere; it can best be felt in the twilight hours of a day in late autumn, if only because at that time of year visitors to Gueberschwihr will actually be on their own.

Pfaffenheim is yet another winegrowing town that is worth visiting simply because it isn't crowded. You should take a look at the moving picture of the vespers in the church of St. Martin. Vine-dressers in the Middle Ages sharpened their knives on its sandstone blocks. The Route du vin leads on to **Rouffach**. This town has been influenced by wine-growing as much as by agriculture and at first glance seems more sober than the picturesque wine towns and villages between Sélestat and Colmar. However, you should not let yourself be disappointed by this first impression. There is hardly another wine village where it is so worthwhile taking a second glance.

It is best to leave a few hours for a stroll through the old quarter between the ramparts (the remains of the old town walls), the Rue du Maréchal

Lefèbvre and the Rue des Bouchers. Here you will find the church **Notre-Dame-de-l'Assumption**, on which the people of Rouffach worked for eight centuries, which is why you can discover all sorts of styles from early Gothic to Classical in the building. There are also many interesting palaces and middle-class houses. Our favourite house, however, is a couple of streets away, **Rue Poincaré No. 23**. It is the Half-Moon House, with its curious outer facade dating from 1623.

To the north of Rouffach is the Isenberg hill, on which a fortress has stood since prehistoric times. Attached to the present castle, the **Isenbourg**, is another legend proving that women in Alsace always were more resolute than their sisters elsewhere. In the 12th century, the lord of the castle kidnapped a beautiful woman from Rouffach. Thereupon the women of the town stormed the castle, and—in those days

even more importantly—they exerted the right to sit on the right-hand side of the church, which had previously been reserved for men.

The castle has since been destroyed. In its place today is a 19th century palace which is not stormed by the townswomen, but has been invaded recently by gourmets. In the hotel Château d'Isenbourg is the Dalibert couple's restaurant **Les Tommeries** (Château d'Isenbourg, 68250 Rouffach, tel. 89 49 63 53). The young chef in this establishment uses the basic ingredients of regional cuisine and prepares them with a great deal of creative imagination (one example of the many delicious dishes—poultry braised in Riesling wine). Those who love *foie gras* will definitely feel at home, if only because, interestingly, goose liver in the Tommeries is served as a main dish, which is not the usual practice.

From Rouffach the route leads on southwards to **Guebwiller**. This town has been greatly influenced by industry than others along the Route du vin—and also by the spirit of the French Revolution (which was largely ignored in most of Alsace). "Live in liberty—or die! In the third year of Liberty!" reads the defiant inscription dating from 1791 on the tower clock of St. Léger. The church itself, much more interesting than the main town church of Notre Dame (an ostentatious Classical building), is one of the best preserved Romanesque churches in Alsace.

From Guebwiller you can drive on to the romantic wine village of Soultz. From here also, it is worthwhile making a short trip to the west to the situated little village of **Jungholtz**. On the way you will pass the **Résidence Les Violettes** (Jungholtz, 68500 Guebwiller) with its attached restaurant. Here, at exorbitant prices, you can eat to your heart's content (try one of the fish dishes, for instance) and thereafter spend the night. The Résidence has

A wine village on the inside..

twelve rooms, each decorated in a different colour.

Passing through **Cernay**, where in 58 B.C. Caesar defeated Ariovistus' German army, you come finally to **Thann** and to the end of the Route du vin.

A memorable legend describes the origins of this town. The sainted Bishop Theobald died in Gubbio in Italy in 1160. Before his death, he left his bishop's ring to his Alsatian servant Frederick. When Frederick tried to take the ring off the dead saint, the whole finger came off the body. Without delay, Frederick took this relic, hid it in the hollow of his pilgrim's staff and made his way home to Alsace with it.

He spent the night in a forest at the entrance to the beautiful Thur valley. He leaned his staff against a fir tree, and overnight it grew onto the tree. At the same time three lights appeared above the fir tree, which attracted the Count of Ferrette, the lord of the nearby castle of Angelsburg. Once he saw this miracle of the staff, both the Count and Frederick the servant decided to clear the forest in this place. This occasion is commemorated today in the *Three Fir Trees Festival*, which takes place every year on 30 June, and the pilgrims' shrine and church built on this spot also goes back to the Count.

The church was dedicated, how could it be otherwise, to St. Theobald—as was the church built here later, **Saint-Thiébault**, the second largest Gothic church in Alsace. Saint-Thiébault is worth visiting in particular for its beautiful windows, and for its unusually (even for Gothic churches) ornamental and decorative sculptures.

The people of Thann themselves are of the opinion that Strasbourg Cathedral may be the tallest, and the cathedral of Freiburg on the other side of the Rhine the broadest, but the most beautiful of churches is that of Thann.

nd from outside.

THE WINES OF ALSACE

The vintners of Alsace still partly market the wines that they produce themselves (on the bottles you can see the labels *Propriétaire-Viticulteur* or *Viticulteur-Récoltant*). They have also formed co-operatives (*Viticulteur-Membre de la Coopérative de ...*) and deliver their wine to the co-operative. There are in addition *Viticulteurs-Négociants* who are contracted to deliver their wines to particular wine merchants or cellars and finally the *Producteurs-Négociants* who in addition to their own vineyards use grapes or finished wine from other producers.

The most important means of differentiating between the various wines of Alsace are the various **types of grapes** and not the geographical location.

You rarely come across **Chasselas** in good restaurants. However, as a light and unassuming table wine, it is served in the traditional taverns and in Alsatian homes.

Sylvaner is a fresh wine, which is unfortunately losing some of its popularity. Drunk young and chilled, it is often an excellent accompaniment to light meals.

Take care with **Edelzwicker** and most especially with plain **Zwicker**. This wine is popular with those drinkers who don't realise that Zwicker is an Alsatian word for "blend". The mixture is composed of Sylvaner on the one hand, Riesling, Pinot or Traminer on the other. The result is quite variable as far as flavour is concerned, so it is a good idea, especially if you want to buy the cheaper Edelzwicker in large quantities, to devote some time to tasting it.

Pinot Blanc or **Clevner** is substantial, harmonious and—in the best cases—elegantly rounded. It is also considered an easily digestible wine and is definitely on the way up.

Pinot Gris is a full-bodied, strong wine and was imported into Alsace more than 300 years ago from Hungary, as its other name, *Tokai d'Alsace*, demonstrates.

Pinot Noir is a fruity and yet extremely dry rosé wine, which finds more and more

Down at the Seilly cellar in Obernai.

204

followers with each passing year. Its darker varieties look like light red wine. However, the Pinots noirs cannot be compared to the few genuine Alsatian red wines, such as the *Rouge d'Ottrott*.

Riesling is aptly considered the king of the wines of Alsace. The consistently dry Riesling is usually fairly full-bodied and has a powerful bouquet, and yet good Rieslings often distinguish themselves by their extraordinary delicacy. This also means that a Riesling can be drunk on many occasions (always assuming that you find the right one for the occasion in question)—as an aperitif, as a drink with many *hors d'oeuvres*, with fish, and with the lighter meat dishes. Nevertheless, to get to know the many secrets of Rieslings, we can only recommend three courses of action for wine lovers: tasting, tasting and tasting.

Muscat d'Alsace, with its strong, partly spicy and partly fruity bouquet, is something for refined tastes, but only rarely is it a suitable table wine. However, the fresher versions in particular make excellent aperitifs. The full, intensive taste of **Gewürz-traminer** is ideal for rather heavy *hors d'oeuvre* and desserts, for *paté de foie gras*, for instance, or the strong Munster cheese.

Last on the list is **Crémant d'Alsace**, a natural sparkling wine which is used in Alsace instead of champagne in the cocktail *Kir Royal*.

Courses for wine lovers (usually as chartered tours) are specially arranged by the Departement du Tourisme Rural (Maison de l'Agriculture, 103, Route de Hausbergen, 67300 Schiltigheim, tel. 88 62 45 09) and the **Centre les Genêts d'Or**, (129 La Chapelle, 68650 Le Bonhomme, tel. 89 47 51 27).

If you want to offer help with the **grape harvest** (for some pocket money, free board and lodging), you can approach and obtain information from the **Comité interprofessionel du vin d'Alsace** (Place de la Lattre, 68000 Colmar).

Please take note that harvesting grapes is hard work. But once you have a hand in it and have experienced for yourself *mal aux reins* (backache from the long hours of bending-over at the vineyard), you are likely to have a wholly new attitude to the wine!

THE MUNSTER VALLEY

You can follow the official course of the **Route du fromage**—the famous cheese route—above the Munster valley as a circular tour, starting from and finishing in the town of Munster. The route we recommend is, however, slightly different and particularly attractive. With a car, it can be followed either as a tour complete in itself (ideally, you should take two days over it) or as a diversion off the main Route du vin. Leave the Route du vin in Kaysersberg and make for the Col du Bonhomme, then turn south before Lapoutroie and (now travelling on side roads) you will come via Orbey and Pairis to Munster. From there, follow the course of the peaceful Fecht valley and, crossing the Col du Platzerwasel, you will come to the Route des crêtes. Follow this south for a couple of miles till you reach Le Markstein. Then drive down the Lauch valley via Lautenbach, and you will return to the Route du vin at Guebwiller.

Fresh farmhouse Munster cheese: The cheese route is named after the two dozen or so farms which make and sell the Munster cheese, famous since the Middle Ages. Sometimes you can watch the production of the cheese: Munster cheese is made with fresh cow's milk, thoroughly ripened, seasoned with caraway or aniseed, stored for at least a month in a well-aired cellar, and then shaped into disks of eight to 18 centimetres in diameter. Some of these farms also belong to the so-called *fermes-auberges*; here you can eat a rustic meal and sometimes even stay overnight, all at reasonable prices. Information (and a complete list of *fermes-auberges*) is available at the helpful tourist office in Munster. It is best to book your stay, if you are holidaying in the countryside with plenty of time, during the holiday season.

You can also explore the countryside around the Route du fromage on foot—indeed there is an excellent network of footpaths with a total length of almost 249 miles (400 km). The best times of year for walking are spring (the flowering meadows are often still in bloom well into June in the uplands) and late autumn. In October, you may have to count on thick morning and evening mist in the Vosges, which lend their particular charm to this harsh landscape, although rainfall is not heavy at this time of year. Still, you should take warm clothes. In the mountains above the valleys of the Weiss, Wolmsa, Feucht and Lauch it is fairly cool all the year round, even in high summer. A good starting point for a walk is the mountain farm of Les Alisiers.

Les Alisiers (5, le Faudé, 68650 Lapoutroie, tel. 89 47 52 82) is a farmhouse extended to include a restaurant and attached hotel-pension. Here the

generously portioned Alsatian specialties such as *choucroute, jarret de porc braisé* (braised pigs' trotters) and the excellent *pommes de terre coiffées au munster fondu* (potatoes au gratin with Munster cheese and onions) are never prepared as a matter of routine, but always with affectionate care.

The nicest thing about Les Alisiers is its location, among high pastures well above the floor of the valley. For this reason alone you should stay at least one night here, if it's at all possible. You can get to Les Alisiers if you travel from Kaysersberg in the direction of Col du Bonhomme, passing by the turn-off to Munster and not taking the N 415 till just before Lapoutroie. In the town itself, take the little mountain road just behind the church (watch out for signs!) to the left and uphill to Les Alisiers.

In **Lapoutroie** itself there is not much to see apart from the church. Here, you can shop around. The distillery **Gilbert Miclo** (next to the eastern exit of the N 415 to Lapoutroie) sells excellent fruit brandies. You can also get very good (some even say the very best) Munster cheese at **Jacques Haxaire's** (18, Rue du Général Dufieux).

Orbey is the next stop on our route. It is not a village as such but a series of hillside farms, some of which have experienced quite an upturn in their fortunes (Orbey, because of its altitude, is reputed for its health resort with excellent fresh air) due to tourism. It is important to remember, in this connection, that the area around Orbey is an island of the Romance languages in Alsace (even the local dialect, Walsh, is a variant of French) and thus more French than German tourists come here. Travellers will notice the difference at mealtimes. In and around Orbey, traditional French cuisine is served, rather than the German-influenced Alsatian cuisine.

Instead of going via Kaysersberg and

The Munster valley: ideal for a vacation in the countryside

Lapoutroie, you can also get to Orbey and the Route du fromage directly from Colmar. In this case, your route will take you through another major health resort, the little town of **Trois Epis**, nine miles (15 km) to the south of Orbey, on the sunny slopes high above a side valley of the Weiss. The Cistercian monastery, founded in 1138, around which the town was built has been destroyed (only one gate and some large sections of the monastery wall survive), but it is still worthwhile stopping here and taking a walk through the occasionally narrow and steep streets. Time and again, the gaps between the walls reveal new delightful glimpses of the upland meadows and forests of the surrounding countryside. Continue via Hohrodberg (nearby is the Vosges peak of Le Linge, scene of heavy fighting during World War I) to the centre of this region and the centre of the Route du fromage.

Traces of war: No matter which ad-joining valley or road you use to get here, the first impression is overwhelmingly disappointing. Munster cannot compete with the charms of the surrounding towns and villages, if only because the precious historic buildings of this town have been completely destroyed in the two world wars. The sparse remains of the Benedictine abbey of Munster (founded as early as A.D. 660 by a monk named Oswald) have nothing much to write home about. It is almost impossible for the modern visitor to imagine that this was for more than 500 years the site of one of the most important spiritual and cultural centres of the European continent.

The active town council tries hard to make Munster attractive to tourists, but it succeeds only once a year, at the end of August, when the bakers of Munster prove, during the *Pie Festival*, that the local culinary talents are not confined to the making of Munster cheese.

aditional *oucroute rnie.*

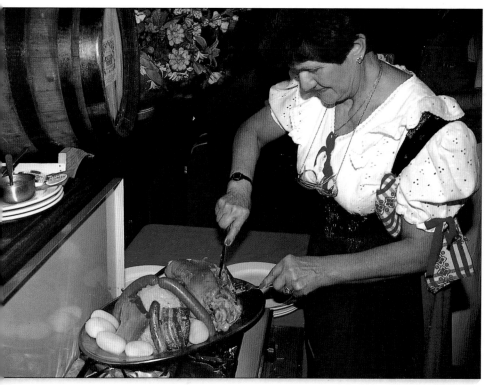

Though the rewards for visitors interested in art and history may be small, the scenic attractions are considerable and may be found in the immediate neighbourhood of Munster itself.

Popular (but not overcrowded, which is why we recommend it) is the walk from **Stosswihr** (the village is only one and a quarter miles (2 km) uphill from Munster on the road to the Col de la Schlucht) to the cave of Dagobert near **Frankenthal**. Those of a nervous disposition should not, however, travel this road at night, and definitely not at full moon. At such times, the local people will tell you, cries and faint gurgles can be heard, coming from the nearby **Dead Lake Marsh**, the last gasps of two villains who once sank into the marsh. The poor souls can find no peace because they once tried to murder King Dagobert, the generous patron of the abbey of Munster. Fortunately, Dagobert became aware of their ambush, saved himself at the last minute by fleeing into a cave (the Dagobert cave mentioned above) and waited there for his followers. He then had the two scoundrels caught, ordered their hands and feet, cut off, and had them sunk into the bog. No wonder the two of them are still screaming and gurgling...

If you drive from Munster through the meadows of the southern Fecht valley, you will regret for staying inside the car. The landscape is so beautiful here that you simply want to get out and finish the journey on foot.

The village of **Muhlbach** offers an excellent opportunity for exercising your legs. When taking a short stroll around the town, make sure that you don't miss the chance to visit one of the most unusual museums in Alsace, the Musée des Schlittages (open from June to mid-September, afternoons only). Here you can see the sledges, mostly original pieces, which the woodcutters have used since the old days to transport the cut trunks (and themselves) from the hillsides into the valleys, often on specially built log-surfaced paths. Even more fun than a visit to this museum is watching a sledge race such as the people of Muhlbach still hold from time to time (information can be had in the Syndicat d'Initiative in Gerardmer).

Carry on to **Metzeral**, an ideal base for small and large circular walks and for visiting two mountain lakes. To get to these, though, you do really have to leave your car. You can drive part of the way on the D 10 VI from Metzeral, but from the point where the valley of the Wormsa winds away northwards into the mountains you can only continue on foot; the walk uphill to the **Fischboedle lake**, possibly the most delightful of the Alsatian mountain lakes, takes a good hour, and from there it is another half hour to the larger **Schiessrothried lake**, surrounded by impressive rocky outcrops and cliffs of stone. (The latter can also be reached from Muhlbach directly

Quenched for now.

212

by car—but the walk up from the south really is much nicer.)

Before getting to the Col du Platzerwasel (you set out, once again, from Metzeral) it is worth making another short trip on foot to the **Schnepfenried peak**. From this high point, particularly on clear autumn days, you can get a beautiful view of the nearby Grand Ballon d'Alsace and the southern fringes of the Black Forest on the other side of the Rhine valley, down to the Alps. The Eiger, Mönch, and Jungfrau, all giants of the Bernese Alps, can also be seen quite clearly with the naked eye from here especially on clear days. (You can get to the peak by turning off right from the D 27 at the crown of the pass of Col du Platzerwasel, driving half a mile (1 km) to the village of Schnepfenried and walking the rest of the way—there and back should not take more than an hour.)

The trail now continues across Platzerwasel and the Route des crêtes to Markstein, from there along the course of the Lauch valley, past the Lauch lake and down into the valley.

Holidays in peaceful Lautenbach: Lautenbach lies in the vicinity of the restless Route du vin and has a very fine Romanesque abbey church, which is however often overlooked, as what is probably the most impressive Romanesque abbey in the whole of Alsace is situated not far away—the church of Murbach, built in the mid-12th century.

It is worth staying in Lautenbach or Murbach, and not only if you're a follower of the fine arts. Ramblers can enjoy the beautiful scenic countryside around the nearby **Petit Ballon d'Alsace**, and those with exclusive culinary tastes will find a visit to the hotel **Saint-Barnabé** (25, Rue de Murbach, 68530 Buhl, tel. 89 76 92 15) worthwhile. Here, once again, there is much more on offer than just Munster cheese.

springs
those
stures on
h ground.

NEUF-BRISACH
TO COLMAR

The **Route vert** is one of the routes that approach Alsace through Germany. It begins at the source of the Danube river, passes Lake Constance, passes the city of Freiburg, and then crosses the Rhine at Breisach. Once on Alsatian soil, it continues via Colmar (from this point it is identical with the Route du fromage) through the Munster valley and through the Col de la Schlucht to Domrémy-La-Pucelle, the birthplace of Jeanne d'Arc.

Vauban's contributions: Just inside the border, crossed by the bridge of Vogelgrün (which offers a lovely view of the river, the countryside and Breisach) you come to **Neuf-Brisach** and its fortifications, which are definitely a masterpiece among the works of the famous architect of defences, Vauban. Commissioned by Louis XIV, he planned Neuf-Brisach and supervised the building, thus fulfilling a dream of long standing. He had already built 300 fortresses and had himself commanded more than 50 sieges, thus discovering all the points that could be improved. Now he had the opportunity to design a fortress according to purely strategic principles, starting from the drawing board with no geological or architectural obstacles to be taken into consideration. The building of this huge fortress had become necessary because Breisach, on the opposite banks of the Rhine (with fortifications also designed by Vauban for Louis XIV), had been returned to Austria after the Peace of Rijswik in 1697.

In order to build the bulwark on the left bank of the Rhine, Vauban had a canal dug for the sole purpose of bringing granite from the Vosges by boat. For the heavy labour he used a gang of convicts who had been promised freedom as their payment. Those who survived

fever in the Rhine marshes, other illnesses and the inhuman effort demanded by work in the quarries could settle down in the new town.

An aerial view of the town makes it appear like a huge star. The inner fortress wall is octagonal, surrounded by a moat. The second star shaped wall is protected by bastions at the outer points and also surrounded by a moat. The walls were once broken by four fortified gates, of which only the Colmar Gate and the Belfort Gate survive today.

Today the exhibition rooms of the Vauban museum, which also contains a relief model of the fortress, are in the Belfort Gate. The outlying entrenchments, which were part of the clever system of exactly calculated interlocking defences, are now lost in the woodlands that surround the town. Inside the fortress, the strict geometrical plan is a reminder of the former military role of Neuf-Brisach. The interior is divided up

like a chessboard into 48 squares by roads crossing at right angles. In the centre of these small squares is the Place d'Armes, once a parade ground, at the side of which the tower of the Classical church of Saint Louis can be seen. In the corners of the rectangular square are the old wells, now filled with flowers.

In earlier years traffic from the Rhine squeezed itself through the town, around the square and through the narrow alleys between the pink houses with their mansards and tiled roofs. Nowadays there is a bypass road, built to bring some order into the traffic chaos. But don't let this practical route tempt you into passing the town by. Apart from its grandiose architecture, Neuf-Brisach has other attractions.

On the first of May there is the *Lily of the Valley Cavalcade*, with processions, floats, music and costumes that are famous throughout Alsace. In summer there are historic parades involving changing of the guard and closing the gates. A walk by the moat below the walls around the Colmar Gate provides an opportunity to examine the system of martial fortification and its most important elements.

If you are not put off by the ugly sight of the huge nuclear power stations, you can make the nostalgic journey from Neuf-Brisach to **Marckolsheim** along the banks of the Rhine in an old train which dates from 1900. In Marckolsheim you can view barracks from World War II or tour the Rhine in a steamship from the 1930s.

Further along the route to Colmar there are many other opportunities for short trips and sightseeing. From Neuf-Brisach the route leads through the Kastenwald forest, which is delightful all the year round and invites you to ramble and relax. You can stop at one of the small villages along the roadside and board at the typical country inn.

The Magin Line (Marck olsheim Museum).

218

Beyond **Andolsheim** (famed for its asparagus) and just before Colmar is **Horbourg**. There are only a few traces visible today of the formidable Roman fortress that once stood on this site, which is now a suburb of Colmar. Later the castle of the Counts of Horbourg stood on the same site. In 1324 the Horbourgs sold their estates to Count Ulrich of Württemberg. The resulting domain of Horbourg-Reichenweier lasted until the French Revolution. The old palace was completely destroyed by Louis XVI, and only remains of the former estate buildings have survived. The old 16th century church was replaced by a new building in 1897.

In the immediate neighbourhood of Horbourg is the community of Weiher auf'm Land, fortified in 1252 by Walter III of Horbourg. Walls with Romanesque elements have survived, parts of the town wall. From 1478 on it belonged to the rulers of Rappolstein. The church

of Saint Michel is particularly well worth seeing, with its choir tower dating from the 12th century. In the early 16th century this single-nave church with its tracery windows was altered. However, the tower suffered only minor changes and was made part of the new building. The interior was painted in 1511 in the manner of Schongauer and contains Gothic wood-carvings. The west entrance, also of late Gothic fashion, is beautifully adorned with the coats of arms of the Rappolstein and Habsburg families.

Before continuing the journey to Colmar, it is worth making a trip to **Jebsheim**, just four miles (7 km) away. This little village with its attractive half-timbered houses was once a resting place on the Roman road. The church, still partly Romanesque in style, dates from the second half of the 15th century and still has its original red facade, not quite typical of Alsace.

ie-cold s: nan wall efs near bourg.

THE RHINE: ENVIRONMENT IN DANGER

"I know not why, but my gladness hath utterly passed away..." Once the many songs and poems which praised the Rhine spoke of the beauty of the river scenery, but nowadays the opening lines of Heine's famous Lorelei poem can be given a different interpretation. The Rhine has become Europe's problem child. In earlier years the river was the most famous communications and transport route in Western Europe, down which Alsatian boatmen could travel to the North Sea, to Denmark, Sweden and England. As early as 1826 the first regular steamship service made it possible for Alsatian goods to be transported upriver as far as Switzerland.

The river has always had its moods, according to the weather and the season, but if in previous years it was "only" the countryside and the villages which vanished

under the floods, it was now the shipping companies and the industries along the Rhine which suffered economically. As early as 1840, therefore, work began on the first scheme to regulate the flow of the Rhine, and in 1920 the Grand Canal d'Alsace had been planned to run parallel to the Rhine from Basle to Strasbourg. This huge project, wider than the Suez Canal, was not intended for tourist boat trips but was also used industrially. By now, the time was past in which the Rhine could be poetically described by Victor Hugo, as a blue-green, crystal-clear river. Conventional hydro-electric and other fueled power stations were installed at all the dams along the river, but these were not enough. In 1971 a nuclear power station came on line in Fessenheim.

Those who lived along the river, at any rate, not only reacted to this concentration of power stations with mixed feelings, but founded pressure groups, making Alsace a pioneer of French environmental issues. In contrast to the rather indifferent attitude to nuclear power current in other parts of France, massive opposition developed in Alsace. Here people did not share the popular opinion that French nuclear power stations were not dangerous because they were the safest in the world (no comparison with the Soviet "corrugated iron huts"). No-one took Sunday boat trips to admire the nuclear reactors. Instead people chose to sit-in at demonstrations on the sites.

Another nuclear power project in Wyhl (in Baden, West Germany) aroused protest, as did a chemical works for the production of bleaches, planned for Marckolsheim by a Munich-based company. Both cases ended with the sites being occupied by demonstrators. Pressure groups from Baden and Alsace formed the Netzwerk Dreieckland (Triangle Network—a reference to the area's situation between Germany, France and Switzerland) and other organisations. After a five-month siege the planning approval for the Marckolsheim site was withdrawn. Solidarity was upheld, and the 21 pressure groups from France, Switzerland and Germany were able to prevent the Wyhl project, probably permanently.

The Greens have remained active in Alsace, as they have almost elsewhere in Europe, and have gained popularity. They put up their first candidate in 1973 in

Causes for concern: stricken trees ...

Mulhouse, and they have won many votes in local and presidential elections. Their share of the vote in the elections in early March 1989 was approximately 12 per cent. The "alternative" scene in Alsace is composed of many small groups. The AFRPN alone is an umbrella organisation for about 100 groups, and though many may criticise the lack of political direction in the movement, it is precisely the breadth of opinion that is covered which is the recipe for its success.

Environmental pressure groups are also very active in getting the message across to the public. Apart from periodic publications, and some books printed partly in-house, there are two radio stations, *Radio Dreyeckland* and *Radio Vert Fessenheim*, which provide the people with information and which enjoy considerable popularity.

However, it is not only the nuclear power stations which cause concern in Alsace. Topping the list of issues by environmental pressure groups is the planned waste incinerator—still being resisted to the end by the city of Strasbourg—and the developing of the countryside.

Between 1935 and 1970 more than 49,420 acres (20,000 hectares) of forest were cut down, with irreparable damage done to flora and fauna. In 1975 new clearances were planned for the Rhine forests; so-called "progress" demanded big industrial estates in the Marckolsheim, Strasbourg and Colmar-Heitern areas.

The Vosges, the "green belt" of Alsace, will have to make way for new roads and recreational facilities. Environmental protection groups have prevented some plans from being carried out. Despite all their efforts 14,826 acres (6,000 hectares) of unspoilt Alsatian countryside have disappeared beneath the concrete in the last few years.

The Alsatians will not stand idly by and watch the destruction of this splendid region, starting with the green Wasigen forest in the Hanau region, where once Hagen of Tronje and Walter of Aquitaine fought over the Huns' treasure, and going on to the gentle hilly landscape of the Sundgau. Hopefully, their courageous example will find followers throughout France.

**nd pollut-
ivers.**

ROUTE DES CRÊTES

This part of the guide is not only for those tourists who are travelling by car, but also for those who have already laced up their walking boots and are impatiently adjusting the straps of their backpacks. We are going to walk the Vosges, under mighty fir trees, over lush meadows, up stony peaks and along winding paths.

Our goal is an area of incomparable scenic beauty—the hills and valleys of the Alsatian Vosges. Here you will be surrounded by a silence which makes you forget that only a few miles away tourists move in crowds through the busy streets. If you should get too lonely deep in the forest, all you need to do is to go downhill in an easterly direction. After a few miles you will be back in one of the lively and attractive villages of the lowlands.

Officially, the Route des crêtes, the road that runs along the crest of the Vosges, runs from Sainte Marie-aux-Mines in the north to Cernay in the south. We have extended the route slightly to the north, for the countryside between Schirmeck and Sainte Marie is just as interesting.

If, for example, you are coming from the Route des châteaux, you will have the opportunity of seeing the nearby interesting scenery and getting on to the Route des crêtes, without having to travel through miles of uninteresting countryside.

Whether you travel by car or by bicycle, the busy stretches of road will bring you near to your goal. If you are walking, you will escape from the crowds of tourists in the attractive towns and villages, but that doesn't mean that in the summer you'll be walking along lonely paths without meeting another human being.

Unfortunately, over the last few years those people who apparently lacked the

energy to walk a short distance have been tearing through the quieter parts of Alsace with four-wheel drive vehicles. It is easy to get to almost all the sights with a four-wheel drive car. Luckily, some areas have been designated as protected sites.

You should try to climb up to at least one summit, and not only because the view is so beautiful, but also because the walk is well worth it. Anyway it can be good for your health to be really out of breath at least once a day. However you organise your itinerary, don't forget that the clouds coming from the west shed their rain on the Vosges, and that the weather in the mountains can always change suddenly. Also, it can be decidedly chilly even in summer at an altitude of nearly 4,900 ft (1,500 m). It is therefore a good idea to take weather-proof clothing at any time of year.

You will also need proper maps in your backpack, so that you don't get

lost. Detailed maps and information about rock climbing possibilities are available from **Club Vosgien** (4, Rue de la Douane, 67000 Strasbourg). The Club Vosgien has laid out paths and circular walks, and the Vosges as a whole have a good network of paths. Hiking trails are marked with holly.

If you want detailed information about hunting and fishing, then get in touch with **Loisirs Accueil** (Relais départemental du tourisme rural), 7, Place des Meuniers, 67000 Strasbourg, tel. 88 75 56 50, and Loisirs Accueil, Haut-Rhin BP 371, 68007 Colmar Cedex, tel. 89 23 21 11.

Are you now properly equipped? Have you got your backpack on? Then let's be off!

First of all, we are heading for the **Bruche valley**. While you are in **Schirmeck**, one of the old centres of the textile industry (which has to make way for international competition and be-

cause it has no future), which has very little to offer the tourist but can act as a base for setting out on the next stretch and for all the preparations, make a little trip to the **Donon pass**, which is not far away, but well worth the journey. There are very few places which offer a more beautiful view than the summit of Donon, if it isn't misty. Unfortunately, it often is in the Vosges.

The central towns in the region south of Schirmeck are **Hohwald** (here you should visit the town hall, which has an exhibition of *Schlitte*, those dangerous-looking giant sledges which once brought the logged wood down into the valley) and the little town of **Villé**, in the heart of the Pays du Kirsch, the home of cherry brandy. There are some ten distilleries producing the strong brandies from all sorts of fruits and berries (wild or cultivated).

It is worth staying here to explore, for this region is of interest to hikers. There

Château de la Roch and smoke from St. John's fires in the background

are beautiful paths through flowering meadows and under huge fir trees. At the Champs du foi and the Col du Charbonniére there are various cross-country skiing routes which curve through the conifer forests, insofar as these have not been cut down to make way for more downhill pistes and for the construction of ski-lifts.

The green hilly landscape in the valley between Ban de la Roche and **Fouday** (here Pastor Oberlin, founder of the education system in Alsace, is buried) is also a popular meeting place for the makers of model aircraft who launch their flying boxes here in good weather. Gourmets will find an excellent hotel and restaurant in the tiny village of Colroy-la-Roche—La Cheneaudière.

The whole area is full of names ending in *la Roche*: Ban de la Roche, St Blaise de la Roche, Donjon de la Roche, Château de la Roche, etc. It's not far from the castle "de la Roche" to

Waldersbach. Apart from a few blocks of stone, all you see is the rock on which the castle once stood. This rock is really remarkable, though. Skilled climbers know how to get up to it safely (take a rope for all eventualities), everyone else has to use a rather steep metal staircase up to the vertiginous viewing terrace, with its view of the broad valley, where many fires burn around the time of the summer solstice.

In **Waldersbach** there is the house of Pastor Oberlin, the cleric whose humane and socially committed work has often been praised and who became famous through Georg Büchner's novella *Lenz* (the work describes how the mentally ill poet Lenz was wandering in the trackless countryside in all kinds of weather and sought shelter in Oberlin's house). The paths here have stretches which offer many fascinating views of the hills and mountains and of the Donon peak.

STRUTHOF

Let us assume that you are travelling on a sunny day along the winding road from Hohwald to Natzwiller through the green, dense forest. Suddenly, and surprisingly, you see the gleaming white memorial of the former concentration camp of Struthof before you. Shortly after you will see a clearing with long, low barracks, hidden behind a hedge, lined up along the steep slope. You can also see watchtowers, a double fence with barbed and electrified wire. In the middle of the idyllic Vosges you are confronted with the traces of one of the worst features of the Nazi rule of occupied France.

Up till now, it all looks quite bearable, even though the silence now seems quite sinister. Then you step into the past which still haunts and inflicts so many. The exhibits and the documents in the barracks are enough to make any visitor sink into horror as though into deep waters. Again and again you hear the same questions: how could human beings be so indifferent to the sufferings of others, how could they display such ingenuity in making these sufferings even worse? This complete lack of compassion towards fellow human beings is unimaginable.

Many Germans visit the former camp, as can be seen from the visitors' book. "I am ashamed to be German" is one of the quotes you can read; another, written in childish scribble, "we never realised how bad it was." No, we don't usually realise how bad it is; it is in our nature to have images of horror in order to even make a guess...

But are all these dreadful acts something "typically German"? Are (or were) Germans the only people capable of acting in this way? Is it really nothing but the past with which we are confronted here? Again and again we are told that the destruction of human life in

this fashion was so abhorrent that it cannot be compared with anything else. A closed chapter of human history, then? Something that only happened here and under Nazi rule?

Indeed, the chapter seems to be closed in Western Europe, if not forgotten. And Struthof is unlikely ever to be anything else than a museum of terror. Some look at it and are ashamed of their German origins. Some look at it and "discover" the capabilities of "others" in inflicting cruelty. But is that all? What about the present age we live in? Is this museum a memory of the past or a warning? If it is a warning, the warning needs to be universal, and how many people will ask themselves the question of what crimes they would be capable of committing, how quickly they would lose pity if they were always surrounded with such suffering?

We all prefer, at least in this situation, to identify with the victim rather than the perpetrator of the crime. Such an identification does not damage our own image as human beings...

Whatever reason you may have for coming here, the confrontation with the past touches all of us, and we all work at it differently. Some push the implications away, snigger and tell jokes. Others comment, examine, observe each detail scientifically and take themselves on a "visual horror trip" into the past. Who knows the reasons which motivate other visitors to the camp? We avoid looking straight into their eyes and at their faces.

Concentration camps within Germany had been operating since the burning of the Reichstag (February 1933), controlled by the SS and SA and holding prisoner enemies of the Nazis (communists, social democrats and others). After the start of World War II, the SS also built concentration camps in those areas occupied by German troops.

In May 1940 the German western offensive began, with the aim of forcing

bed and
ctrified.

229

a hasty military decision in northern France. Many French resistance fighters were imprisoned in Struthof by the occupying powers. Forced labour in the quarries led to many prisoners dying painful deaths or suffering permanent damage to their health.

Not all visitors will realise that they are in a place once of cruelty and horror. Many may want to make their way to drink beer under the sun umbrellas of the "Struthof" bar and restaurant. Was it thoughtlessness on the part of the administration to put the sign *La chambre à gaz* right next to it? At any rate, the restaurant is the older of the two, and even the shady paths look as if nothing unusual ever happened here.

The creation of the Vosges and their climate: The most impressive part of the Vosges massif lies between Sainte-Marie-aux-Mines in the north and the Grand Ballon in the south. The lower slopes with their typical beech and conifer forests are symptomatic of a very damp oceanic climate (never go out without waterproofs!). In contrast, the climate on the peaks of the massif, which drops down abruptly on the Alsatian side and gently towards Lorraine, is similar to that of those in the Alpine regions which have peaks around the 6,500 ft (2,000 m) mark. Although Alsace does not have peaks as high as those in the Alps, the flora and fauna and the volume of rainfall are quite similar in both areas.

Some 600 million years ago, central Europe lay under an ocean. The first massifs of gneiss and granite, such as the Vosges and the Black forest, were already surfacing in this age. Some 300 million years later volcanic activity and the deposition of sediment in the shallows left traces such as the rock layers in the Bruche valley. Lush vegetation was gradually washed down to the valleys, later to form coal deposits.

Left, the church of Ranrupt Below, Château de la Roch

Two hundred million years ago the massif was flooded again and received "new" deposits, among them the coloured sandstone typical of the Vosges. During this time, the course of the Rhine broke through the massif.

Some 25 million years ago the landscape developed to somewhat like an open book. Between the Vosges in the west and the Black Forest in the east, the waters of the Rhine flowed in a bed 22,000 yards (20,000 m) across and formed the Alsatian Plain in the west, the lowlands of Baden in the east. Over the last two million years, when cold, hot and temperate periods alternated, and after the Ice Age, the massif of the Vosges evolved into its present form.

Looking from the west, you see the peaks of the Vosges range forming gentle waves on the horizon. Looking from the Alsatian side, the picture is quite different. Here there is a drop of 2,625 ft (800 m) over three miles (5 km)—no gentle waves here! On the Alsatian side the glaciers, which only disappeared 10,000 years ago, have left deep basins in which the Alpine flora survives. The glaciers flowed away fairly quickly towards the east, eroding the ground and leaving behind the mountain lakes typical of the Vosges.

Its north-south alignment makes the massif a real watershed for all weather systems coming from the west. For this reason it is not surprising that a fresh breeze in the heights can rapidly turn into a hurricane with speeds of 60 to 90 miles per hour (100 to 150 km per hour). This is also reflected in the plant life.

Up to the 3,300 ft (1,000 m) mark, the slopes are covered with beech and conifers. Higher up, only the conifers can withstand the fog and the wind, growing to 4,000 ft (1,200 m) before the lumberjacks came with their axes and saws.

The higher the altitude at which the trees grow, the smaller and more

untain n: gh and athered.

twisted they become, eventually leaving the field to scrub and bilberries. Up here, it is essential to treat the weather seriously. In the winter the temperatures are around the 4° Celsius mark, and the wind whistles through the scrub at 52 miles per hour (83 km per hour). These winter storms, however, are most important for the plant life in the mountain basins. They blow the snow down off the summits into the basins, where it sometimes lies more than 66 ft (20 m) deep. Even in summer, the masses of snow keep these regions damp and cool. Otherwise, the Alpine flora would have vanished long ago.

The "official" Route des crêtes: Sainte Marie-aux-Mines is a small town still dominated by the textile industry. Once there were mines here, particularly for silver and quartz. You can learn more about the past of Sainte Marie in the **Musée minéralogique, minier et des traditions locales** (70, Rue Wilson,

open daily during July and August from 10–12 am and 2–6 pm). The old silver mine, the **Ancienne mine d'Argent**, is also worth a visit. Enquire about the visiting hours, which change throughout the year—tel. 89 58 72 28.

One interesting fact is that the language border runs through the middle of this town. The inhabitants of the left bank of the Liepvrette river spoke French and were Catholic, those on the right bank spoke an Alemannic dialect and were Protestant.

In early July there is a mineral fair, which attracts great crowds of visitors. From Sainte-Marie-aux-Mines you can get to the Col du Bonhomme. It is still, as it was in times of war, an important "strategic" point, although only for leisure and recreation today. The name of the pass is due to St. Dié, a hermit who is said to have lived in the area. "*Bonhomme*" means "good man".

Here there are more beautiful foot-

Left and below, from the forests of Vosges to the factory.

paths, such as the one which leads from Saint-Pierre-sur-Hâte to the Brézouard, a "Ballon" 4,029 ft (1,228 m) high, which in good weather will give you a view of the Donon pass, Strasbourg and the Mont Blanc massif.

Easily reached from the Col du Bonhomme are the Black and White Lakes (Lac Noir, Lac Blanc). Lac Blanc covers 69 acres (28 hectares) and is five miles (8 km) away, at an altitude of 3,445 ft (1,050 m), to the southwest. No-one will swear to it being white. The rocks of the glacier basin in which it lies make it seem more of a steely grey in colour. At 230 ft (70 m) it is the deepest of all Alsatian lakes.

From the dam of the White Lake there is a path (follow the red-white-red square) to the **Château de Hans**, a strange tower-shaped rock. From here you have a view of the whole area. Botanists can find rare Alpine plants here, such as the sulphur-coloured

hawkweed and unusual types of ferns.

If you are travelling with children and are no expert on plants, stop your off-springs from picking the flowers. Flowers such as foxgloves, and many other very pretty flowers with bright colours, are very poisonous.

There is a shorter way (2 miles/3 km) across country from lake to lake, by the longer way (5 miles/8 km) across the "Gazon de Faing" bog, the spring and the Reisberg forest is worth taking. This forest was once cleared by human agency and is now being reforested with pines from abroad.

The Black Lake looks sinister. Especially when the sun is hiding behind the clouds, the round, tree-encircled lake gives quite a spooky impression, a complete contrast to the many mountain lakes which can be reached by one of the many footpaths (there is a wide choice).

Continue on to the Col de la Schlucht. This part of the Route des crêtes is

233

crowded at weekends. Apart from nature lovers, skiers also come here, drawn by the ideal snow conditions.

The pass (*col*) at an altitude of 3,737 ft (1,139 m), is the highest in Alsace and is an important crossroad. The roads leading to Colmar, Géradmer (Lorraine) and Munster all meet here.

You will need good hiking maps at the **Col de la Schlucht**. The footpaths through the ancient granite range are beautiful and varied, but often suitable for experienced trekkers only, as the routes are fairly long. For the amateurs, there is a chair lift to the tower on the summit of **Montabey**.

The scenery around the Col de la Schlucht offers a variety of panoramic views. This is one of the reasons for the area's popularity. A footpath leads to the **Lac Vert** (Green Lake), which owes its name to the water plants that cover it. On the way, you pass through great fields of bilberry bushes. According to local lore, the fruit will make you drunk if taken in great quantities.

Let us take a closer look at one of the footpaths: the **Sentier des Roches**, surely the most famous but also the longest trail. The *sentier* starts 219 yards (200 m) beyond the pass (in the direction of Munster—follow the blue triangle) and leads you not just through impressive rock formations, but also through pine forests untouched by human hand (the nature of the ground makes logging difficult) and a wildflower reserve with the greatest variety of species in the Vosges. Thanks to the undisturbed growth cycles of the plants there are many kinds of insects here, which would have far less to eat in other "tidier" forests, where dead wood is hardly ever left lying around. Where there are insects, there are also birds. The *sentier* is a miniature paradise for amateur ornithologists.

The path goes on through mixed for-

The grain fields of summer

est (largely beeches) and widens out into a broad forest path leading towards Frankenthal. If you follow this path, you will come to a bog in a glacial basin. The bog was once a mountain lake, of which only a pond is left. It owes its existence to the the avalanches from St. Martin's Wall, which regularly "dig over" the floating parts of the bog. Here too you can see wild flowers, especially in spring. But once again, caution is needed. Among the daffodils there are many poisonous plants.

The **Frankenthal** is one of the most beautiful valleys in Alsace and has a glacial basin in which Alpine flora flourishes more than anywhere else in Alsace. Here all the plants are protected by law, and it is an offence to pick or pull up any plant to take home with you. It would be safer to take a photo!

A small, steep path (follow the yellow disk) rises in daring curves up to the **Col du Falimont**, 984 ft (300 m) higher.

From here, you can follow a flat (and restful) path through bilberries and gentians back to the Col de la Schlucht.

The Hohneck is the third highest peak in Alsace (4,461 ft/1,360 m). On top is a toposcope which will explain the view to you, insofar as it isn't hidden by mist.

In the north you will see the Donon, in the south the Ballon d'Alsace, in the east the Kaiserstuhl, and if it's really frosty but clear, you can just make out the shape of Montblanc, which is after all 155 miles (250 km) away. Officially, the Route de fromage follows this same stretch between Hohneck and the Markstein, for this is where the *hautes chaumes* are, the high pastures to which the cattle are driven in spring (see also the Route Joffre). Many of the *marçaireries*, the dairy farms which made cheese on a small scale, are now *fermes-auberges* offering food and lodging.

These lush hilly meadows between the Route des crêtes and the eastern

erlooking ̣ Noir.

course of the Route du fromage also have a great variety of hiking trails and footpaths. The most beautiful upland pastures are to be found between Metzeral and Mittlach. If you do have some time available, you can visit a sawmill in this region—in Steinabrück.

The route continues, past the Lac du Schiesroth, an artificial lake in idyllic surroundings at the foot of Hohneck, past **Kastelberg** (with its nice *ferme-auberge*), past Altenweiher and Hus, up the Col de Hahnenbrunnen and the Markstein, a skiing area not exactly known for its breakneck pistes. In fact, it's a ski centre more for families.

However, the **Markstein** in particular is an example of crime against nature. The winter sports area has driven out the capercailzies, which once occupied a privileged position in the locality.

There are many walking and hiking trails in the Markstein. Here the route to Guebwiller crosses the Route des crêtes

and leads to the Lac de la Lauch and the source of the Lauch river. This is a pleasant place to stop for rest and recreation in the middle of the forest.

Carry on to the Grand Ballon, the site of bitter fighting in World War I between French and German armies. This peak is the highest point of the Vosges (4,469 feet/1,423 m). There is another popular skiing area along its slopes. Also there is a great view of the Black Forest, of the hills and valleys of the area where a very beautiful hiking trail runs as far as the Lac d'Alfeld.

Along the route is the Vieil Armand. This place is also well known. In World War I, it was the site of one of the big battles. Around 60,000 soldiers died here. At the Col du Silberloch there is a memorial with a crypt. The bones of more than 12,000 unknown soldiers are housed in the crypt. Among the crosses and tombs is a path leading 3,137 ft (956 m) to the mountain top.

This is a sad end to a visit to the Route des crêtes. But there were battles all along it (the same is true of the Route Joffre) during World War I. Nonetheless, true nature lovers visit this stretch more than once. You can see a small part of the route during the holidays or over a weekend. Don't be disappointed if time runs out before you've seen everything. You may have the opportunity to come back!

Now we have arrived in **Cernay**, our last stop—and we are back on the wine route. This small town suffered much in World War I. You can still see the gate **Porte du Thann**, once part of the old town wall, which houses a small museum. Fate struck hard at Cernay once before: in 58 B.C. when Ariovistus fought the Romans here. A tourist sight is the little old train which comes from Sentheim through the Doller valley (see the Route Joffre) and ends here.

So let us continue through the south of Alsace, along the Route Joffre and into the Sundgau...

Left, Col du Bohomme. Right, across the Ballon d'Alsace, and beyond Following pages, lone parachuter braves the wintry cold.

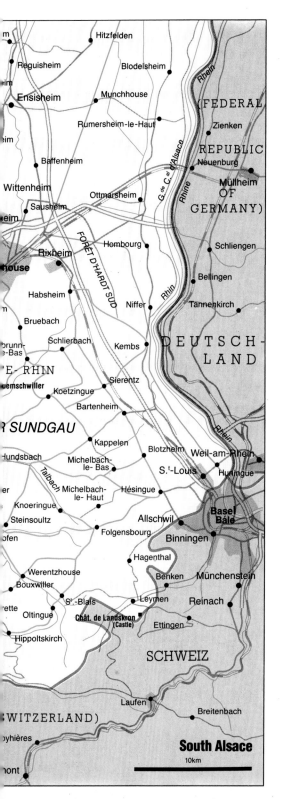

THE SOUTH
OF ALSACE

If you came from the north, you have now seen the greater part of the Alsace that is popular with tourists. However, if you started your journey in Mulhouse or near the Swiss border, you still have the beauty of Alsace as before and you can read the book from back to front, or from "south to north".

Whichever way you may have taken, you are someone who appreciates the beauty of nature, you have followed us along the Route des crêtes, and you are now on your way to get to know the Route Joffre, one that is best experienced in hiking boots and with a backpack. Or you have been making your way through the fleshpots of the wine route as far as Thann, have eaten and drunk more than you have walked, and would now like to discover the south of Alsace and the Sundgau.

We have not chosen any specific route through the Sundgau. Follow the road signs along the Route de la carpe frite or the signs that direct you to the towns mentioned in the article on the Sundgau. But whichever way you travel through this area, you will soon experience the delights of Alsace at close quarters again: the plate of delicious food, the glass of light Riesling, the nature reserve which invites you to rest and relax, the historic town, the Romanesque chapel, the romantic castle ruins, or simply the apple tree under which you are at liberty to take a well-earned nap after fishing a weighty carp out of the pond, or pedalling through valleys and over the hills on your trusty bike.

It could also be that you have just looked at the sights of Altkirch in uncomfortable new shoes or have taken a comfortable, if not very healthy, drive in the car to digest your lunch...

The Sundgau is worth visiting—if only because of the apple trees!

ROUTE JOFFRE

For years, the crowds of tourists streaming along the winding road around the Rossberg and on south to the Sundgau or up to the Ballon d'Alsace have been a common sight. The visitors may be interested only in the spectacular view from the summit, or they may have decided to walk one of the many trails around the Rossberg.

However, there is no getting around the martial side of Alsatian history, not even here. Did the Alsatians want to issue a warning by pointing to their war-torn past, or was it a sign of their untroubled faith in military authority?

At any rate, the Route Joffre is named after a field marshal. Under the command of this Maréchal Joffre, French soldiers built this nine mile (15 km) stretch of road during World War I, purely for strategic reasons. It was intended to provide a quick supply route between the Thur and the Doller valleys. In World War II, too, the Route Joffre played a none too glorious part in the conquest of Thann. Today, however, it fulfils quite different demands. Round every bend a surprise lies in wait for the many peaceful holidaymakers, whose hunger for ever-varying scenery can finally be sated.

Once you get to Thann, there are two signs to Masevaux. Be sure you follow the one with the additional words "Route Joffre". Otherwise, you will end up on less attractive roads with hardly tourist traffic, and which run along the foot of the hills, although those looking for peace and quiet will find placid scenery along these roads.

The actual Route Joffre, though, runs along the southeastern slopes of the Rossberg and begins in the little town of **Bitschwiller-les-Thann** (travelling in the opposite direction, you turn off left in the middle of the town of Masevaux). Here Franciscan monks from Freiburg,

Basle and Neuenbourg once settled. From 1479 on the abbots of **Murbach**, who obviously had a remarkable talent for making money throughout the whole region, were in charge of iron mines here, and in the 18th century they even had their own smelter.

Both were given up in the 19th century, yet various small machine manufacturing industries and a few foundries have survived today. The steam whistle on locomotives is believed to have been invented in one of the foundries here.

The situation is similar in **Bourbach-le-Haut**, the next town along this stretch, which was first inhabited by woodcutters from Tyrol, with the makers of wooden clogs, wagon builders and charcoal burners following after. From here, footpaths lead into the forest of Masevaux and up the Rossberg to the dairy pastures and cheesemakers.

If you happen to be in the area around 24 June, it is worth making the trip to

Bourbach-le-Bas, where you can see the St. John's fires that are still widespread in this region. Here it is combined with a traditional celebration (on the Saturday closest to St. John's Day). Before you get to Bourbach, the road crosses a small pass, 2,454 ft (748 m) up, the **Col de Hunsrück**. From here you have a magnificent view of the Alsatian Plain, the **Burgundian Gap** through which the Rhine originally flowed into the Mediterranean, and across to the Grand Ballon. It is worth going a few steps on foot—perhaps along part of the great European trail from Holland to the Mediterranean, which runs through here—to admire the Alpine-looking flora. An hour's walk from here will take you to the **Thanner Hubel**, where you'll be a few feet higher up and right in the middle of the upland pastures. There are impassioned mountain hikers who like it so much up here that they simply set up their tents on the *Col*. It's a suitable place, apart from the fact that the pass is popular with the Alsatians, for weekend excursions and is therefore crowded.

If you follow Marshal Joffre's road further and come round the final bend, you will arrive in **Masevaux**, a charming town on the Doller river. Imagine yourself in the year 730. Count Maso, the wealthy owner of the castle of Ringelstein, has one eight year old son, whom he loves more than anything. St Odile, who had only recently joined the ranks of Heaven and was probably still throwing the odd look back down at her old home, saw the boy one day in the company of his father and his aunt, the father's sister. The thought that this tender child would be subjected to many ill-fortunes in his life seemed so unbearable to her that she begged God to take him now, in all his childish innocence, into the divine presence.

The Heavenly Father agreed to this

Left, sandstone church in Masevaux. **Right**, the steadfa Silberman organ.

suggestion, and as a sign of His coming intervention in the fate of these people, the saint, according to the legend, appeared to them as they walked in the forest, so that they went on their knees in awe. A few days later the little boy fell into the Doller river and drowned, which made the father so sorrowful that he lost all interest in worldly power and in his possessions.

He had a convent built and a minster erected over the tomb of his only child—Maso's Minster, around which the present town later grew, and which soon became very rich due to its weaving and the metalworking industry.

The Benedictine order which moved into the convent had founded many schools, in which the highest nobility had their children educated—the Tsarina Catherine II was a pupil of the Benedictines—but it was dissolved during the French Revolution. The buildings were almost completely destroyed, so that very little remains of the abbey church today.

Apart from a well dating from 1768 and the 18th century town hall, there are a few canons' houses, built by the famous Kléber before his appointment as general in the service of Napoleon. The present church of St. Martin has two organs which are worth seeing. Every year there is an international organ festival and a passion play here.

The peaceful little town may have few sights to offer today, but it is an ideal base for many walks. A gravel road leads away from the heavy tourist traffic to **Sewen**, which is very suitable for a half-day excursion on foot or by bicycle, for boat trips on the Doller or fishing trips.

If you are travelling with children, it is worth taking a trip to **Sentheim**. Located here is an inviting little zoo with native animals to visit—**la Perle de la Doller**—and just next to it is a restaurant which is a favourite with trippers. It is a rather sad thing to pay a visit to the Alsatian storks, which are confined here in the park all year round and no longer travel south in the winter. The building of highways has progressed at a hectic pace to improve tourist facilities, and power cables and generally increased noise levels have not spared Alsace either, so that the storks have been driven from their ancient home. Sadly, a questionable form of "progress" has made the region poorer by losing one of its natural attractions.

There is a hiker's map by the station in Sentheim, and here too you can choose between many paths of varying distances, among them a geological trail, for which the community offers a folding map (ask for it in the restaurant).

And if you're already fed up with driving, you can always board a small train which will take you to Cernay via **Guewenheim** and **Aspach-le-Bas**, the Chemin de fer touristique de la Vallée de la Doller.

orlorn
ter
orosa
ich
presses.

"THIS IS THE ESSENCE OF THE VOSGES..."

Over the last few years more and more winter sports fans have discovered the Vosges, where they experience pleasures which are either missing or forgotten in urban dwelling. Along the trails (about 125 miles/200 km of them) left by the Club Vosgien—formed in the 19th century on the model of the Alpine clubs—you find isolation, peace and quiet, the feeling of wide horizons, an almost unknown flora and fauna, varied types of scenery and farm life.

The following description holds true especially in autumn, but not only then, when the Vosges seem to have been dipped in yellow paint and a harsh wind blows over the "Ballons": "This is the essence of the Vosges: areas of reddish-brown spread out in the sun and slopes full of scree and the wonderful play of line and form... Everywhere there are bilberries, some blue and some still as red as redcurrants. There are anemones and grey scabious in the clearings. Centaury, Swedish clover, musk mallow and yellow wort sprinkle the slopes. There are brambles sprawling over sunny places, and the blackberries are of unimaginable sweetness. Deadly nightshade, with its heavy black fruit, shinier than Japanese lacquer, is mixed up with them... The beech trees rise a little higher. But then all is meadow and rock, spread out in the sun, wonderfully strong, lonelier than ever, as the *fermes* have all been closed since Michaelmas and the sound of cow bells has slipped down to the valleys."

Many of the plants listed by Kasimir Edschmid in his flowery language are still—just about—waiting for the visitor in the forests rich in beech, fir and pine trees, or in the broad pastures: aquilegia and arnica (for instance around the Rossberg in July and August), blue lupins, yellow St. John's wort, spotted orchid, mint, primula and other orchids (in the Sewen region),

saxifrage, forget-me-not, willow herb, even whole stretches of heather (such as those around the Col du Bussang). Around the Ballon d'Alsace you can find the yellow gentian, which is protected by law. It needs to grow for ten years before it flowers for the first time. Gentian brandy is distilled from the roots, which grow to a metre long.

You can walk across the *hautes chaumes*, the grassland and upland dairy pastures. The traditional dairy and cheese-making country lies around Bourbach-le-Haut on the Rossberg and on the Thanner Hubel, about a mile's walk from the Col de Hunsrück.

In May the herds are driven to the high pastures, which the herdsmen rent for the summer. Usually, they pay the owner the price of 50 kilos per cow, with a cow producing on average 10 kilos of butter and 80 kilos of cheese per season. Up till Michaelmas (29 September) they are responsible for their "protegées". The calves born before St. John's Day (24 June) belong to the owner, calves born between St. John's Day and St. Bartholomew's Day are shared equally between the herdsman and the owner, those born after St. Bartholomew's Day belong wholly to the herdsman. It is obvious why the fertility rites of the St. John's or solstice fires are emphasised in this region.

Travellers need not fear starvation, as there are *fermes-auberges* around (some open in the winter). You can try good home-cooking, goat's cheese, bilberry pancakes and quiche Lorraine. The plain surroundings, however, don't usually put off the landlord from charging city rates. And normally, he has a bed or mattress to spare.

The Vosges can still arouse enthusiasm in city dwellers when they see the exotic (for them) environment. However, pollution of the environment has threatened the fairly sheltered Vosges, though they are by no means as threatened as the Black Forest on the opposite bank of the Rhine. Let us hope the Vosges will be spared this fate!

247

AROUND THE BALLON D'ALSACE

The **Ballon d'Alsace** and the surrounding area have much to offer nature lovers—for instance walks around the Rossberg, south to the Baerenkopf, the Trémontkopf, Sumpfenkopf, the Ballon itself, the Tête des Perches or north in the direction of Kruth or Ventron. This is also an area of old mines, early industrialisation and legends.

In Niederbruck the copper and brass works dating from 1804 can still be seen. Their former director, Josef Vogt, discovered potash in Alsace. From here it's not far on foot to the *ferme-auberge* **Bruckenwald**.

There is a legend about a mine of precious stones in **Kirchberg**. It belonged to a gentleman in Vienna. Every year he came here, disguised as an old man, to fill his coffers. Unfortunately, no details of the place or its valuable treasure have been discovered yet!

From here, and also from Masevaux, a walk of several hours will take you to the **Lachtelweiher** lake. There have been stories about this southern Vosges lake. The mentality of the lonely herdsmen may be one reason for the sinister nature of the stories. Like the tale of a dreadful spirit that lives in the depths and lures people to it by calling, whistling and singing, or by playing a flute. Whenever such an unfortunate creature lands at the bottom of the lake, you can hear devilish laughter in the hills. The water swirls around until it foams, and the body is washed up on the shore. The restless soul, however, is doomed to wander about the area. But even evil spirits can be bribed by the glitter of gold. If a compassionate person throws a golden plate into the deep, the spirit is mollified and the poor soul is liberated.

Carry on via **Wegscheid** to Ober-

Mini tourist train (below) runs from Sentheim (left) to the Doller valley

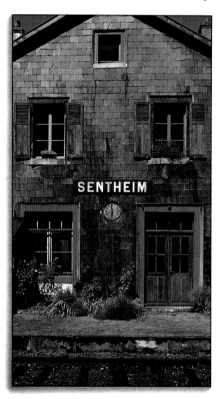

bruch, where the Doller and the Rimbach rivers join. The old farmhouses in Dollern—the source of the Doller lies nearby—make it a worthwhile stop.

In **Sewen**, at the Assumption of the Virgin Mary (on 15 August), there is a great traditional festival, when the *Maison des Jeunes* and the local choir put on plays in the local dialect. Sewen is a good starting point for many splendid circular walks. Even if you are travelling by car, you can enjoy the Lac de Sewen, which is a nature reserve.

Bed and breakfast is offered in the splendid villas along the way. You can stay and examine the many rare plants or the cemetery chapel dating from the 16th century with its charnel.

The Lac d'Alfeld, dammed in the 19th century, covers 23 acres (9.2 hectares) and is one of the major reservoirs of the Vosges. It is popular for excursions and suitable for water sports.

At long last the snaking curves lead you to the top of the Ballon d'Alsace, 4,101 ft (1,250 m—the exact measurement has not been established to this day!) high. There is nothing left here of the loneliness of the Vosges, especially in winter. Ten ski-lifts and 25 miles (40 km) of pistes attract crowds (especially on the west side). However, skiing fans cannot be blamed by nature lovers on one point. In contrast to the Alps, the forests on the upper slopes of the "Ballon" were not cut down because of the increasing popularity in skiing, although they had been cleared many years before, by the tenants of the famous convent of Masevaux and the counts of Ferrette. In recent years the Ballon d'Alsace has become more and more popular among hang-gliders too. There is a landing site on the southeastern wing behind the *ferme-auberge*, by the road. If the weather is favourable, you will find it worthwhile coming here even if you don't care for hang-gliding—you can still enjoy the view and make out Mont Blanc in the distance.

Driving down the Ballon, you will come to the town of **St. Maurice-sur-Moselle**, once a thriving weaving industrial centre but now a quiet holiday and winter sports resort. St. Maurice is already over the border in the Moselle valley (Lorraine) and lies at the entrance to the charcoal burners' valley, **Vallée des Charbonniers**, once infamous because of its rough inhabitants. The charcoal burners were believed to have descended from Swedish and German families who were brought in by Duke Charles of Lorraine in the 17th century to work in the copper and coal mines. Cut off from the outside world, these immigrant families formed a small community over the years and lived in relative autonomy according to their own customs and laws. Even when mining was no longer economically viable and had to be suspended altogether, the group stayed on in the valley and lived off the resources of the forest:

wood, charcoal and resin, paying little or no attention to property rights and forestry laws. The obstinate charcoal burners were only subdued in 1832 after a bitter war.

From St. Maurice you can walk via the **Jumenterie** (a former stud farm of the Dukes of Lorraine, now a holiday home) to the Ballon (it takes two hours). You can return via the Ferme-Auberge du Ballon d'Alsace via the **Col de Stalon**, the watershed between the Rhine and the Rhône. Just before the Stalon pass, on Route D 465, is the **Monument des Démineurs**, a memorial to those who lost their lives in defusing mines.

From **Bussang**, another winter sports resort, there is a road leading in a northerly direction to an old glassworks, where a footpath leads to the hermitage of Brother Joseph Formet, who did not flee from medieval darkness but from the light of the Enlightenment. On all the surrounding hills you will notice, if you are here before 24 June, wood stacked for the St. John's bonfires.

It is also worthwhile to tour the surroundings of the **Great Neuweiher lake** and the **Lac des Perches**, one of the most beautiful in the Vosges, left behind by prehistoric glaciers. Here too people have let their imagination run wild and relate how the lake got its German name *Sternsee* (Lake of Stars). Once a little boy is said to have seen a shooting star fall into the lake. He followed the trail of the glittering mass and bent over the waters at the lake, and saw thousands of stars which mirrored themselves on the surface. He wanted to touch them and so bent further, but unfortunately he lost his balance, fell in the lake and drowned.

In **Urbès**, the next town along our way back from the Ballon along the Moselle, we are back in Alsace. The little town was once part of the copper industry which was widespread throughout the area (copper mines and smelting). But it also played a part in the horrors of Hitler's dictatorship—there was a branch of the Dachau concentration camp here, and a memorial plaque acts as a reminder. Between Urbès and Fellering, on the left side of the N 6, is a small but interesting nature reserve, the **Lac d'Urbès**, a peat bog created by glaciers and water courses. The footpath leading from the car park by the road offers you yet another opportunity to enjoying Nature's peace. If you have the patience and are lucky, you can see teal, wagtails and other waders, herons and shrikes. The tourist office in St. Amarin and a few hotels in the area distribute an informative leaflet.

Finally our round trip takes us to **St. Amarin**. Its origins belong to legend than to history. There is no saint named Amarin, so it is assumed that the name goes back to Marinus, who is believed to have withdrawn in the 7th century to the *Doroangus de Thoro* (the inhabitable country along the Thur).

Village vivacity.

250

It is evident that the town was already flourishing under the Romans. Nearby, in the Malpersbach area, the remains of a Roman road can be seen. The town flourished even more once the St. Gotthard Pass was opened in the 13th century, linking Flanders with Italy. One of the abbots of Murbach, that abbey which was active in its efforts to secure a worldly income, soon raised a road toll, with the approval of Frederick II. Frederick was indebted to the abbey, as it had actively supported his crusade. This led to a six-year war with the Count of Ferrette, who saw his toll-raising privileges in Vieux-Thann threatened, and finally had to give in.

In 1480 St. Amarin received the right to hold a market and, until the Revolution era, it administered all the villages of the lower valley. It is also the starting point for several walks. Above **Merbechel** a small nature reserve is signposted, the trail GR 532 leads to the Route des crêtes and to the Grand Ballon. Also worth seeing is the small private museum **Musée Serret** with its militaria dating from World War I, its religious exhibits from the 15th and 16th centuries, its objects from forgotten and surviving crafts and works of art from the former glass factory of **Wildenstein**, the oldest in Alsace.

Finally we pass through the historic **Willer-sur-Thur**, where the once-busy Murbach abbey met with strong resistance from the people when its smithy used up too much charcoal that they feared for the survival of the forest. In 1789 the time for uprising and revenge had arrived: the abbey buildings in Guebwiller were attacked.

In **Bitschwiller-les-Thann** you will have to decide: either to follow the Route Joffre back to Masevaux, or to carry on to Thann. You can use the highway which begins here to get to the Sundgau, your next stop.

emn
minder at
il Armand.

THE SUNDGAU

The Sundgau can offer neither the varied range of Alsatian cuisine nor the sensational art and architecture nor the beautifully preserved villages of the northern regions. Yet this area south of the river Thur has great charm which delights its visitors. In earlier years, the term Sundgau (=southern lands) was applied to all of Upper Alsace. Nearly every village has its own individual charm and hides secret treasures which are perhaps not readily obvious to everyone. There is practically nowhere else where you can roam so freely, whether you explore the meadows and forests or sit by a pond to fish.

Water is the basis of the countryside in the Sundgau, more than in almost any other region. The landscape is formed by the river beds of the Largue, the Teil, the Birsig, the Ill (most importantly) and a network of little streams and waterways which covers the whole area and gives it its particular charm. It is not just the gentle, hilly landscape that owes its shape to water, but the people and their culture have been influenced by water until very recently.

The distribution of the villages and towns generally follows the courses of the rivers. However, early settlers respected the moods of the rivers and built their dwellings at the mouths (Hirsingue, Hirtzbach, Carspach) or high above the water (Hochstadt, Didenheim, Froeningen) to escape the frequent flooding. Indeed a high water level could be catastrophic if it coincided with the hay harvest and the waters either washed the hay away or flooded the dry grass. But usually, the water was a blessing, bringing fertility to the fields and meadows. It meant that the water meadows produced plenty of fodder even in times of drought, a fact which explains the practice in many villages of having the priest to bless the

waters. You can find discarded wirings, evidence that earlier generations of farmers knew how to deal with the water wisely and understood the principles of regulating the flow.

The Ill was also a source of energy. There were water wheels turning in their side channels, powering flour and oil mills, saws, paper presses, textile mills and hammers. If you drive through the area, you can still see the odd rotting water wheel, in stark contrast to the now fashionable "nostalgic" mill restaurants. In the past the intervention of human beings did no harm to the purity of the water. The Ill has been able to maintain its original course and still flows through the famous orchards and "grass gardens", meandering through lush green meadows which readily soak up the water.

Unfortunately, agribusiness is moving into the area too, and small farmers are being pushed out by maize monoc-

ceding
les,
r the
in harvest
he
idgau.
t,
n's
ourite
rt.
ht,
< on
Rhine.

ultures which require plenty of fertiliser—and we know by now what that means for the water! Approximately two out of every six families still make their living exclusively from agriculture, and many of them work in Mulhouse or in Switzerland. These circumstances alienate local people more and more from their environment. For this reason, there has always been insufficient outcry about the sewage which flow into the Ill, damming, "regulating", or channelling and covering up for questionable building enterprises.

The results came all too soon. In May 1983 there were disastrous floods. However, public opinion is beginning to change. People are now more aware of the need to respect the natural attributes of the river, of the importance of saving the flood-prone areas, and of preventing the occurrence of the same mistakes. The Ill is still an active river, and together with the Largue, Thalbach and Birsig, feeds many fishing ponds (*étangs*) which have been a feature of the Sundgau and the Largue valley in particular since the Middle Ages.

Crab, trout, minnow, gudgeon, perch, pike, tench and carp may no longer be available in large numbers. Nevertheless, fishing is still a popular sport for the local folks as well as for tourists.

Young people meet frequently after work for an hour or two at the pond, many equipped with fishing rod and folding stool. Especially popular are the ponds around the friendly little town of St. Ulrich and Altkirch. The ponds are not always easy to find, and some are reserved for private angling clubs. You need, in all cases, an angling permit, which you can obtain in most of the towns and villages. Even if you're not particularly enthusiastic about fishing, the waters of the Sundgau are an attraction in itself if you are looking for an oasis of peace and quiet.

Staggering sight: villa houses in the Sundga

ALTKIRCH

St. Morand, a priest from Altkirch who had studied in Worms, stopped off in Cluny on a pilgrimage to Compostela. Hugue, the abbot of Cluny, sent him to the Auvergne, where he was to take charge of a parish. When Frédéric de Montbéliard presented St. Christopher's church in Altkirch to the Cluny movement, Hugue placed monks in Altkirch, but they soon ran into serious difficulties because they could not speak the Alemmanic language. Hugue remembered Morand and transferred him from the Auvergne to Altkirch.

Morand, who died in 1115, was believed to have been a very kind man, ever cheerful, patient, thoughtful, discreet and considerate, and on top of all those qualities, he was a pleasant conversationalist. His talents were soon put to the test in his new parish, as the people of Sundgau stuck to their old superstitions and heathen beliefs. Even the age of technology and science has not been able to do much about that. The isolated village of Willer is still considered a centre of superstition. Morand is the patron saint of the Sundgau and is often portrayed as a vintner with pruning knife and grapes. The new church and the hospital in the valley are named after him. Altkirch is the capital of the Sundgau region, and it has a busy market and also many small industries.

It is better to park outside the town and to pass through the 14th century town gate in the walls dating from 1215 on foot. Go up a flight of steps and you will come to the **Place de la République**, which has a fountain in the Neo-Gothic style of Napoleon III. The town hall with its fine wrought iron balcony was designed by Kléber before he embarked on his military career.

Strolling through the town, you will discover many little gems, such as the **Tourelle de la Pomme** (Apple Tower),

a staircase tower in the **Rue de la Cure**, or a Renaissance house. Altkirch is an unassuming but friendly little town.

If you are interested in history and in the famous people of the Sungau, visit the Sundgau **museum** and look at the collection of paintings by the Sundgau artists Léon Lehmann and Jacques Henners, as well as the archaeological and the historical collections with their charters, seals, a contract with the Altkirch executioner, and documents and photographs about the history of the Gilardoni family. This family made their contribution in the 19th century towards industrialised building methods, and manufactured tiles for half-timbered houses, roof tiles and fire-proof tiles—the best in the world, it was said. Also among their products were tiled stoves, fayence, stones, floor tiles, flues and sewage pipes.

The chapels around Altkirch: The site of the chapel of **St. Afre** was a place of

e town hall
Altkirch,
signed
Kléber.

baptism until this century, because the spring which rises here is believed to possess healing powers. Sick children were dipped three times into the spring of St. Afre while prayers were made to the Trinity. The spring and its stream are contaminated with petroleum, but unfortunately all attempts to filter it out have so far failed.

St. Morand, on one of his frequent trips to convert the neighbouring communities, was once caught in a thunderstorm and sought shelter beneath a rock. The rock suddenly arched itself up over his head to form a shallow cave, offering him rest and comfort during the storm. To commemorate that occasion, a small chapel was later built at this spot: the Chapelle de repos de St. Morand. Pilgrimages on Whit Monday still take place here today. The *Litten* chapel near Aspach is a reminder of the poor people, lepers or *litten* in the local dialect. The *Vierge merveilleuse* is believed to have been carved by a leper.

The walls of the **chapel of St. Morand** in the valley of Altkirch were covered with paintings by Guiseppe Appiane, who came from Milan. Appiane founded an art academy in Mainz. His works can be seen in Lindau, Althau-sen, the palace of Meersburg on Lake Constance and in St. Peter's in Mainz. The oldest chapel is in Burnkirch. In the 15th century it was painted all over with frescoes, which still survive, quite well-preserved, in the choir.

Altkirch is a starting point for many tours, long or short, through the Sundgau. At first glance you may not know which way to drive, but in case of doubt, follow the Route de la carpe frite, which reveals the most beautiful places in the region. It is reassuring to know that the Sundgau is blessed with delightful scenery. There is particularly pleasant, indeed charming scenery around Willer, where many ancient traditions have survived: customs, tales and legends and old farming methods— and, as mentioned earlier, superstition.

You can also take a trip to **Hitzbach**, with its **Château de Reinach**, a real treasure. It was destroyed during the Revolution, but was rebuilt at the end of the 19th century. The house of Reinach belongs to one of the oldest Alsatian families. The Reinachs are documented as *chevaliers* (knights) as early as 1210. Opposite the château is a park which makes good use of the river.

If you feel the need for refreshments after a trip through the Sundgau, we recommend the **Mill of Kaegy** (1565) at **Steinbrunn-le-Bas**. It is a gourmet restaurant with princely prices. Try to get hold of the popular but rare red wine in **Luemschwiller** as a souvenir. If you can't, just console yourself with art. The church here dates from the 13th century. The paintings at the rear of the altar are believed to be an early work by Hans Baldung Grien.

Castle entrance in Ferrette.

FERRETTE

In Ferrette—or, to give it its German name, Pfirt—one of the most interesting walks is the one to the two castle ruins, passing through the Rue du château to look at some fine Renaissance houses. The upper castle was built in the 12th century for the Count of Bar-Montbéliard and inhabited by a branch of the family which, as Counts of Ferrette, played a leading role in all the affairs of Upper Alsace for a long time. In 1324 one of the counts married into the Habsburg family, and ever since then the ruling dynasty added "Count of Ferrette" to its list of titles. In 1648, after the Peace of Westfalia, the county went to the French, and finally to the Italian Grimaldis, who descended from the Mazarins. The last Count of Ferrette, therefore, is no less a person than Prince Rainer of Monaco.

The upper castle was destroyed in 1633 by the Swedes, the lower by the enraged populace during the French Revolution. From the wild and romantic ruins you can get a good view of the Vosges and the Swiss Jura.

After half an hour's brisk walk from Ferrette you will come to the Wolf Caves. Here in the rock chambers, centuries ago, a community of dwarfs is believed to have dwelled, using silver tools for working in the fields and gardens. The dwarfs never aged, and were—according to "eyewitnesses"!—beautiful and delicately built, with remarkably shining eyes. They lived all together, childless, and often went among human beings in pairs, learning their language and rendering considerable help during the hay and grain harvests. For the people of the Sundgau, it was soon taken for granted that every household had a pair of dwarfs working and living with them. The dwarfs took part in festivals and funerals, and were generous at giving away presents. In return, the people showed their respect and gratitude by reserving the best seats at the feast table and the tastiest food and wine for the dwarfs. There was one thing that was hard to bear: the dwarfs imposed a limit to human curiosity. They wore long robes, so that no-one knew what their feet looked like.

Of course, there were a couple of particularly impudent girls whose boundless curiosity put an end to this idyllic way of life. They sprinkled sand on the rocky platform at the entrance to the Wolf Mill, and then hid behind the bushes. At sunrise, the dwarfs hopped across the rock on their way to the forest and left their footprints in the sand—the prints of goat hoofs. Upon seeing the imprints, the girls laughed out loud. The dwarfs heard the laughter, turned around, and saw the girls in hiding. Feeling very hurt and sad, they went back into their caves and were never seen again.

ht,
ng
veller
ws off
venir
n.

If you drive from Altkirch towards Ferrette, you will pass **Feldbach**, an unassuming place, at the crossroad with the D 463 to Basle. Feldbach offers an insight into the war-torn and troubled history of Alsace. Around the year 1144 Count Frederick I of Ferrette founded a Benedictine convent here, which was entrusted with the duty of praying for his soul after his death. The convent became one of the most important Cluniac houses in the Sundgau. The nuns came from noble families of southern Alsace and Switzerland. The chapter general of Cluny put in Feldbach a prior who was also familiar with the German and Alemmanic languages.

When Ferrette became part of the Habsburg domain the convent lost its importance. It lay unprotected at a crossroad and was plundered several times—by the English in 1370, by the Armagnacs in 1444, by the armies of Basle in 1446. The priory too was plundered and burned down during the Peasants' War. The nuns fled to Basle, and after that the estates of the convent were administered solely by a prior.

The success of the Revolution also meant the end of the priory. Ever since then, the church has been the property of the community and is therefore nothing more than a parish church. It is worthwhile visiting this gem of Romanesque architecture. Interestingly, the nave in the church is divided in two parts: one for the convent and one for the parish. If you go back up the road a short distance from the church and then turn left round the corner, you will find the old priory house dating from 1542, with its broad roof and staircase tower.

On your way to **Leymen** and **Landskron** on the Swiss border, you pass through the pretty village of **Oltingue**, where you should stop to admire the architecture of the old Sundgau farmhouses. The former capital of the Sundgau Jura, it is still the most important village in the southern part, as is

evident not least from the farmhouse museum. Its collection is due to the efforts of a parish priest and advocate of peasant tradition, who collected the items used daily in his homeland and wanted them preserved for posterity. Before he died, he left his collection to the museum in Mulhouse with the proviso that it must not be removed from the area and that it must be preserved in Oltingue. Thanks to him, visitors can take a close look into the well-known Sundgau *Stub* or parlour, the kitchen, the bakery and also at folk art.

Also praiseworthy are the efforts of the *Maisons paysannes d'Alsace* and the *Chrétien pour la paix*, who in 1984 here rebuilt an old half-timbered house threatened by decay. Similar work has been done in **Feldbach** and especially in **Gommersdorf**, where a row of old but beautiful half-timbered houses have been restored.

On the second Sunday in September, **The chapel of Aspach.**

there is a great festival in Ferrette, with historical processions and folk dances from all over the Sundgau. There are also many stalls selling local specialties. Among these stalls, local craftsmen (particularly wooden clog makers) exhibit their work.

If you are travelling to look at works of art, you should go and see the Gothic Madonna dating from the 15th century in the church of St. Marc or the Gothic pilgrim church in the cemetery.

In **Folgensbourg**, too, art lovers will find what they are looking for. This is the centre for ceramic arts. Every year in July there is a great potters' festival, with products from various regions of Alsace and also of France. Folgensbourg also has its orchards to offer, and its many traditional half-timbered houses, as does **Michelbach**, where you can find a restored mill.

The scenery to the west of Ferrette is quite different. It will delight the heart of every angler with its many ponds— which are also inviting if you want to swim. Here along the Largue lies a broad landscape of bogs and marshes. Finally, we come to Lucelle, the highest and most southerly village set in the midst of beautiful scenery. Unfortunately, there is not much left of its former Cistercian abbey—it was already destroyed as early as 1355 by a powerful earthquake.

However, a few of the treasures of the monastery have found refuge in the area around **Lucelle**, and art lovers can put the jigsaw together again themselves. The massive high altar and the statues of St. Nicholas and Pope Leo IX are in **Koestlach**, two side altars in **Winkel**, two more in the church of **Bouxwiller**, the Trinity Altar and the altar of St. John the Baptist. Of the abbey itself, only the estate buildings and guest houses remain and these have been converted into a family hotel.

ght,
uctures
power:
t of the
ctrical
wer
tion.
low,
ndscape
h rowan
e.

THE APPLES OF SUNDGAU

The Sundgau landscape is not only formed of forests, meadows and fields. The mild climate between the river Thur and the Swiss Jura is also favourable for growing fruit. The scenario of the whole region is particularly delightful in spring, when the cherry and apple trees blossom in the many orchards by the roadside.

The peaceful landscape is hardly imaginable without its apples, even though many an exotic and fine-sounding name has already been forgotten. Have you heard of the *Borovitzky*, the apple from the land of the Tsars, which was planted along the roadsides here in the last quarter of the previous century? What about the *Bell* apple from Switzerland, which lay on the farmer's table until Easter? And incidentally, do you know anything about the *Bean* apple, which was an early feature of the landscape? It was a juicy apple par excellence. The *Bean* was the source of the farm cider (*cidre de ferme*), which was sometimes mixed with wine from Rouffach or perhaps from another place even further away.

That, however, was during the period when the vines of Alsace did not flourish as they do now and were not rivals for the "peasants' wine". There can hardly be a single orchard without its *Grey Reinette* or *Winter Rambour*, two types of apple which are still popular today for cooking or for taking a bite at. Although apple trees were hardly cosseted, they formed part of the landscape, filled the cellars and quenched people's thirst for generations.

Over the years, tastes changed, and *Boskop, Ontario, Winter Gold Pearmain (Reine de Reinettes)* found their place, and finally grafting began: Gravenstein apples and the *Reinette de Blenheim*, the "Queen of the Patisserie". The flesh swells when cooked and is especially suitable for flans and for baked apples, which have been stuck at the top of the tiled stove when the family sit comfortably together in the parlour.

But then the city dwellers got to know the Golden Delicious and began to despise the speckled fruits of yesteryear in favour of this spotless super-breed. Soon the orchards were no longer in tune with the times, the old apple trees by the side of the narrow country roads got in the way of traffic; many an old tree got ill and quietly died.

It may be that one of the young farmers, specialising in maize or root monocultures, sniffed the fruit during childhood and was filled with the desire for a "real" apple. Perhaps people have read the signs of the times and are heeding the call for natural food. At any rate, there is a new generation of tree planters and brandy distillers arising in the Sundgau, and they have remembered the old juice presses (particularly in the area around Didenheim). The old cider has not been rediscovered , but apple juice has made a comeback on many tables, and the smell of cider vinegar is becoming popular. It is even rumoured that people will travel long distances to enjoy the taste of an original apple, and that they no longer bother about a few brown spots on the fruit!

Gravenstein, probably because of its beautiful flowers and fine fruit, now adorns many a barren garden with frequently-mown lawns and is gradually replacing the popular conifers. Along the communal roads it is no longer the policy to plant quick-growing poplar trees. Even among bureaucratic circles there is obviously a growing feeling that the Sundgau would lose part of its soul if it lost its apples.

At any rate, the Sundgau now blooms again in spring as it did of old, and in the spring of 1983 an orchard was planted in Michelbach-le-Haut with nearly 150 different types of apple trees.

Right, just ripe for the picking! Following page, golden grapes add special touc to wine bar signboard.

TRAVEL TIPS

GETTING THERE

BY AIR

It is only worth flying directly to Alsace if you are short of time, e.g. you are taking a weekend break. You can land at one of the following two airports:

Aéroport de Bâle-Mulhouse: A number of daily flights from European cities use this airport. Buses leave the airport nearly every hour for Mulhouse rail station.

Aéroport de Colmar-Houssen: Inland flights only. Enquire on up-to-date flight schedules, tariffs and special offers at your travel agent's office or at the respective airline information counter.

BY TRAIN

There is an excellent network of rail routes connecting Alsace with various French and other European cities. Enquire at the French Government Tourist Office:

178 Piccadilly
London W1V 0AL
Tel: 01-491 6911

or at the British offices of the French state railways:

SNCF
179 Piccadilly
W1V 0BA
Tel: 01 493 9731.

BY CAR

There is an extensive road network in France, so you can choose between using your own car or hiring one to gain maximum freedom of movement. If you use the motorways, note: you have to pay toll on French motorways, and you must conform to the speed limits: 80 mph (130 km/h) on motorways, 68 mph (110 km/h) on dual carriage-ways, 56 mph (90 km/h) on national and département roads. The speed limit for built-up areas is 37 mph (60 km/h). Keep your seatbelts on, as this is a traffic regulation.

The distribution of lead-free petrol stations is getting better all the time. Ask for an information leaflet from the French Government Tourist Office.

In Alsace, the routes with fine scenery are specially marked. Recommended are the "Route verte" along the western slopes of the Vosges to Col de la Schlucht, via Soultzeren and Munster to Colmar; the "Route des crêtes" from Mulhouse via Munster, Colmar or Kaysersberg and the "Route du vin" which leads to the wine villages over a stretch of 93 miles (150 km).

TRAVEL ESSENTIALS

PASSPORTS & VISAS

To visit France, you need a valid passport or British Visitor's Passport. Children under the age of 16 need passports or if not their names must be listed in their parents' passports. Your stay in France is limited to three months unless you obtain a special visa.

MONEY MATTERS

One French franc (FF) has 100 centimes, which are available in the following coins: 5, 10 and 20 centimes. Francs are available in 1/2, 1, 2, 5, and 10 franc coins and in 10, 20, 50, 100, 200 and 500 franc notes.

You can bring into the country any currency in any amount, but large amounts should be reported. On leaving France, you may not take out more than 5,000 francs.

HEALTH

Travellers from Britain should fill in Form E 111, available from post offices, before they leave. This will entitle them to essential medical treatment. If you want to be absolutely certain of receiving treatment, arrange a private insurance scheme before you go. (Note: Immunisation is not required.)

CUSTOMS

There are some restrictions on goods which you can take into France. Strictly prohibited are narcotics, weapons (except for sporting equipment) and, unless you have a prior arrangement with the French state bank, gold bars. Small amounts of food or flowers can be brought in without problem. Those above the age of 15 from other EEC countries (Belgium, Denmark, Federal Republic of Germany, Great Britain, Greece, Ireland, Italy, Luxembourg, Netherlands, Portugal and Spain) can bring in goods up to a limit of £250 in value, as well as the following goods:

Alcoholic drinks
Spirits over 22 per cent proof	1.5 litres
Spirits under 22 per cent proof	3 litres
Liquor, sparkling wine	3 litres
Other wines	5 litres

Coffee
Roast coffee	1000 grammes
Coffee extract	300 grammes

Tea
Tea	200 grammes
Tea extract	60 grammes

Perfumes and Toiletry
Perfumes	75 grammes
Toiletry	0.375 litres

Tobacco and cigarettes
Cigarettes	300
Cigarillos	150
Cigars	75
Tobacco	400 grammes

GETTING ACQUAINTED

GOVERNMENT & ECONOMY

France is a republic. Presidential elections are held every seven years. The president appoints the prime minister who is responsible for the government and the ministries. The National Assembly and the Council of the Republic form the two houses of parliament. France is divided into 22 regions and 96 départements: Bas-Rhin (Lower Alsace) and Haut-Rhin (Upper Alsace) are the two départements of Alsace.

France has the fifth largest economy in the world, is a member of the European Community and is an important producer of wine, wheat and other agricultural products for world markets. Equally important are the steel and machine industries.

Five types of industry dominate the Alsatian economy:

the *timber* industry in the Vosges, where forests still cover about half the range. Directly dependent on this industry are the building construction industry, paper and cellulose manufacture and the carton packaging industry;

the *textile* industry, which was well developed in the 19th century, thanks to continental tariffs. Conditions in Alsace were ideal, as the artificial lakes in Vosges valleys provided the necessary power. Today, jute, cotton and wool textiles are still produced here. However, automation and the increasing numbers of takeover of small companies by larger ones have led to the closure of more and more mills;

the *chemical* industry based on the controversial potash mining in Mulhouse (Upper Alsace). Here potash is mined and refined and fertilisers are produced, using the most modern methods. Oil is produced in Pechel bronn (Lower Alsace) and refined locally to produce petrol, asphalt, paraffin, lubricating oil and other by-products;

the *metal and machine manufacturing* industries; and

the *transport* industry. The port of Strasbourg has developed into the fifth largest in France. The closely-linked network of canals between the rivers Rhine and Rhône allow products manufactured in Alsace to be shipped to destinations within France and to those in neighbouring countries.

GEOGRAPHY & POPULATION

Alsace, situated in the east of France, is part of the Upper Rhine Plain, which begins from the bend in the Rhine at Basle and stretches as far as Bingen (West Germany). Its geographical boundaries are formed by the Rhine to the east, the Jura mountains to the south, the crest of the Vosges to the west and the Pfälzer Wald to the north. Geologically speaking, Alsace forms a long, mild depression surrounded by mountains.

Many peoples and tribes have settled in Alsace at one time or another and contributed to the population growth. First there were the Celts, followed by the Romans, the Alemanni and the Franks, and in more recent years the French and the Germans. The influence of the various types of tribes and nationalities has on the one hand led to the development of a markedly individual people with an independent culture, on the other to the preservation of some traces of earlier cultures. For instance, a strong Alemannic influence is still noticeable in Strasbourg, and there are Celtic traces around Labaroche and also signs of Frankish influence around Wissembourg. In Alsace, the way of life, customs, building architecture, traditional dress, social customs and gastronomical items differ noticeably from town to town and even from village to village.

Alsace is the third most densely populated region among the regions of France.

CLIMATE

The weather fronts which pass along the western coast of Europe with their depressions have a formative influence on the climate of Alsace. The climate is an oceanic one, without extremes in temperature, wet in the mountains and dry in the lowlands.

Alsace is therefore an ideal country to visit at any time of year. In the summer, you can go hiking or enjoy water sports, and in the winter you can visit the Vosges which is an ideal centre for winter sports.

TIME ZONE

In Alsace, as in the rest of France, Central European Time is in use: summer time begins in early April and lasts until the end of September.

ELECTRICITY SUPPLY

The national power supply is 220 volt AC, but in certain places you may find 110 volt. If you want to be sure that your personal shaver or hair-dryer, do remember to bring along an adaptor.

BUSINESS HOURS

There is no official rule to the opening and closing times of **shops** in France. Usually, shops open for business between 9 am and 7 pm. Markets and food shops often open earlier and close later, but have longer lunch breaks, often until 4 pm. Supermarkets normally open till 10 pm. Many shops and markets open on Saturdays and Sundays but close on Mondays. On the two Sundays before Christmas, shops in Strasbourg open their doors for last-minute shopping.

There is no universal set of business hours for **banks** either, though the usual opening hours are from 9 am till 4.30 pm, and banks in rural areas tend to close at lunch-time.

Post offices are open Monday to Friday from 9 am to 7 pm, and on Saturday till 4 pm. In rural areas, they take a lunch break.

Government offices are open to the public Monday to Friday from 9 am to 12 noon and from 2 pm to 5 pm.

PUBLIC HOLIDAYS

* 1 January (New Year's Day)
* Good Friday
* Easter Monday
* 1 May (Workers' Day)
* Ascension Day
* Whit Monday
* 14 July (Bastille Day)
* 15 August (Assumption of the Blessed Virgin Mary)
* 1 November (All Saints' Day)

* 11 November (Armistice Day, 1918)
* 25 December (Christmas Day)
* 26 December (St. Etienne)

FESTIVALS

Altkirch:
Spring festival (end of April), flower market (May), Kilbe (festival and fair—the last two Sundays in August).

Ammerschwihr:
Great Wine Market (April), Käfferkopf festival/wine festival (August).

Barr:
Wine market and folk festival (14 July), craft week (first week in August), gingerbread festival in Gertwiller (end of August), wine festival (first Sunday in October), music weeks (November through to May).

Benfeld:
Tobacco festival (end of August).

Bergheim:
Cherry festival in Thannenkirch (July).

Bischwiller:
Pfiffertag/Musician's Day (August), folk festival (October).

Bouxwiller:
Folk festivals (summer), village festival (September).

Brumath:
Country festival (June), onion fair (September).

Cernay:
Kilbe (festival and fair—last weekend in June and first week in July).

Colmar:
Fête de Colmar (June), wine festival (mid-August), Sauerkraut Day (October).

Colroy-la-Roche:
Solstice festival (June).

Dabo:
Marathon and majorettes festival (May), fox festival (August), patron saint festival (July).

Dambach-la-Ville:
Wine festival (early August).

Eguisheim:
Festival of St. Leo (19 April), patron saint festival and procession of St. Peter and St. Paul (29 June), wine festival (late August).

Erstein:
Sugar festival (September).

Feldbach:
Procession (February), Kirmes (festival and fair—September), St. Martin's festival (November).

Guebwiller:
Foire aux Vins (Ascension Day), solstice festival (24 June).

Gunsbach:
Solstice festival (24 June).

Haguenau:
Charcoal burners' festival in Schirrhein (July), hop festival (early September).

Hohwald:
Fire Day (May).

Hunawihr:
Fête de l'Ami Fritz (the Sunday before and the Sunday after 14 July).

Hunspach:
Fête de l'Harmonie (July), village festival (St. Martin's Day, 11 November).

Ingwiller:
Schieweschlawe (shooting festival—February), village festival (August).

Kaysersberg:
Folk festival (July), folk concerts (summer), grape harvest festival (September).

Lapoutroie:
Trout festival in Fréland (May).

Lauterbourg:
Fried chicken festival (July).

Marckolsheim:
Pâté en croute days (July), Ascension Day festival in the chapel at Mauchen.

Marlenheim:
Wedding of Ami Fritz (August), wine festival (October).

Marmoutier:
Flower festival (first Sunday, September).

Masevaux:
Amateur passion play (Lent), organ festival (July).

Molsheim:
Patron saint festival, St. George (23 April), wine market (1 May), Western festival (end of June), Bugatti festival (September), wine festival (second Sunday in October), St. Nicholas festival (6 December).

Mulhouse:
Carnival (February/March), Bach festival (June), annual fair (last Sunday in July till the 3rd Sunday in August).

Munster:
Snail race in Osenbach (April), solstice festival (June).

Neuf-Brisach:
Lily of the Valley Festival (1 May).

Neuwiller-les-Saverne:
Shot putting (Easter), folk festival (September), procession (Sunday before Christmas), Christmas festival in the forest, arts and crafts festival (September), village festival (October).

Obernai:
Antiques market (May), grape harvest festival (October).

Orbey:
Solstice festival (24 June).

Ribeauvillé:
Kougelhopf festival (June), wine festival (July), Pfiffertag (traditional musician's festival—first Sunday in September).

Riquewihr:
Solstice festival (June), Festivale Folklore Alsacien (July), organ concerts (summer), Almond Tree Festival in Mittelwihr (August), grape harvest festival (October), St. Nicholas festival (6 December).

Rosheim:
Torchlight procession (first Sunday in September), flower festival (second Sunday in September).

Saint-Amarin:
St. John's Fire (24 June).

Saint-Jean-Saverne:
Angling competition (Whitsun), village festival (June).

Saint-Marie-aux-Mines:
Textile fair (spring and autumn).

Saverne:
Carnival (February/March), art exhibition and festival in the palace (early June), Rose Festival (June), festival in the palace (14 July), folk festival (August), Messti/fair (September).

Schwerwiller:
Solstice festival (24 June).

Schiltigheim:
Beer festival (mid-August).

Sélestat:
Wine market (April), flower festival and traditional procession (second Sunday in August), onion festival (late August/early September).

Seltz:
Carnival (February), fishing competition (March), solstice festival (June), fireworks (14 July).

Sigolsheim:
Traditional procession (June), sauerkraut festival (early September), nut festival (October).

Strasbourg:
Film festival (March), international music festival (June), fireworks (14 July), traditional folk festivals (summer), "Son et Lumière" in the Cathedral (summer), boat races on the Ill (July/August), Musica: international festival of contemporary music (September/October).

Thann:
St. John's Fire and folk festival (30 June).

Villé:
Crafts festival (24 July).

Wasselonne:
Cherry festival (late June/early July), *Ami Fritz* in Marlenheim (15 August).

Wissembourg:
Traditional Kermess (fair and festival—Whit Monday).

COMMUNICATIONS

MEDIA

Radio and television provide up-to-date information on current events, world affairs and road conditions. In Alsace you can receive the three channels of French TV, TF 1, Antenne 2, FR 3, as well as regional stations, such as the Strasbourg station, which sometimes broadcast in German.

The French are avid newspaper readers, a fact which obviously answers the need for a wide variety of daily papers at the newsstand. The most important Alsatian papers are *Dernières Nouvelles d'Alsace* and *L'Alsace*, having German language editions as well. If you don't happen to speak French, you can buy international newspapers and magazines on the newsstands of the larger cities and in the major hotels.

The only paper published in Alsatian dialect is *Uss'm Folk*, an interesting variation for students of dialect. Unfortunately *Le nouvel Alsacien* had to cease publishing in 1986, as the number of people speaking dialect continually kept on decreasing.

POSTAL SERVICES

Post offices are marked with signs saying PTT or P-et-T.

In general, post offices are open Monday to Friday from 9 am to 7 pm, and Saturday from 8 am to 4 pm.

You can find out about the cost of postage at any post office counter. You can also often buy stamps at the tobacconist's.

TELEPHONE

Unfortunately, tourists visiting Alsace all too frequently discover that the public telephone booths don't work. It is therefore a good idea to make your phone call from your hotel, a post office, or from a restaurant. However, if you should come across a working telephone booth and want to make several trunk calls, it is easier to buy a Télécarte at the nearest post office, which will give you either 40 or 120 units.

If you want to phone abroad, dial 19 first, then add 44 for Britain. Then dial the dialling code of the place you are calling (leaving out the initial 0), followed by the number of the person. The best times to phone are from 7.30 pm to 8 pm Monday to Friday and from 2 pm on Friday till 8 am on Monday. If you phone between these times you can save either 50 per cent (within France) or 30 per cent (within the European Community) on each call.

Useful local telephone numbers:
–Telephone information 12
–Telegrams 02 11 11

EMERGENCIES

SECURITY & CRIME

France is considered a safe country for holidaymakers, but here too the pickpockets are active. For this reason it is advisable to make a note of your passport number before leaving and to keep that at home. It is also safer to keep your documents in the inner pocket of your clothing. Be wary of children who beg in the streets; they can be very shrewd and might just win you over.

It is advisable for female tourists not to linger in districts favoured by prostitutes and to avoid hitch-hiking in the dark, even if the poor public transport connections makes you want to try it. Some useful contacts:

For **Bas-Rhin:**
Gendarmerie Départementale
Groupement Bas-Rhin
2, Rue de Molsheim
67000 Strasbourg
Tel. 89 32 53 68.

For **Haut-Rhin**:
Gendarmerie Nationale
56, Rue Cavalerie
68000 Colmar
Tel: 89 41 42 00.

Police (police) 17
Fire brigade (pompiers) 18
Breakdowns 87 69 12 39

LOST & FOUND

Lost and found property offices are *Bureaux des objets trouvés* in French. The communal offices of the *gendarmeries* are responsible for lost property (see above for addresses and phone numbers). If you have left something on public transport, please contact the appropriate company, e.g. SNCF or the taxi ranks.

MEDICAL SERVICES

If really necessary, you may contact the emergency medical service (*permanence médicale*) or go directly to the local hospital.

There are no universally agreed opening hours for pharmacies. If the pharmacy is closed, it will display a notice on the door giving the name of the pharmacy which operates an emergency service and which is also listed in the local paper. Further information can be obtained by ringing the following telephone numbers:

Colmar   89 41 08 00 & 89 41 14 00
Mulhouse   89 59 59 11
Strasbourg 88 32 99 08 & 88 36 09 93

GETTING AROUND

ORIENTATION

The following list of tourist offices in Alsace will help you to obtain information and find your way about:

68130 Altkirch
Syndicat d'Initiative
Tel: 89 40 02 90

68770 Ammerschwihr
Syndicat d'Initiative
Tel: 89 47 12 24

67140 Andlau
Syndicat d'Initiative
Tel: 88 08 93 01

67120 Avolsheim
Town Hall

67140 Barr
Syndicat d'Initiative
Tel: 88 08 94 24

67230 Benfeld
Town Hall
Tel: 88 74 42 17

68750 Bergheim
Town Hall
Tel: 89 73 63 01

67660 Betschdorf
Town Hall
Tel: 88 54 48 00

67240 Bischwiller
Town Hall
Tel: 88 63 50 11

67113 Blaesheim
Town Hall
Tel: 88 68 80 24

68650 Bonhomme
Auberge du Vallon
Tel: 89 71 22 80

67330 Bouxwiller
Town Hall
Tel: 88 70 70 16

67130 Bruchetal
Syndicat d'Initiative
de Schirmeck
Tel: 88 97 00 02

67170 Brumath
Town Hall
Tel: 88 51 02 04

68700 Cernay
Office de Tourisme
Tel: 89 75 50 35

67730 Châtenois
Town Hall
Tel: 88 82 02 74

67160 Cleebourg
Town Hall
Tel: 88 94 52 23

68000 Colmar
Office de Tourisme
4, Rue d'Unterlinden
Tel: 89 41 02 29

67420 Colroy-la-Roche
Syndicat d'Initiative
Town Hall
Tel: 88 47 20 10

67850 Dabo
Syndicat d'Initiative
Tel: 87 07 47 51

67650 Dambach-la-Ville
Syndicat d'Initiative
Tel: 88 92 41 05

67430 Diemeringen
Town Hall
Tel: 88 00 40 54

67160 Drachenbronn-Birlenbach
Town Hall
Tel: 88 94 14 55

67600 Ebersmunster
Town Hall
Tel: 88 85 71 66

68190 Eguisheim
Town Hall
Tel: 89 81 02 25

67150 Erstein
Syndicat d'Initiative
Tel: 88 98 07 06

67400 Eschau
Town Hall
Tel: 88 64 03 76

68640 Feldbach
Town Hall
Tel: 89 25 80 55

68480 Ferrette
Syndicat d'Initiative
Tel: 89 40 40 01

68240 Fréland
Town Hall
Tel: 89 47 57 13

68500 Guebwiller
Office de Tourisme
Tel: 89 76 10 63

68970 Guemar
Town Hall
Tel: 89 71 83 12

67500 Haguenau
Office de Tourisme
Tel: 88 73 30 41

67140 Hohwald
Syndicat d'Initiative
Tel: 88 08 30 90

68150 Hunawihr
Town Hall
Tel: 89 73 60 42

67250 Hunspach
Town Hall
Tel: 88 80 59 39

68150 Illhäusern
Syndicat d'Initiative
Tel: 89 73 62 22

67340 Ingwiller
Town Hall
Tel: 88 89 47 20

68240 Kaysersberg
Office de Tourisme
Tel: 89 78 22 78

67600 Kintzheim
Syndicat d'Initiative
Tel: 88 82 09 90 & 88 82 04 97

68650 Lapoutroie
Town Hall
Tel: 89 47 50 10

68610 Lautenbach
Town Hall
Tel: 89 76 32 08

67630 Lauterbourg
Syndicat d'Initiative
Tel: 88 94 80 18

67510 Lembach
Syndicat d'Initiative
Tel: 88 94 43 81

67390 Marckolsheim
Syndicat d'Initiative
Tel: 88 92 56 98

68610 Markstein
Town Hall
Tel: 89 82 60 53

67440 Marmoutier
Town Hall
Tel: 88 70 60 08

68290 Masevaux
Office de Tourisme
Tel: 89 82 41 99

67250 Merckwiller-Pechelbronn
Syndicat d'Initiative
Tel: 88 80 77 85

67520 Merlenheim
Syndicat d'Initiative
Tel: 88 87 51 09

68380 Metzeral
Town Hall
Tel: 88 38 52 00

67120 Molsheim
Syndicat d'Initiative
Tel: 88 38 52 00

68100 Mulhouse
Office de Tourisme
Tel: 89 45 68 31

68140 Munster
Office de Tourisme
Tel: 89 77 31 80

68600 Neuf-Brisach
Syndicat d'Initiative
Tel: 89 72 56 66

68220 Neuwiller
Town Hall
Tel: 89 68 50 11

67330 Neuwiller-les-Saverne
Town Hall
Tel: 88 70 00 18

67110 Niederbronn-les-Bains
Office de Tourisme
Tel: 88 09 17 00

67210 Obernai
Office de Tourisme
Tel: 88 95 64 13

67510 Obersteinbach
Town Hall
Tel: 88 09 25 06

68830 Oderen
Office de Tourisme
Tel: 89 82 60 01

68270 Orbey
Town Hall
Tel: 89 71 20 07

68490 Ottmarsheim
Town Hall
Tel: 88 26 06 42

67530 Ottrott
Town Hall
Tel: 88 95 87 07

67350 Pfaffenhofen
Town Hall
Tel: 88 07 70 55

68150 Ribeauvillé
Office de Tourisme
Tel: 89 73 62 22

68340 Riquewihr
Office de Tourisme
Tel: 89 47 80 80

67560 Rosheim
Town Hall
Tel: 88 50 40 10

68250 Rouffach
Office de Tourisme
Tel: 89 78 53 15

67420 Saales
Syndicat d'Initiative
Tel: 88 97 60 66

68550 Saint-Amarin
Office de Tourisme
Tel: 89 82 60 01

68590 Saint-Hippolyte
Town Hall
Tel: 89 73 00 13

68300 Saint-Jean-Saverne
Town Hall
Tel: 89 91 10 83

68160 Sainte-Marie-aux-Mines
Syndicat d'Initiative
Tel: 89 58 74 04

67700 Saverne
Office de Tourisme
Tel: 88 91 80 47

67130 Schirmeck
Syndicat d'Initiative
Tel: 88 97 00 02

67600 Sélestat
Office de Tourisme
Tel: 88 92 02 66

67470 Seltz
Syndicat d'Initiative
Tel: 88 86 52 64

67770 Sessenheim
Town Hall
Tel: 88 86 97 04

67620 Soufflenheim
Town Hall
Tel: 88 86 61 10

68360 Soultz-Haut-Rhin
Syndicat d'Initiative
Tel: 89 76 82 44

67000 Strasbourg
Palais de la Musique et des Congrès
Tel: 88 35 03 00
By the Europa Bridge
Tel: 88 61 39 23
Place Gutenberg
Tel: 88 32 57 07

68800 Thann
Office de Tourisme
Tel: 89 37 96 20

68410 Trois-Epis
Syndicat d'Initiative
Tel: 89 49 80 56

68230 Turckheim
Town Hall
Tel: 89 27 18 08

67220 Villé
Office de Tourisme
Tel: 88 57 11 69

67710 Wangenbourg
Syndicat d'Initiative
Tel: 88 87 32 44

67310 Wasselonne
Syndicat d'Initiative
Tel: 88 87 17 22

67160 Wissembourg
Syndicat d'Initiative
Tel: 88 94 10 11

MAPS

In addition to the maps in this book, we would suggest that you ask at any of the tourist offices listed above for information and tourist brochures/maps, which are often complimentary.

For hikers we recommend the Folex maps, which confine to an area of 37 miles (60 km) surrounding the town in question. You can buy them at any newsstand in Alsace.

WATER TRANSPORT

Alsace is criss-crossed by rivers and canals, on which canoe and kayak trips are particularly popular. Houseboats, of course, allow you to enjoy the wonderful scenery at especially close quarters.

If you are interested, contact

Syndicat National des Loueurs des Bateux de Plaisance
Port de la Bourdonnais
F-75007 Paris.

PUBLIC TRANSPORT

There are several ways to explore Alsace and enjoy the sights. Use the form of transport which is most convenient to you to get the most out of your journey.

BY RAIL

The *Société Nationale de Chemin de Fer* (SNCF) has a large network of rail routes. For further information contact:

SNCF
179 Piccadilly
London W1V 0BA
Tel: 01 491 9731.

You can also get information on various special offer tickets like those listed below:

Inter Rail Card: valid throughout Europe, gives the right to travel unlimited miles for a fixed price.

Carte Jeune and *Carré Jeune:* (young people's railcard) are valid for those under 26 and offer reductions of up to 50 per cent.

Carte Vermeil: (senior citizen's railcard) gives pensioners the right to reduced fares, but only on local trains.

France Vacance: (holiday railcard) allows you to travel on all routes within a fixed time limit.

Billet de séjour: (tourist's railcard) is valid for two months and entitles you to reduced fares for distances over 621 miles (1000 km).

Group tickets entitle you to reductions of up to 40 per cent.

BY BUS

Alsace has a closely-knit network of bus routes. More details can be obtained from the respective tourist office. Don't forget to buy a ticket from the driver before boarding, or in advance from the newsstand or a tobacconist's store, otherwise you risk a fine of up to 65 FF for fare dodging.

Apart from the normal scheduled buses, special bus tours are offered. Private operators (whose addresses can be obtained from the tourist offices) offer day tours, and the SNCF offers half and all day tours. Information is found in the leaflet *Indicateur Tourisme*, obtainable from the ticket offices of rail stations.

SELF-DRIVE

There is a well-developed network of roads in France, thus providing convenient links between Alsace and the cities and also easy accessibility within the local region.

ROADS AND SPEED LIMITS

Here is a classification of different types of road, and the corresponding speed limits:
–*autoroute* (A), motorway with toll payable, 80 mph (130 km/h), 68 mph (110 km/h) in wet conditions.
–*route nationale* (N), 68 mph (110 km/h)
–*route départementale* (D), equivalent to a B road, 56 mph (90 km/h), in wet conditions 50 mph (80 km/h)
–*chemin vininal/voie ordinaire* (V or VO), local road, 37 mph (60 km/h)

HIGHWAY CODE

In France the same traffic rules generally apply to driving as in other European countries. You should note, though, that you are allowed to drive at night with the sidelights switched on only in places with good street lighting, that parking in the blue zones (*zones bleues*) is only allowed if you have a permit, and that a driver who has been in possession of a driving licence for a year or less is not allowed to drive faster than 56 mph (90 km/h).

FUEL

The French road network is basically well provided with petrol kiosks, but in Alsace particularly it is advisable to travel with an emergency spare can of petrol.

Lead-free petrol, *super sans plomp*, is unfortunately not easily available as yet, but you should be able to find it along the motorways and the larger routes nationales.

BREAKDOWNS

The emergency breakdown services (*touring secours*) can be reached from the emergency telephones:

Round the clock: Paris 1/45 02 14 50
7 am to 11 pm: Metz 87 69 12 39.

CAR RENTAL

Note that a driver must be above 21 years of age and should possess a driving licence for a least a year.
Some useful addresses:

Colmar
Avis, 9, Rue de la Garde. Tel: 89 23 21 82
Hertz, Place Rapp et App. Tel: 89 24 11 80

Mulhouse
Europcar, 81, Av. Général-de-Gaulle, tel: 89 67 15 65
Hertz, 26, Rue de Bâle. Tel: 89 46 23 21
Avis, 68 Rue Nordfeld. Tel: 89 45 75 57

Strasbourg
Avis, Galerie Marchande, Place de la Gare. Tel: 88 32 30 44
Europcar, 31 Rue Course. Tel: 88 22 18 00
Hertz, 14 Rue Déserte. Tel: 88 32 57 62

Apart from the main car rental companies, there is also the *train et auto* service operated by the state railways SNCF.

CYCLING

Cycling is one of the nicest ways of discovering the Alsatian countryside. You can either take your bicycle with you on the train —for a small fee it can travel as luggage—or you can make use of the bicycles for hire at the railway stations (*train et velo*).

WHERE TO STAY

HOTELS

The following list offers a few suggestions and makes no claims to be complete. The numbers within brackets refer to the number of rooms available.

Altkirch
Auberge Sundgovienne (31), Route de Belfort. Tel: 89 40 97 18.
La Terrasse (20), 44-46 Rue du 3e Souave. Tel: 89 40 98 02.

Ammerschwihr
L'Arbre Vert (12), 7, Rue des Cigognes. Tel: 89 47 12 23.
Aux Armes de France (10), 1, Grand-Rue. Tel: 89 47 10 1. Excellent restaurant.
Aux Trois Merles (20), 5, Rue de la 5e D.B. Tel: 89 78 24 35.

Andlau
Au Canon (10), 2, Rue des Remparts. Tel: 89 08 95 08.

Barr
Château d'Andlau (25), 113, Vallée St Ulrich. Tel: 88 08 96 78.
Hotel-Restaurant La Couronne (10), 4, Rue des Boulangers. Tel: 88 08 25 63.
Maison Rouge (13), 1, Avenue de la Gare. Tel: 88 08 90 40.
Du Manoir (18), 11, Rue St Marc. Tel: 88 08 03 40.

Bergheim
A la Vignette (13), 14, Route de Thannkirch. Tel: 89 73 63 42.
Le Parc (15), 14, Route du Vin. Tel: 89 73 63 07.

Betschdorf
Hotel-Restaurant La Couronne, 20, Rue du Dr Deutsch. Tel: 89 54 42 49.

Blaesheim

Hotel-Restaurant Au Cygne (7), 171, Rue du Maréchal Foch. Tel: 88 68 86 81.

Bonhomme

Au Lion d'Or (12), 64, Rue Principale. Tel: 89 47 51 11.

Hotel-Restaurant La Poste (21), 48, Rue du 3e Spahis Algériens. Tel: 89 47 51 19.

Bouxwiller

Hotel-Restaurant Au Soleil (15), 71, Grand-Rue. Tel: 88 70 70 06.

Heintz (14), 84a, Grand-Rue. Tel: 88 70 72 57.

Brumath

A la Ville de Paris (14), 13, Rue du Gl. Rampont. Tel: 88 51 11 02.

L'Ecrevisse (21), 4, Ave. de Strasbourg. Tel: 88 51 11 08.

Cernay

Hotel-Restaurant Hostellerie d'Alsace (10), 61, Rue Poincaré. Tel: 89 75 59 01.

Châtenois

Hotel-Restaurant Dontenville, 94, Rue du Maréchal Foch. Tel: 88 92 02 54.

Cleebourg

Au Tilleul (12), 94, Rue Principale. Tel: 88 94 52 15.

Colmar

Altea Champs de Mars (75), 3, Ave. de la Marne. Tel: 89 41 54 54.

Colbert (50), 2, Rue des Trois Epis. Tel: 89 41 31 05.

Maréchal (40), 4-6, Place des Six Montaignes Noires. Tel: 89 41 60 32.

Park Hotel (50), 52-54, Av,. de la République. Tel: 89 41 34 80.

Terminus Bristol (85), Place de la Gare. Tel: 89 23 59 59. Excellent restaurant *Au Rendez-Vous de Chasse.*

Colroy-la-Roche

La Cheneaudière (28). Tel: 88 97 61 64.

Dambach-la-Ville

Hotel-Restaurant Aux Deux Clefs (5), 1, Rue des Remparts. Tel: 89 92 40 11.

Hotel-Restaurant Au Raisin d'Or (11), 28, Rue Clémenceau. Tel: 88 92 40 08.

Eguisheim

Hotel-Restaurant L'Auberge alsacienne (20), 12, Grand-Rue. Tel: 89 41 50 20.

Erstein

Hotel-Restaurant Au Brochet (31), 94, Rue du Général-de-Gaulle. Tel: 88 98 03 70.

Eschau

Hotel-Restaurant Au Cygne (20), 38, Rue de la 1ère D.B. Tel: 88 64 04 79.

Ferrette

La Bonne Auberge (20), 5, Rue Léon Lehman. Tel: 89 40 40 34.

Geispelsheim

Hotel-Restaurant Campanile (47), 20, Route de l'Ill. Tel: 88 66 74 77.

Guebwiller

Hotel-Restaurant Alsace (29), 140 Rue de la République. Tel: 89 76 83 02.

Château de la Prairie (23), Allée des Maronniers. Tel: 89 74 28 57.

Hotel-Restaurant Lac, (23), Rue de la République. Tel: 89 76 63 10.

Haguenau

Hotel-Restaurant Europe (83), 15, Ave. Professeur Leriche, tel: 88 93 58 11.

Les Pins (22), 112, Route de Strasbourg, tel: 88 93 68 40.

Hohwald

Hotel-Restaurant Grand-Hôtel (74). Tel: 88 08 31 03.

Hunawihr

Hotel-Restaurant Le Cigogne (8), 26, Rue du Nord. Tel: 89 73 60 14.

Ingwiller

Hotel-Restaurant Aux Comtes de Hanau (15), 139, Rue du Géenéral-de-Gaulle. Tel: 88 89 42 27.

Kaysersberg

Hotel-Restaurant Chambard (20), 9-11, Rue du Général-de-Gaulle. Tel: 89 47 10 17.

Les Remparts (29), 4, Rue de la Flieh. Tel: 89 47 12 12.

Tonneau d'Or, (5), 13 Rue du Général Rieder. Tel: 89 78 24 74.

Kintzheim
Hotel-Restaurant L'Abbaye d'Alspach (20), Rue du Général-de-Gaulle. Tel: 88 82 31 42.

Lapoutroie
Aux Vieux Moulins (20), 57. Rue du Général Dufieux. Tel: 89 47 56 55.
Hotel-Restaurant Étang du Devin (6), 68, Rue du Général Dufieux. Tel: 89 47 20 29.

Lautenbach
Hotel-Restaurant de Lautenbach, (11), 68, Rue Principale. Tel: 89 76 32 03.

Lauterbourg
Hotel-Restaurant Au Cygne (7), 3, Rue du Général Mittlehauser. Tel: 88 94 80 59.

Lembach
Relais du Heimbach (14), 15, Rue de Wissembourg. Tel: 88 94 43 46.
Vosges du Nord (8), 59, Route de Bitche. Tel: 88 94 43 41.

Marckolsheim
Hotel-Restaurant A l'Aigle (18), 28, Rue du Maréchal Foche. Tel: 88 92 50 02.

Markstein
Hotel-Restaurant Belle Vue (14). Tel: 89 82 61 82.
Les Crêtes (107). Tel: 89 82 61 81.
Hotel-Restaurant Wolf (21). Tel: 89 82 64 36, 89 82 61 80.

Marlenheim
Hotel-Restaurant Hostellerie du Cerf (20), 30, Rue du Général-de-Gaulle. Tel: 88 87 73 73.
Hotel-Restaurant Hostellerie Reeb (35), 2, Rue du Dr Schweitzer. Tel: 88 87 52 70.

Marmoutier
Hotel-Restaurant A la Couronne d'Or (10), 1, Rue Général-de-Lattre-Tassigny. Tel: 88 70 60 32.
Hotel-Restaurant Aux Deux Clefs (15), 30, Rue du Général Leclerc. Tel: 88 70 61 08.

Masevaux
Hotel-Restaurant A l'Aigle d'Or (9), 9, Place Clémenceau. Tel: 89 82 45 25.
Hotel-Restaurant Hostellerie Alsacienne (9), 16, Rue du Maréchal Foch.

Tel: 89 82 45 25.
Hotel-Restaurant Relais de la Poste (10), 16, Fossé des Flagellants. Tel: 89 82 46 30.

Merckwiller-Pechelbronn
Hotel-Restaurant Engel (39), 1, Route de Lobsann. Tel: 88 80 70 11.
Hotel-Restaurant A l'Etoile (25), 1, Route de Woerth. Tel: 88 80 71 80.

Molsheim
Hotel-Restaurant Cheval Blanc (13), 5, Place de l'Hôtel de Ville. Tel: 88 38 16 87.

Mulhouse
Hotel-Restaurant Altea-Frantel (96), 4, Place Charles-de-Gaulle. Tel: 89 46 01 23.
Hôtel Bâle (31), 19, Passage Central. Tel: 89 46 19 87.
Hôtel Europe (50), 11, Ave. Foch. Tel: 89 45 19 18.
Hôtel Musée (43), 8, Rue d l'Est. Tel: 89 45 47 41.
Hotel-Restaurant Du Parc (76), 26, Rue de la Sinne. Tel: 89 66 12 22.

Munster
Hotel-Restaurant La Schlucht (20), 4 Rue de Luttenbach. Tel: 89 77 32 48, 89 77 55 26.
Hotel-Restaurant Au Val Saint-Gregoire (30), 5, Rue St. Gregoire. Tel: 89 77 36 22.

Neuf-Brisach
Hotel-Restaurant Au Cerf (30), 11, Route de Strasbourg. Tel: 89 72 56 03.
Hotel-Restaurant France (21), 17, Rue de Bâle. Tel: 89 72 56 06.
Hotel-Restaurant Au Soleil (25), 6, Rue de Bâle. Tel: 89 72 51 28.

Neuwiller
Hotel-Restaurant Wunenburger, 7, Rue d'Allschwill. Tel: 89 68 51 08.

Obernai
A la Cour d'Alsace (30), 3, Rue de Gail. Tel: 88 95 07 00.
Hotel-Restaurant Le Grand Hôtel (24), Rue Dietrich. Tel: 88 95 51 28.
Hotel-Restaurant Le Parc (33), 169, Rue du Général Gourard. Tel: 88 95 50 08.

Obersteinbach
Hotel-Restaurant Anthon (7), 45, Rue Principale, tel: 88 09 25 01.

Orbey
Au Bois le Sire (12), 20, Rue Charles-de-Gaulle. Tel: 89 71 25 25.
La Croix d'Or (18), 13, Rue de l'Eglise. Tel: 89 71 20 51.
Le Saut de la Truite (22), Remomont. Tel: 89 71 20 04.
Hotel Wetterer (18), Basses Huttes. Tel: 89 71 20 28.

Ottmarsheim
Hotel-Restaurant La Couronne (9), 17, Rue du Général-de-Gaulle. Tel: 89 26 05 12.

Ottrott
Hotel-Restaurant Beau Site (9), 1, Rue du Général-du-Gaulle. Tel: 88 95 80 61.
Hotel-Restaurant Le Moulin (21). Tel: 88 95 87 33.

Pfaffenhofen
Hotel-Restaurant A l'Agneau (17), 3, Rue de Saverne. Tel: 88 07 70 55.
Hotel-Restaurant Le Pichet (10), 11, Rue Principale, La Walck. Tel: 88 72 58 58.

Petite Pierre
Hotel-Restaurant Auberge d'Imsthal (23), Route Forestière. Tel: 88 70 45 21.
Hotel-Restaurant Aux Trois Roses (48); 189, Rue Principale. Tel: 88 70 45 02.
Hotel-Restaurant Vosges (30), 30, Rue Principale. Tel: 88 70 45 05.

Ribeauvillé
Hotel-Restaurant Clos St.Vincent (11), Route de Bergheim. Tel: 89 73 67 65.
Hotel-Restaurant La Pépinière (19), Route de Sainte-Marie-aux-Mines. Tel: 89 73 64 14.
Hotel-Restaurant Les Vosges (16), 2, Grand-Rue. Tel: 89 73 61 39.

Riquewihr
Hotel-Restaurant Saint-Nicholas (34). Tel: 89 49 01 51.
Hotel-Restaurant Le Sarment d'Or (10), 4, Rue du Cerf. Tel: 89 47 92 85.

Rosheim
Hotel-Restaurant Hostellerie du Rosenmeer (20), Ave. de la Gare. Tel: 88 50 43 29.

Rouffach
Château d'Isenbourg. Tel: 89 49 63 53.

Hotel-Restaurant Ville de Lyon (40), 1, Rue Poincaré. Tel: 89 49 62 49.

Saverne
Hotel-Restaurant Au Boeuf Noir (14), 22, Grand-Rue. Tel: 88 91 10 53.
Hotel-Restaurant Chez Jean (27), 3, Rue de la Gare. Tel: 88 91 10 53.
Hotel-Restaurant Geiswiller (38), RN4 Route de Paris. Tel: 88 91 18 51.

Sélestat
Hotel-Restaurant Vaillant (47). Tel: 88 92 09 46.

Seltz
Hotel-Restaurant L'Arbre Vert (18), 43, Rue Principale. Tel: 88 86 51 15.
Hotel-Restaurant L'Homme Sauvage (7), 40 Rue Principale. Tel: 88 86 50 60.

Sessenheim
Hotel-Restaurant La Croix d'Or (9), 1, Rue Goethe. Tel: 88 86 97 32.

Saint-Hippolyte
Hotel Munsch (40), 16, Route du Vin. Tel: 89 73 00 09.
Hotel-Restaurant Aux Vieux Remparts, 31, Rue du Collège. Tel: 89 73 02 75.

Saint-Jean-Saverne
Hotel-Restaurant Kleiber (17), 37, Grand-Rue. Tel: 89 91 11 82.

Sainte-Marie-aux-Mines
Hotel-Restaurant Les Bagenelles (15), 15, La Petit Liépvre. Tel: 89 58 70 77.
Hotel-Restaurant Grand Hôtel Cromer (40), 185, Rue du Maréchal De Lattre. Tel: 89 58 70 19.

Sainte Odile
Hotel-Restaurant Hostellerie du Mont Sainte-Odile (132),. Tel: 88 95 80 53.

Strasbourg
Arcade (245), 7, Rue de Molsheim. Tel: 88 22 30 00.
Bristol (38), 4-5, Place de la Gare. Tel: 88 32 00 83.
L'Industrie Hotel (119), 223, Route de Colmar. Tel: 88 79 22 10.
Hannong Hotel (70), 12, Rue du 22 Novembre. Tel 88 32 16 22.

Holiday Inn (170), 20, Place de Bordeaux.Tel: 88 35 70 00.

Horloge Astronomique, (14), 2, Rue de la Rape. Tel: 88 35 22 11.

Le Pax (119), 24-26 Rue du Fg.-National. Tel: 88 32 14 54.

Port du Rhin (29), 59, Route du Rhin. Tel: 88 61 19 00.

Suemar

La Clarière (25), 46, Route d'Illhaeusern. Tel: 89 71 80 80.

Thann

Hotel-Restaurant Kléber (15), 39, Rue Kléber. Tel: 89 37 13 66.

Hotel-Restaurant Parc (20), 23, Rue Kléber. Tel: 89 37 10 98.

Trois-Epis

Hotel-Restaurant La Croix d'Or (12). Tel: 89 49 83 55.

Hotel-Restaurant Grand Hotel (50). Tel: 89 49 80 65.

Hotel-Restaurant Marchal (43). Tel: 89 49 81 61.

Turckheim

Hotel-Restaurant Auberge du Brand (16), 8, Grand-Rue. Tel: 89 27 06 10.

Hotel-Restaurant Les Deux Clefs (49), 3, Rue du Conseil. Tel: 89 27 06 10.

Villé

Hotel-Restaurant Freppel, 28, Route de la Libération. Tel: 88 57 17 05.

Hotel-Restaurant A la Ville de Nancy (20) 6, Rue du Mont St. Odile. Tel: 88 57 10 10.

Wangenbourg

Hotel-Restaurant Belle Vue (270), 16, Route de Dabo, Obersteigen-Wangebourg. Tel: 88 87 32 39.

Hotel-Restaurant Parc Hotel (250), 39, Rue du Général-de-Gaulle, tel: 88 87 31 72.

Wasselonne

Hotel-Restaurant Au Saumon (18), 69, Rue du Général-de-Gaulle. Tel: 88 87 01 83.

Wissembourg

Hotel-Restaurant L'Ange (8), 2, Rue de la République. Tel: 88 94 12 11.

Hotel-Restaurant A la Cave de Cleebourg (20), Rue de Lobsann-Rott. Tel: 88 94 52 18.

CAMPING

Basically, camping is permitted, even away from camp sites, wherever it is not expressively prohibited and providing sanitary and police regulations are met with. A list of camping sites is available from:

Fédération Française de Camping et Caravanning
78 Rue de Rivoli
F-75004 Paris.

Touring Club de France
Agence Acceuil Touring
11, Rue de la Division Leclerc
F-67000 Strasbourg
Tel: 88 32 72 63.

YOUTH HOSTELS

Colmar
7, Rue Saint Nicholas
Tel: 89 41 33 08.

Mulhouse
37 Rue de l'Illberg
Tel: 89 42 63 28.

Sainte-Marie-aux-Mines
21, Rue Reber
Tel: 89 58 75 74.

Schirmeck
Les Minières in Grandfontaine, five miles (7 km) to the northwest.

Strasbourg
Montaigne Verte district
9, Rue de l'Auberge de Jeunesse
Tel: 88 30 26 46.

OTHERS

Bed and gourmet board: Alsace is famous for its gourmet cuisine, and these organisations list addresses of places that offer both accommodation and *haut cuisine*.

Office départemental du Tourisme du Bas-Rhin
Maison du Tourisme
9, Rue du Dôme, BP 53
F-67061 Strasbourg Cédex
Tel: 88 22 01 22 / telex: 880198.

Association Départementale du Tourisme Haut-Rhin
Hôtel du Département
F-68006 Colmar Cédex
Tel: 89 22 68 00, 89 23 21 11
Telex: 870530.

You can obtain information about accommodation in private residences and farmhouses from:

Loisirs Acceuil
Relais Département du Tourisme Rural
F-67000 Strasbourg
Tel: 88 75 56 50.

FOOD DIGEST

CUISINE

Alsatian cuisine is famed far and wide for its excellence. Many a gourmet is prepared to travel long distances to experience the delights of a *haut cuisine* paradise. In Alsace, the best food is often found in plain inns and restaurants in remote places, far away from the star-studded prestige restaurants. The size of the meal does justice to the skill of the cooks. An aperitif prepares the stomach, the *hors d' oeuvres* lead on to a second course, mainly fish. The main course, which is the highlight of the meal, is usually meat and vegetables. The whole meal is usually rounded off by a sweet dessert and/or cheese. A digestive is recommended to aid digestion afterwards.
Among the specialties of Alsace are:

Hors d'oeuvres: *Foie gras* (goose liver), *Quiche Lorraine* (a savoury flan), *Tarte à l'oignon* (onion flan), *Flammekueche* (cream cheese on thin pastry).

Main courses: *Baeckoffa* (layers of potato and various kinds of meat), *Coq au Riesling* (chicken in Riesling wine), *Schif-*
fala (smoked shoulder of pork in a horseradish sauce), *Choucroute garnie à l'alsacienne* (sauerkraut with various kinds of meat and sausage).

Desserts: *Kougelhopf* (a yeast-dough cake), *Tarte alsacienne* (fruit tart with vanilla cream), Munster cheese.

RESTAURANTS

Many of the hotels in Alsace also house excellent restaurants with fine service. The following list of restaurants is by no means complete, and it is mainly intended as a suggestion for the visitor.

Andlau
Au Boeuf Rouge 6, Rue du Dr Stoltz. Tel: 88 08 96 26.

Benfeld
Au Zoll Route du Rhin. Tel: 88 74 43 08.

Blaesheim
Au Boeuf 183, Rue du Maréchal Foch. Tel: 88 68 81 31.

Colmar
Caveau de Saint Pierre 24 Rue de la Herse. Tel: 89 41 99 33.
Le Fer Rouge 52, Grand-Rue. Tel: 89 41 37 24.
Maison des Têtes 19, Rue des Têtes. Tel: 89 24 34 34.
S' Pariser Stewwele 4, Place de Jeanne d'Arc. Tel: 89 41 42 33.
Schillinger 16, Rue Stanislas. Tel: 89 41 43 17.
Unterlinden 2, Rue Unterlinden. Tel: 89 41 18 73.

Ebersmunster
Aux Deux Clefs 72, Rue du Général Leclerc. Tel: 88 85 71 55.

Eguisheim
Caveau d'Eguisheim 3, Place du Château. Tel: 89 41 08 89.

Hunspach
La Cave Fruitière. Tel: 88 80 42 32.

Illhaeusern
Auberge de l'Ill . Tel: 89 71 83 23.

Lauterbourg
La Poêle d' Or 35, Rue du Général Mittelhauser. Tel: 88 94 84 16.

Lembach
Auberge du Cheval Blanc 4, Route de Wissembourg. Tel: 88 94 41 86.

Mulhouse
Auberge Alsacienne du Zoo 31, Avenue de la 9e D.I.C. Tel: 89 44 26 91.
Le Belvedère 80, Ave. de la 1ère D. B. Tel: 89 44 18 79.
Moulin de Kaegy Steinbrunn-le-Bas, Habsheim. Tel: 89 81 30 34.
Relais de la Tour 3, Boulevard d'Europe. Tel: 89 45 12 14.

Niederbronn-les-Bains
Les Acacias 35, Rue des Acacias. Tel: 88 09 68 88.

Rosheim
Auberge du Cerf 120, Rue du Général-de-Gaulle. Tel: 88 50 40 14.
La Petite Auberge 41, Rue du Général-de-Gaulle. Tel: 88 50 40 60.

Sélestat
Vieille Tour 8, Rue de la Jauge. Tel: 88 92 15 02.

Soufflenheim
Le Pichet 39, Rue Haguenau. Tel: 88 86 66 79.

Strasbourg
L'Alsace à Table 8, Rue des Francs-Bourgeois. Tel: 88 32 50 62.
Ami Fritz 8, Rue des Dentelles. Tel: 88 32 80 53.
Aux Armes de Strasbourg 9, Place Gutenberg. Tel: 88 32 85 62.
L'Arsenal 11, Rue de l'Abreuvoir. Tel: 88 35 03 69.
Au Boeuf Mode 2, Place Saint Thomas. Tel: 88 32 39 03.
Buerehiesel 4, Parc de l'Orangerie. Tel: 88 61 62 24.
Au Crocodile 10, Rue de l'Outre. Tel: 88 32 13 02.
Gutenberg 8, Place Gutenberg. Tel: 88 32 82 48.
Kammerzell 16, Place de la Cathédrale. Tel: 88 32 42 14.

Maison des Tanneurs 42, Rue Bain-aux-Plantes. Tel: 88 32 79 70.
La Rivière des Parfums 3, Rue des Dentelles. Tel: 88 32 31 19.
La Table Aquitaine 13, Place de la Cathédrale 8, Fossé des Tailleurs. Tel: 88 32 86 95.

DRINKING NOTES

Good wine belongs to a good meal, and there is no lack of good wine in Alsace. To list only a few of the fine wines available: the light table wine *Chasselas* or *Knipperle, Silvaner, Pinot, Riesling* or *Traminer*. There is more information on this subject in other chapters of this book, particularly in the section on the Route du vin.

THINGS TO DO

GUIDED TOURS

Setting out on your own to discover a town will obviously give you a personal impression of the place and at the same time offer the greatest flexibility. However, if you want to learn something about the country and its people, there are various guided tours on offer:

Colmar
During the summer (mid-June to end of September) the Office du Tourisme (address in the GETTING AROUND section, page 272) arranges guided tours of the city with the *Petit Train*, starting at the Tourist Office.

Strasbourg
Here, too, the Tourist Office is responsible for arranging guided tours. Among those on offer:

Tours of the old city with the Mini-Train
Meeting point: Place de la Cathédrale
Daily every hour from 9 am to 11 pm.

You can get an excellent view of the city from a boat trip on the Rhine or on the Ill:

Tour of the Port of Strasbourg
Meeting point: Promenade Dauphin

Boat trip on the Ill
Meeting point: in front of the Château des Rohan. Daily 10.30, 11 am, half-hourly after 1pm up until 7 pm

Night boat trip on the Ill
Meeting point: in front of the Château des Rohan.

CULTURE PLUS

MUSEUMS

Most urban museums are open at the following times: April-September, daily 10 am to 12 noon and 2 pm to 6 pm; October to March, daily 2 pm to 4 pm except Tuesdays; also on Sundays from 10 am to 12 noon.

Altkirch
–Musée Sundgavien (regional museum)
Place de la République
Tel: 89 40 00 04
15 June to 15 September daily 3 pm to 5.30 pm except Mondays; all year round Sundays 3 pm to 5 pm. Entrance fee FF 4.50.

Barr
–Musée de la Folie Marco
30, Rue du Docteur Sultzer
Tel: 88 08 94 24.
July-September 10 am to 12.30 pm and 2.30 pm to 6 pm daily except Tue: June/October, Sat/Sun, 10 am to 12.30 pm and 2.30 pm to 6 pm. Entrance fee FF 4.50

Colmar
–Musée Bartholdi (history of the city, life of the sculptor Frédéric Auguste Bartholdi)
30, Rue des Marchands

Tel: 89 41 90 60
April-October 10 am to 12 noon and 2 pm to 6 pm, November-March, Sat/Sun 10 am to 12 noon and 2 pm to 5 pm. Admission: FF 5.
–Musée d'Unterlinden (Isenheim Altarpiece)
Place d'Unterlinden
Tel: 89 41 89 23
April-October 9 am to 12 noon and 2 pm to 6 pm, November-March 9 am to 12 noon and 2 pm to 5 pm except Tue. Entrance fee children FF 12, adults FF 15.

Echery
–Musée de l'Ecole
School building near the Catholic chapel
Tel: 89 58 75 24
July-September 2 pm to 6 pm; guided tours by appointment.

Ensisheim
Ecomusée de Haute-Alsace/Maisons Paysannes d'Alsace (open air museum).
Ungersheim
Tel: 89 48 23 44
June-August daily 10 am to 8 pm; May/September 10 am to 7 pm, other months, 10 am to 6 pm. Entrance fee: children FF 6, adults FF 20.

Haguenau
–Musée d'Alsace
Place J. Thierry
Musée Historique
9, Rue du Maréchal-Foche.

Marckolsheim
–Mémorial-Musée de la Ligne Maginot du Rhin
Tel: 88 92 50 01.
Mid-June to mid-September 9 am to 12 noon, 2 pm to 6 pm, other months only on Sundays and public holidays. Entrance fee: children FF 1, adults FF 2.

Mulhouse
–Albert Schweitzer House (house of Albert Schweitzer's birth and cultural centre)
Rue du Général-de-Gaulle
Easter, May-October 10 am to 12 noon and 2 pm to 6 pm.
–Musée des Beaux Arts
4, Place Guillaume Tell
10 am to 12 noon, 2 pm to 6 pm except Tue, Thur 8.30 pm to 10.30 pm.

—Maison de la Céramique
25 Rue Josue Hofer
Tel: 89 43 32 55.
Tue-Sat 9 am to 12 noon.
—Musée de la Chapelle Saint-Jean
Grand-Rue
May-September 10 am to 12 noon and 2 pm to 5 pm except Tue.
—Musée Français du Chemin de Fer (railway museum)
2, Rue Alfred de Glehn
Tel: 89 42 25 67.
April-September daily 9 am to 6 pm, October-March daily 10 am to 5 pm. Admission: children under 16 FF 10, adults FF 25.
—Musée Historique
Place de la Réunion
Tel: 8945 68 31.
15 June–September 10 am to 12 noon and 2 pm to 6 pm except Tue, Thur 8.30 pm to 10.30 pm; October–14 June 10 am to 12 noon and 2 pm to 5pm except Tue. Entrance fee FF 5.
—Musée de l'Impression sur Etoffes (printed textiles)
3, Rue des Bonnes Gens
Tel: 89 45 51 20.
10 am to 12 noon and 2 pm to 6 pm except Tue. Entrance fee FF 18.
—Musée National de l'Automobile
192 Ave. du Colmar
Tel: 88 42 29 17.
Daily 10 am to 6 pm except Tue. Entrance fee children FF 17, adults FF 27.
—Musée du Papier Peint (wallpaper)
28, Rue Zuber, Rixheim.
10 am to 12 noon and 2 pm to 6 pm.

Pfaffenhofen
—Musée de l'Imagerie Peinte et Populaire (folk painting and art)
38, Rue du Dr Albert Schweitzer
Tel: 88 07 70 23.
Wed, Sat and Sun 2 pm to 5 pm. Entrance fee FF 4.

Saverne
—Musée Municipal (archaeology collection)
Château des Rohan, south wing
Place du Général-de-Gaulle
Tel: 88 91 18 51.
July, August Tue-Sat 2.30 pm to 6 pm, Sun 2.30 to 6 pm; May, June, September Sat 3 pm to 5 pm, Sun 10 am to 12 noon. Entrance fee FF 6.

Sainte-Marie-aux-Mines
—Musée Mineralogique
70, Rue Wilson
Tel: 89 58 75 50.
July/August 10 am to 12 noon, otherwise by appointment. Entrance fee FF 3.

Schiltigheim
—Kronenbourg brewery
68, Route d'Oberhausbergen
Tel: 88 29 90 00.
Guided tours Mon-Fri 9 am, 10 am, 2 pm and 3 pm.

Strasbourg
—Musé Alsacien
23, Quai St Nicholas
Tel: 88 32 48 95.
Guided tours Fri 8.30 pm. Entrance fee FF 3.70
—Musée d'Art Moderne
Ancienne Douane
1, Rue du Vieux Marché aux Poissons
Tel: 88 32 46 07.
Entrance fee FF 3. 70.
—Musée Historique
3, Place de la Grande Boucherie
Tel: 88 32 25 63.
Guided tours Mon 8.30 pm. Entrance fee FF 3.70.
—Musées Municipaux
2, Place du Château
Tel: 88 32 48 95.
—Musée de l'Oeuvre Notre-Dame
3, Place du Château
Tel: 88 32 06 39.
Guided tours Wed 8.30 pm. Entrance fee FF 3.70.
—Musée Zoologique
29, Boulevard de la Victoire
Tel: 88 36 32 21.
2 pm to 6 pm, Wed and Sun 10 am to 12 noon and 2 pm to 6 pm. No entrance fee.
—Planétarium de Strasbourg
4, Rue de l'Observatoire
Tel: 88 36 12 50.
Entrance fee: children FF 10, adults FF 20.

Wissembourg
—Musée Westercamp
3, Rue du Musée
Tel: 88 94 14 55.
Mon, Tue, Thur-Sat 10 am to 12 noon and 2 pm to 5 pm, Sun 2 pm to 5 pm. Entrance fee: FF 5.

The following is a list of the most important theatres all of which have a varied programme.

Colmar
–*Théâtre Municipal*
Rue Kléber
Tel: 89 41 29 82.

Mulhouse
–*Centre d'Animation Culturelle*
7, Rue Alfred Angel
Tel: 89 45 63 95.
–*Théâtre Municipal*
39, Rue de la Sinne
Tel: 89 45 26 96.

Strasbourg
–*Centre Culturel de Strasbourg*
13, Place André-Maurois
Tel: 88 26 12 66, 88 26 16 55.
–*Les Drapiers–Centre Théâtrale Rhenan*
31, Rue Louis Apffel
Tel: 88 36 67 49.
–*Théâtre Municipal*
18, Place Broglie
Tel: 88 36 43 41.
–*Théâtre National du Strasbourg*
1, Rue du Général Gourand
Tel: 88 35 63 60.

ARCHITECTURE

Altkirch
–church (1845-50), neo-Romanesque, fine view
–Hôtel de Ville
–Saint-Morand, half a mile (1 km) to the east, place of pilgrimage
–Romanesque high relief on sarcophagus

Ammerschwihr
–church of St Martin
–Fool's Tower (1535)
–Porte-Haute (13th century)

Andlau
–church of St Richardis
–crypt (12th century), Romanesque west portal, frieze (1130-40)
–church of St. André (c. 900), bell tower (15th century), frescoes (15th and 18th centuries).

Avolsheim
–Bruche canal (1681)
–church (1911-13), Romanesque processional crucifix
–Domus Petri, about half a mile (1 km) to the south (11th century)

Barr
–Hôtel de Ville (1640)
–church of St Martin (1850), Romanesque tower with friezes
–Truttenhausen, remains of a late Gothic church

Bergheim
–town walls
–upper gate (14th century), fortified towers
–basilica (1347)

Châtenois
–church (1760)
–bas-reliefs (16th century)
–Hôtel de Ville (1493)

Colmar
–old city quarter around the river Lauch
–*La Petite Venise*
–Ancienne Douane (old merchant house, 1480)
–Dominican church, *Madonna among the Roses* in the choir
–church of St Martin (1230-1370), Gothic style, three aisles
–Maison Pfister (1537)
–Maison des Têtes (1609), facade decorated with heads
–Quartier des Tanneurs

Dambach-la-Ville
–chapel of St Sébastian
–Château du Bernstein (11th century)

Eguisheim
–Eguisheim castle
–chapel (1186-94), museum

Ensisheim
–Hôtel de Ville (1533-47), Renaissance style, meteorite

Ferrette
–Château de Ferrette (12th-14th century)
–Hôtel de Ville (1572), Rhineland Renaissance style

Guebwiller
–Benedictine abbey of Murbach
–church of Notre-Dame (1760-85), Classical, choir seats with reliefs
–church of St Léger (12th century), choir seats (1775-9)

Haguenau
–parish church of Saint-Croix
–pillared basilica, portal and nave (13th century), altarpiece (1511-59)
–chain well (1618)

Kintzheim
–chapel of St-Félix-et-St-Régule (12th-15th century)
–castle of Schwendistein
–eagle reserve in the castle ruins
Tel: 88 92 84 33, open April–September from 2 pm
–Montaigne aux Singes
Tel: 88 92 11 09, open April–September Mon-Sat 10 am to 12 noon, 2 pm to 6 pm, Sun 2 pm to 7 pm.
–stork reserve
Tel: 88 92 84 56.

Marmoutier
–abbey church (12/13th century), chancel (16th century), Silbermann organ (1710).

Molsheim
–Jesuit church (1617), *Madonna of the Crescent Moon* (1515).

Mulhouse
–Hôtel de Ville, fresoes
–church of St. Stephen, stained glass
–Place de l'Europe, marble slabs with the coats of arms of European cities

Neuf-Brisach
–outline of the town
–fortifications

Neuwiller-les-Saverne
–church of St. Adelphe (12th century)
–church of St-Pierre-et-St-Paul (11th century), two-storeyed chapel

Obernai
–Hôtel de Ville
–church of St-Pierre-et-St-Paul (19th century), glass windows, churchyard with Calvary chapel

–Place du Marché (market square)
–fountain of St. Odile

Ribeauvillé
–Hôtel de Ville (18th century)
–church of Notre-Dame

Riquewihr
–Dolder house (1291)

Rosheim
–church of St-Pierre-et-St-Paul
–Maison Paienne (heathen house, 12th century)

Rouffach
–Hôtel de Ville (16th–18th century)
–church of Notre-Dame-de-l'Assumption (11–14th century), stone front (15th century)
–Corn Hall (1569)
–Tour des Sourcières (Witches' Tower)

Saint-Marie-aux-Mines
–Hôtel de Ville (1833)
–church of Sainte-Madeleine (1757)
–Mine Saint-Berthélémy (silver mine)
Tel: 89 58 72 28.

Sainte-Odile
–convent, pilgrim hall, convent church, chapel of the Holy Cross (11th century)
–*Mur Paien* (Heathen Wall)

Saverne
–Château des Rohan
–church of Notre-Dame-de-la-Nativité
–Maison Katz
–Rose gardens

Schirmeck
–Mémorial National de la Déportation, Tel: 88 97 00 02.

Sélestat
–Ancien Arsenal Sainte-Barbe (14th century)
–Bibliothèque Humaniste
–church of Saint-Foy, crypt
–church of Saint-Georges, Renaissance chancel, glass windows
–Tour d'Horloge (Clock Tower, 14th century)
–Tour des Sourcières (Witches' Tower, 12th century)

Soultz-Haut-Rhin
–church of Saint-Maurice (13th–15th century), Renaissance chancel, wood carvings, Silbermann organ
–moated castle of Bucheneck (14th–17th century)

Strasbourg
–old city
–Cathédrale, portals, late Gothic chancel, stained glass, astronomical clock, angel pillar
–Château des Rohan (1730-41)
–citadel
–Kammerzell house
–church of St-Pierre-le-Jeune (13th–15th century), Romanesque cloisters church of St. Thomas
–Orangerie
–Palais de l'Europe (seat of the European Parliament and the Council of Europe)
–Palais de l'Université (1879-84)
–Place Kléber
–La Petite France
–tanners' quarter
–Pharmacie du Cerf
–Ponts Couverts
–St-Pierre-le-Vieux
–St. Thomas
–Synagogue de la Paix

Thann
–Collégiale Saint-Thiébaut, portals, glass windows

Turckheim
–church of Sainte Anne

Wissembourg
–Wooden Apple
–church of Saint-Jean (1523-33)
–church of St-Pierre-et-St-Paul, stained glass (13th century), frescoes (13th century), cloisters
–Maison du Sel (1450)

NIGHTLIFE

The best-known and most popular nightspots are obviously worth visiting. This list is confined to Strasbourg, Alsace's most visited city.

BARS

Le Bar des Aviatuers
12, Rue des Soeurs
Tel: 88 36 52 69.

Bugatti Bar
Hilton Hotel
Ave. Herrenschmidt
Tel: 88 37 10 10
(piano music from 6 pm onwards)

DISCOTHEQUES

Le Chalet
Route de la Wantzenau
Roberston
Tel: 88 31 18 31.

Charlie's
24, Place des Halles
Quai Kléber
Tel: 88 22 32 22.

La Péniche (on board a boat)
Ponts Couverts
Tel: 88 36 22 90.

SHOPPING

SPORTS

Alsace is visited by people from countries around the world, and souvenirs can be found in many shops in the tourist centres The souvenirs come in every imaginable shape, size and quality, from plastic stork's nests to dolls in regional dress. To avoid buying a souvenir from Hong Kong instead of one made in Alsace, look for the label *"Souvenir de France Alsace authentique"*, which means the product was not mass-produced abroad.

You can also find many good pieces, such as antiques, prints, porcelain or one of the culinary delights.

In many villages and towns there are weekly markets and fleamarkets offering a variety of goods. You can browse at the goods on display and enjoy the produce of the harvests from various regions.

The Marché du Canal Couvert (Rue Arisitide Briand) is a special experience. It is held on Tuesdays and Thursdays starting at 8 am, and also on Saturdays, when it looks more like a Middle-East bazaar. The goods on offer range from fruit and vegetables to clothings and even exotic birds. This spectacle is accompanied by a colourful mixture of languages.

Other interesting regular markets in Strasbourg are:

–*Marché du Boulevard de la Marne*
Tuesdays and Saturdays 7 am to 1 pm
–*Marché Sainte-Marguerite*
Wednesdays and Fridays 7 am to 1 pm
–*Marché de la Krutenau*
Wednesdays 7 am to 1 pm and the Christmas market in the Place Broglie from 1 to 24 December.

Alsace offers many opportunities to visitors who look forward to an active and exciting holiday. Here are a few suggestions.

FISHING

Before casting your line, you must obtain a permit from the appropriate tourist office, or contact the following address:
Fédération Départementale des Associations de Pêche et de Pisciculture du Bas-Rhin
1, Rue de Nomény, 67000 Strasbourg.

HANG-GLIDING

The heights of Alsace are a positive invitation to take to the air. Information about schools, clubs and equipment hire can be obtained from tourist offices or from:

Comité Départementale de Vol libre au Haut-Rhin
M. Pierre Woerth
35, Rue Jean-Martin, 68200 Mulhouse
Tel: 89 59 18 39
Ligue de l'Este de Vol libre
M. Petitdemange
4, Rue Strauss-Durkheim,
67000 Strasbourg
Tel: 88 36 49 38.

RIDING

If you prefer a pony to Shank's variety, you will get to know the many different facets of the countryside in a very special way. Information about the various riding centres may be obtained from:
Association Alsacienne de Tourisme Equestre
78, Rue de l'Oberhardt, 68000 Colmar
Tel: 89 79 38 48.

SPECIAL INFORMATION

LANGUAGE

FOR THE DISABLED

In Alsace as well as elsewhere architects and town planners are increasingly making provisions for the special requirements that make travelling easier for the disabled. Specific information on accommodation and events can be obtained from:

Loisir-Vacances des Handicapés
Centre de Documentation et d'Information
Chambre de Commerce et d'Industrie
1, Place de la Gare
68000 Colmar
Tel: 89 23 99 40.

A hotel guide specially for the disabled is available from:

Association des Paralysés de France
Délégation de Paris
22, Rue du Père Guérin
75013 Paris.

Throughout Alsace French is the official language. However, many of the inhabitants of the border regions are also familiar with German.

Since a few decades ago, the German dialect used in Alsace became less frequently spoken for a variety of political and social reasons. Fortunately this dialect has been revived more recently over the last few years and it is now encouraged and promoted as part of the region's cultural heritage.

Apart from the official French names, the German versions of place names are still sometimes used. The French and German equivalents of the most important place names are as follows:

Ammerschwihr - Ammschweier
Bouxwiller - Buchsweiler
Châtenois - Kestenholz
Cernay - Sennheim
Dabo - Dagsburg
Ferrette - Pfirt
Lièpvre - Leberau
Marmoutier - Maursmünster
Masevaux - Masmünster
Mulhouse - Mülhausen
Neuf-Brisach - Neubreisach
Obernai - Oberehnheim
Ribeauvillé - Rapportsweiler
Riquewihr - Reichenweier
Saint-Hippolyte - Sankt Pilt
Saint-Jean-Saverne - Sankt Johann bei Zabern
Sainte-Marie-aux-Mines - Markirch
Sélestat - Schlettstadt
Soultz-les-Bains - Sulzbad
Trois Epis - Dreiähren
Villé - Weiler
Wasselonne - Wasselnheim
Wissembourg - Weissenburg

Art/Photo Credits

Astier, Patrice	3, 9, 20/21, 29, 30R, 33, 36R, 37, 44, 45, 48, 49, 50, 51, 52, 53, 57, 58, 59, 74, 75, 82, 84, 85, 86, 87, 90, 92, 93, 99, 100, 102, 103, 104L& R, 105, 107L& R, 111, 112, 113L, 114, 115L& R, 116, 117, 118L& R, 119, 120, 121, 127, 133, 134/135, 138L&R, 139, 141, 142, 143, 144, 145, 147, 148, 149, 150, 151, 152, 154/155, 156L, 157, 160, 161L&R, 162, 164, 166/167, 171, 172, 173, 174, 176, 177, 178, 179, 180, 182, 183,186, 187, 189, 190, 191, 192, 193, 194, 195, 200, 202, 203, 204, 205, 206/207, 208, 209, 210, 211, 212, 216, 217, 218, 219, 221, 222/223, 224, 225, 226, 227, 228, 230L& R, 231, 232L& R, 233L& R, 235, 236, 237, 244L&R, 245, 248L, 249, 251, 252/253, 254, 255, 256, 257, 258, 259, 260, 261L& R, 264
Bildagentur Anne Hamann	16/17, 25, 28, 60, 61, 64/65, 66/67, 68/69, 70/71, 78, 101, 165, 170, 181, 184/185, 196, 197
Bildagentur Mauritius	cover, 42, 43, 54, 88, 89, 199
Eckhardt, Karl Heinz	214/215
Franz, Fremdenverkehrsamt Ffm.	76
Gockel, Gabi	63, 83, 238/239
InterFoto	41, 55, 96, 113R, 112/123, 128, 163, 234, 246
Lebemann	22/23, 46, 94/95, 126, 129, 130, 131
Museés de la ville de Paris	40
Pfeiffer, Gerd	263
Strasberg, Jans	91

INDEX

293

Z